D0490376

CREATIVE CAMERA TECHNIQUES

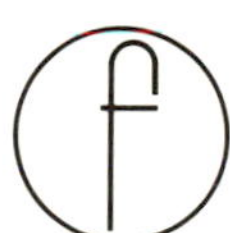

FOCAL PRESS LIMITED,
London
FOCAL PRESS INC.,
10 East 40th Street,
New York, NY 10016
Associated Companies:
Pitman Publishing Pty Ltd
Melbourne
Pitman Publishing New Zealand Ltd
Wellington

CREATIVE CAMERA TECHNIQUES

Axel Brück

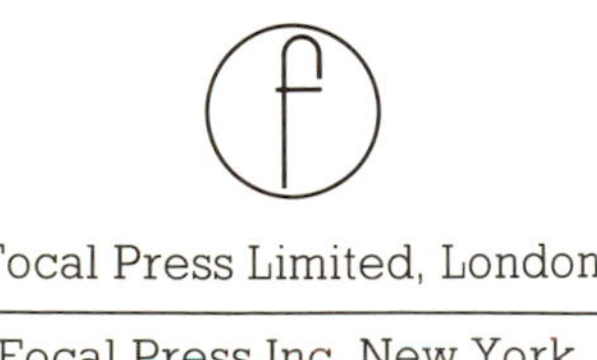

Focal Press Limited, London

Focal Press Inc, New York

BL British Library Cataloguing in Publication Data

Brück, Axel
Creative Camera Techniques
1. Photography
I. Title
770'.28 TR146

ISBN 0 240 51106 9
American Library of Congress Catalog No 80-41402

First Edition 1981

Phototypeset in Great Britain by
Tradespools Limited, Frome, Somerset, England

Printed and bound in Great Britain by
A. Wheaton & Co, Exeter
Jacket and book design by Roger Kohn

CONTENTS

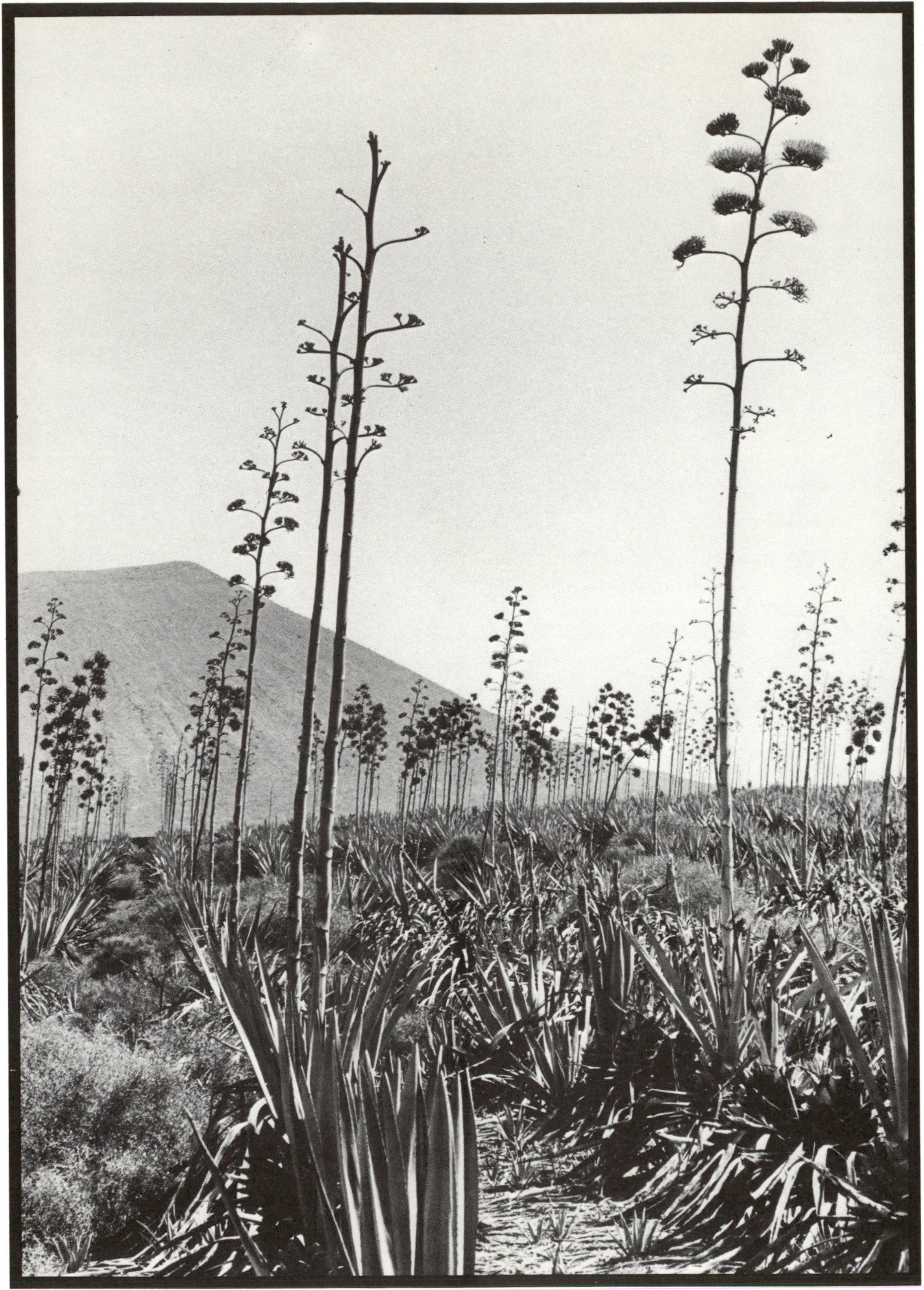

FOREWORD

Photographic technique and pictorial composition are two aspects of one theme, because images are constructed by employing photographic technique in a very particular way. How photographic apparatus and procedures can be used and how their use contributes to the effect of pictures—this is the concern of the first part of this book.

It starts quite simply with a home-made pinhole camera, and continues with 'photography with spectacles' and on to a detailed survey of interchangeable lenses, their properties and use. Other topics include filters and trick lenses, multiple exposure, and the representation of movement. In the final section of the first part there follows a full account of exposure measurement and its uses.

The basic concern of the book is not so much with the explanation of technical or structural details, but rather with 'creation'. The reader learns about what can be achieved with his camera and its accessories (including much that is not included in the instruction booklet), and which photographic possibilities exist beyond the simple 'point and shoot' procedure. This extends from such basic questions as 'what happens when I alter the aperture?' to opportunities for influencing the picture in a more advanced way with directed lighting.

As this book builds on fundamentals, and as each chapter is furnished with informative visual examples, it may be read with profit by the interested beginner. I believe, however, that for the advanced worker it will also supply many suggestions and ideas.

In the middle of the book there is a section, in which I have tried to give some advice about the acquisition of a photographic outfit.

The second part of the book views the theme of visual creation from another aspect. Based on three major thematic groups (landscape, people and the close-up), this part explains to the reader how other non-technical factors play a significant role in pictorial creativity. This is a wide-ranging theme. It extends, for example, from the problem of how lighting for portraiture should be arranged to the question of what a portrait actually is. It deals too with matters such as the particular advantages of a wide-angle lens in landscape photography, and which characteristics of a landscape photograph make it interesting to the observer.

The book is not, however, concerned with an encyclopaedic enumeration of themes or techniques, but rather with those ideas which underlie photographic activity, and hence how these concepts may be represented in practice as pictures. This is amplified by many illustrations, and—as far as necessary—by clear technical advice.

Axel Brück

1: PHOTOGRAPHY—AN AUTOMATIC PROCESS?

You do not need to be a precision engineer, electronics expert or a physicist with special optical skills to be able to take photographs with a modern camera. On the contrary, an appreciable part of the effort that is nowadays devoted to camera construction is directed specifically towards simplifying the control and handling of equipment, and hence making life easier for the photographer. Echoing the words of a publicity statement from the early days of amateur photography, you could say: 'you press the button—the camera will take care of the rest.'

Although you can rely on this claim in most circumstances of your photographic career, do not overlook the fact that the camera can be expected to take over only a part of the photographic task—never the task of thinking. 'Thinking photographically' does not of course imply that, before and during every exposure, you have to engage in profound meditation and intricate mathematical calculation. The latter at any rate should be accomplished for you by the camera. Thinking photographically constitutes rather an important element in 'visualising'. In other words, to be able to take good photographs, at the moment of exposure you must have a clear mental image of how the eventual picture will look. This in turn is possible only if you know exactly what the automatic mechanism of the camera will do when you press the button. This should be self-evident. If at the moment of exposure you still do not know how the final image will look, obviously it is pure chance whether the picture will be satisfactory or not.

Take as an example the measurement of exposure. A camera with an automatic system ensures that a correctly exposed picture is obtained when the release is pressed. In fact, after several years of working with single-lens reflex cameras, I am still astonished at the ability of the automatic system to produce correctly exposed images in nearly all situations. But—and this 'but' applies to every sort of automatic system in every make of camera—it has to be said that the automatic system has been programmed for an average lighting effect. Since the camera is unable to think, it cannot automatically allow for deviations from this average effect. In unusual lighting conditions the photographer must himself decide whether or not he should make any adjustment.

This matter is discussed fully in Chapter 17. At this stage, for the benefit of the reader who has had only limited photographic experience, *Fig 3* shows an example of a situation where the automatic system should be overriden.

It may be readily accepted, with regard to direction of lighting and allocation of dark and light areas, that the subject in *Fig 3* is by no means an average one. Indeed, here the camera's automatic system on its own would not have produced a usable negative. The automatically indicated value had to be corrected by over 1.5 stops in order to obtain any sort of detail in the darker areas of the picture.

To come to this kind of decision it is necessary to have at least a general idea of what occurs during exposure, of how you can modify this process, and how such a modification affects the picture.

If you examine a sectional drawing of a modern high-performance camera (*Fig 1*), you will certainly have the feeling that the whole business is highly complicated. But this is not the case. It is important to remember that to a large extent the intricate mechanism and electronics of such a camera are designed specifically to simplify your photography. It is not the purpose of this book to embark on a course in photographic electronics. Instead, it is the aim to deal with facts which are important for photography in practice. It is a matter of basic principles. So let us have a close look at the schematic diagram in *Fig 2*.

When you view a subject with your camera, the light from this subject enters the lens, the converging rays are then directed by the mirror into the viewfinder, and from there to the eye. In the viewfinder a portion of the light is diverted for the purpose of exposure measurement.

As the shutter release is pressed, the

1

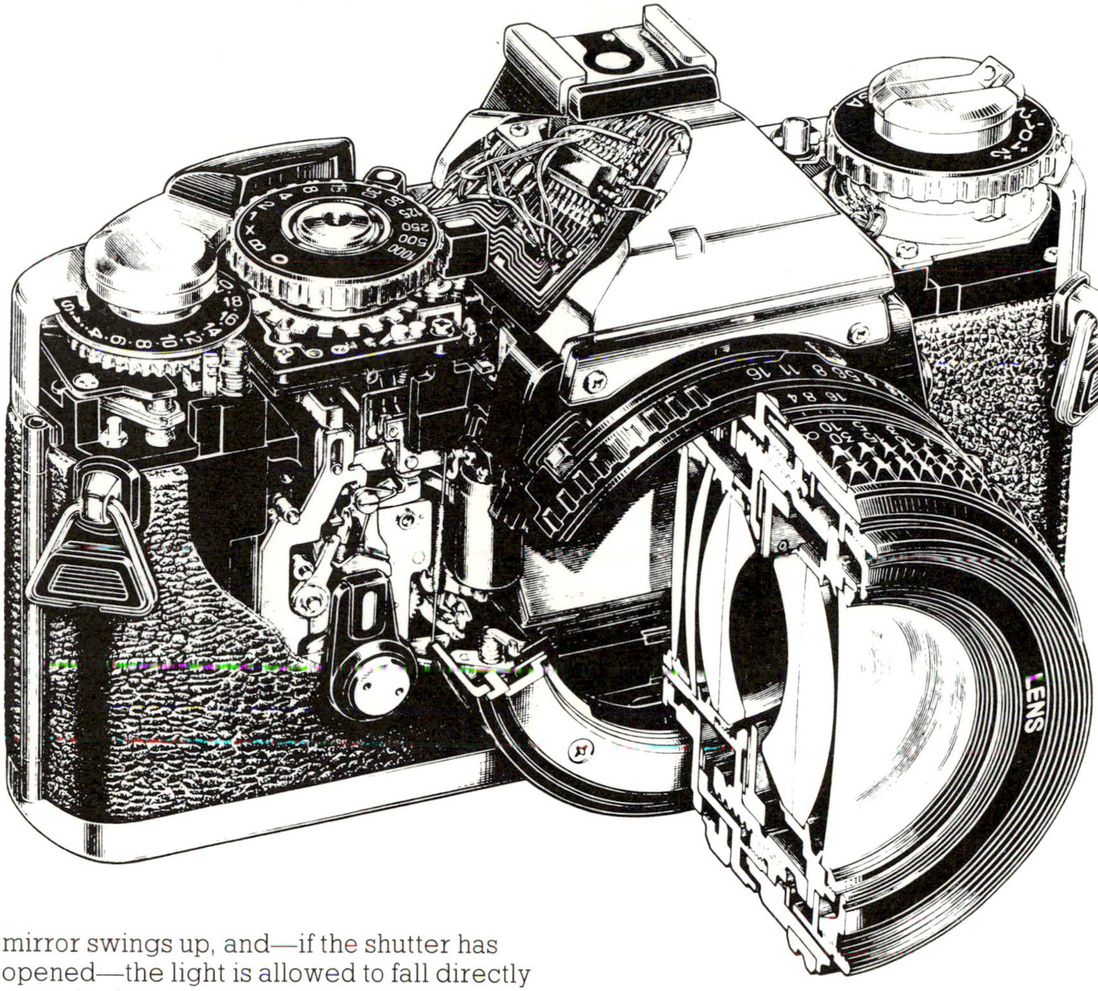

mirror swings up, and—if the shutter has opened—the light is allowed to fall directly on to the film. Thus the amount of light reaching the film is determined by two factors: firstly, by the time during which the shutter is open, and secondly by the extent of the aperture through which the light enters. The factors which are essential for the production of a picture are listed below:

1 the light-sensitive material itself (the film)
2 the light-tight box in which it is contained (the camera body)
3 the aperture through which the light enters (the iris)
4 the lens
5 the shutter.

If any one of these five factors is altered it causes a change in the image, and also affects the structure of the picture. For this reason the succeeding chapters are devoted to considering these points in detail.

2

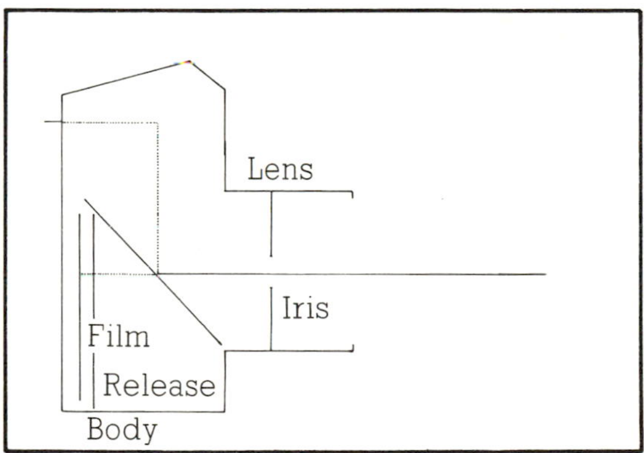

3

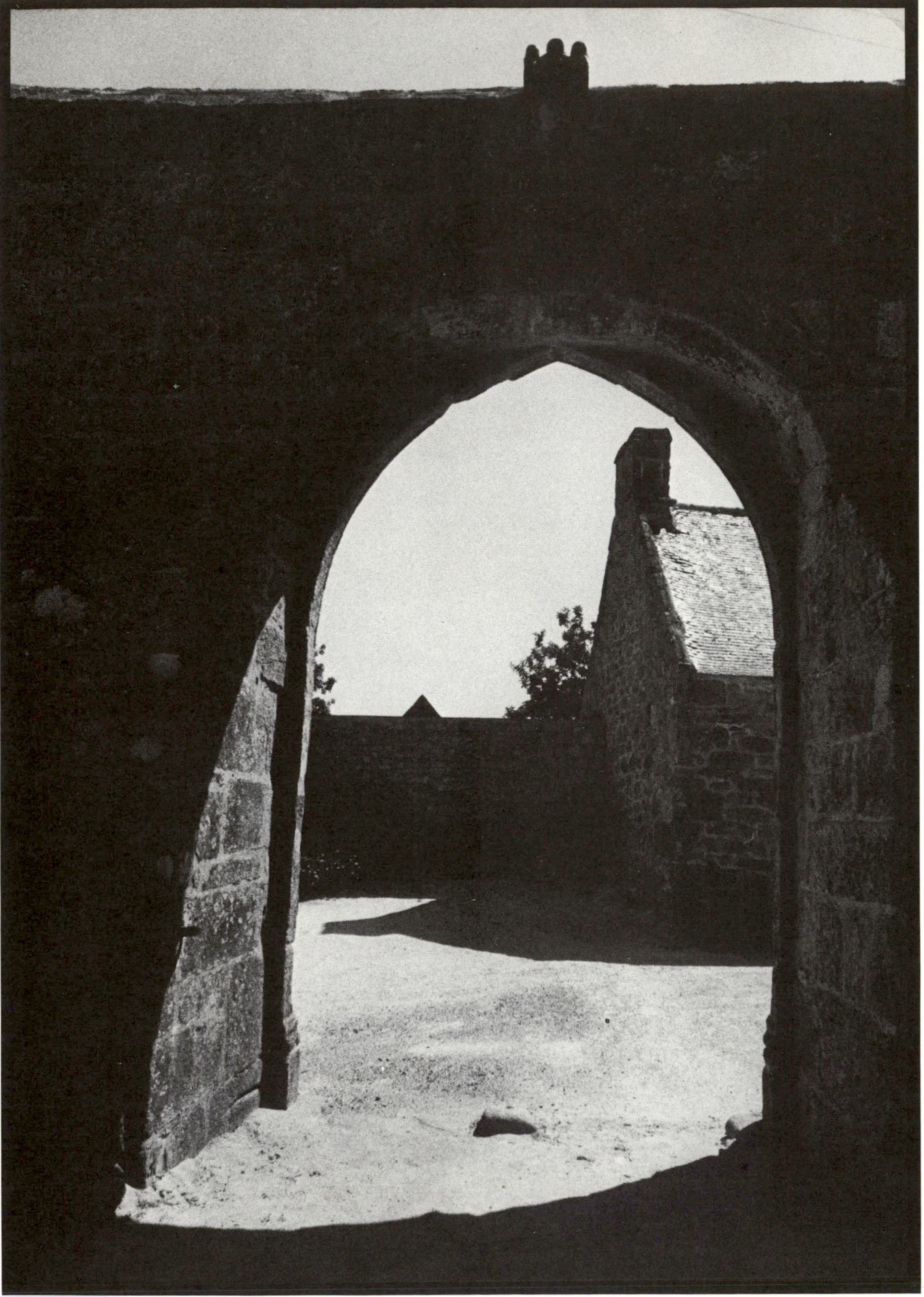

2: THE PINHOLE CAMERA

The role played by the various components of the camera, and their influence on the picture, may best be discovered by trying to manage without them. For instance, it is possible to dispense with every part of a modern camera and yet produce photographs. Not only that, it is even possible to make pictures in that way which can be produced by no other method.

The pinhole camera, the very simplest of all types of photographic apparatus, is able to encompass a viewing angle of about 120° with a distortion-free image, and its depth of field extends from the near foreground to infinity. On the other hand, unfortunately, it is inevitable that pictures taken with a pinhole camera cannot be as sharp as those produced by a normal camera, and that accordingly they cannot be enlarged.

By taking a closer look at this subject, certain basic items of knowledge about the photographic image will emerge, which will prove useful as a basis for further investigations into phototechnique.

Let us start, then, with a question. How does the image occur in the pinhole camera?

At any given time, only a very narrow ray of the light reflected from each part of a subject can pass through the aperture. If this ray is accepted on a 'screen' (the negative film), it creates a circular image of the subject. By reference to *Fig 4a*, it is easy to appreciate that the representation of the subject becomes sharper as the aperture becomes smaller. (For scientific reasons which are too complicated to explain in detail here, an extreme limitation of the aperture would cause the sharpness to decrease again.)

Thus when a ray of light is reflected from every part of the subject through the aperture of the pinhole camera, the picture of the object on the 'screen' (the negative film) consists of a circular image representing all the individual parts of the subject (*Fig 4b*). The size of the image is altered also if, while the focal length remains constant, the subject distance (the distance between subject and aperture) is changed (*Fig 6*).

To construct a pinhole camera you require a light-tight box of convenient size, for example, a large cigar box or a shoe box. (If neither of these is to hand, it is possible to construct a box out of black cardboard.) The size of the box naturally controls the size of the negative format to be used. Bearing in mind the fact that it is impossible to make enlargements, 12 × 9 cm (5 × 4 in) is recommended as a minimum format. Ideally, however, it is best to use a format of 24 × 18 cm (10 × 8 in), with a focal length of about 12 cm (5 in). Film of this size may simply be ordered from a main photographic dealer, although even in monochrome it is expensive. The back of the box must be removable, as the film is attached to it. In the precise centre of the front side, cut a hole (between 2 × 2 cm (1 × 1 in) and 3 × 3 cm (1½ × 1½ in)), in which the aperture is to be situated.

The aperture should be made in a piece of household aluminium foil. The best way to accomplish this is by placing a suitable, large piece of foil on as hard a base as possible and firmly pushing a pin against the foil. Then rotate the foil slightly, in order to ensure that it has been fully penetrated by the pin. The aperture should be fixed with black adhesive tape over the hole in the front of the box in such a way that light can enter the box only through the aperture.

Finally, you require another piece of black cardboard, with which to cover the aperture when desired. This piece of cardboard can be secured with a length of adhesive tape as a hinge on the front.

After you have painted the pinhole camera inside—and, for a deluxe model, outside too—matt black, you can place a negative inside and search for a subject. (It goes without saying that the negative should be inserted in darkness—attaching it to the back of the box with pieces of adhesive tape—and also the box kept tightly shut until the photograph has been taken!)

The main difficulty of the entire process, without a doubt, is in the determination of exposure time. At any rate, it will be of a very long duration. For *Fig 7* it amounted to about 5 minutes (diameter of aperture 0.3 mm, focal length about 12 cm, ASA 400/

4

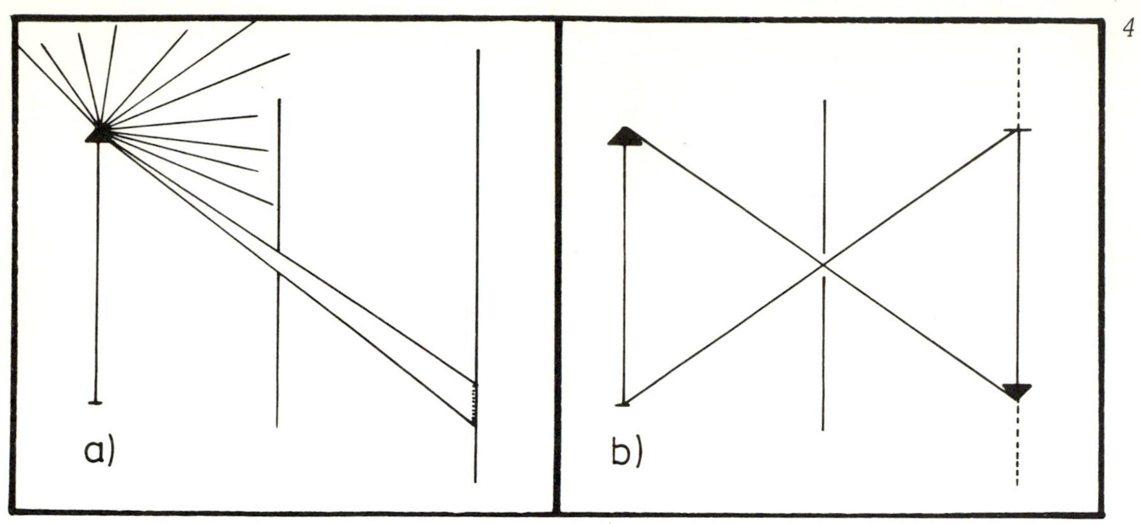

5

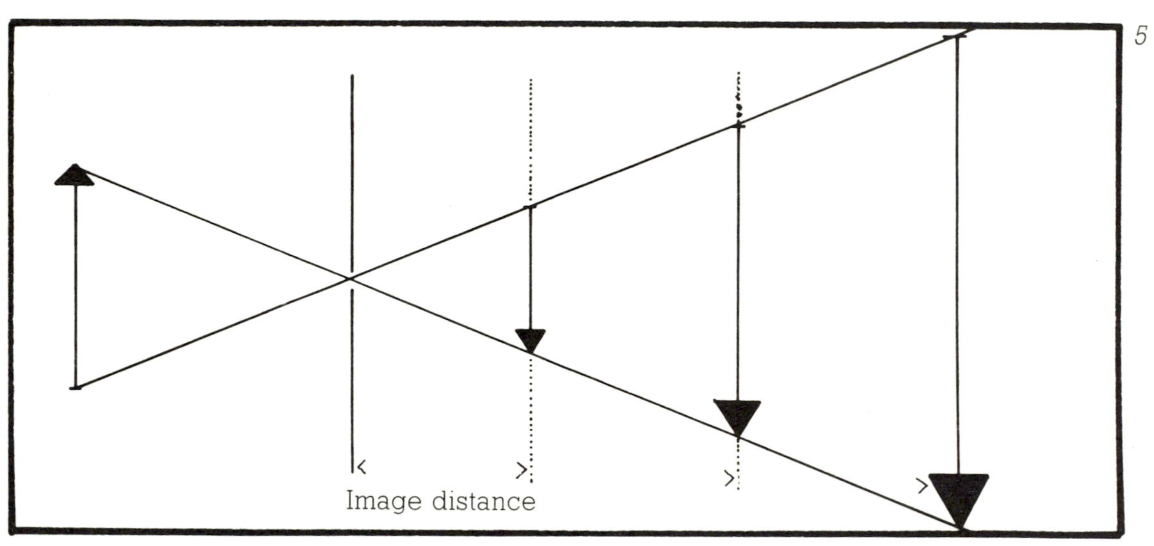

6

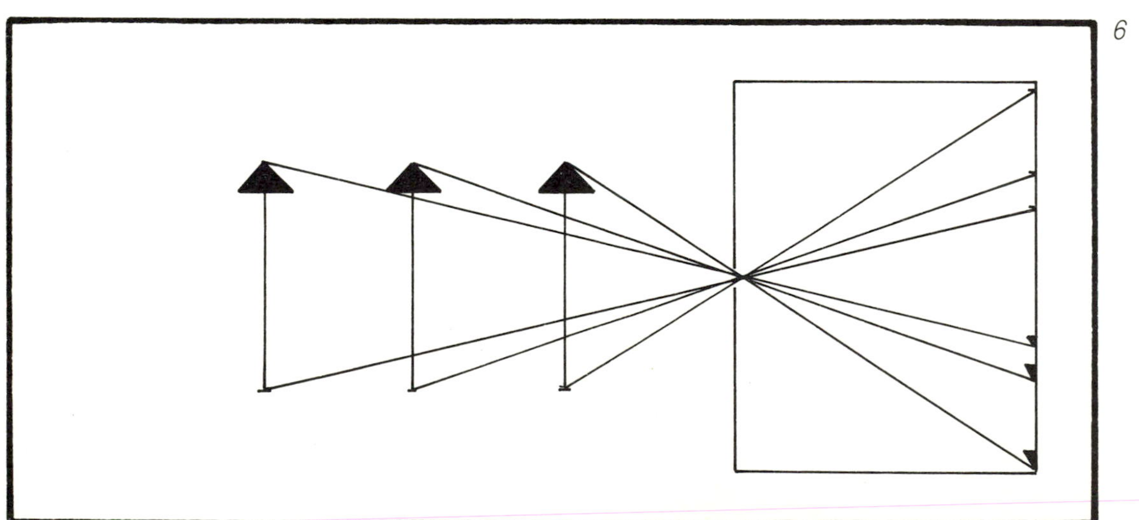

27 DIN film, 24 × 18 cm [10 × 8 in]).

If you wish to use your pinhole camera frequently, take a note of the exposure times for the first test photographs, as shown on a light meter, at a chosen aperture. If, for example, with an exposure time of 5 minutes, you obtain a correctly exposed negative, and if the light meter indicated 1/30 sec at an aperture of *f*8, then for another photograph, if the light meter indicated 1/60 sec at aperture *f*8, the exposure time would be halved to 2½ minutes.

By preparing a table on which the respective halving and doubling of exposure time is entered, derived from the values obtained in test lighting conditions, experimentation with the pinhole camera is greatly simplified. This should then become a pleasurable activity rather than a mathematical labour.

7

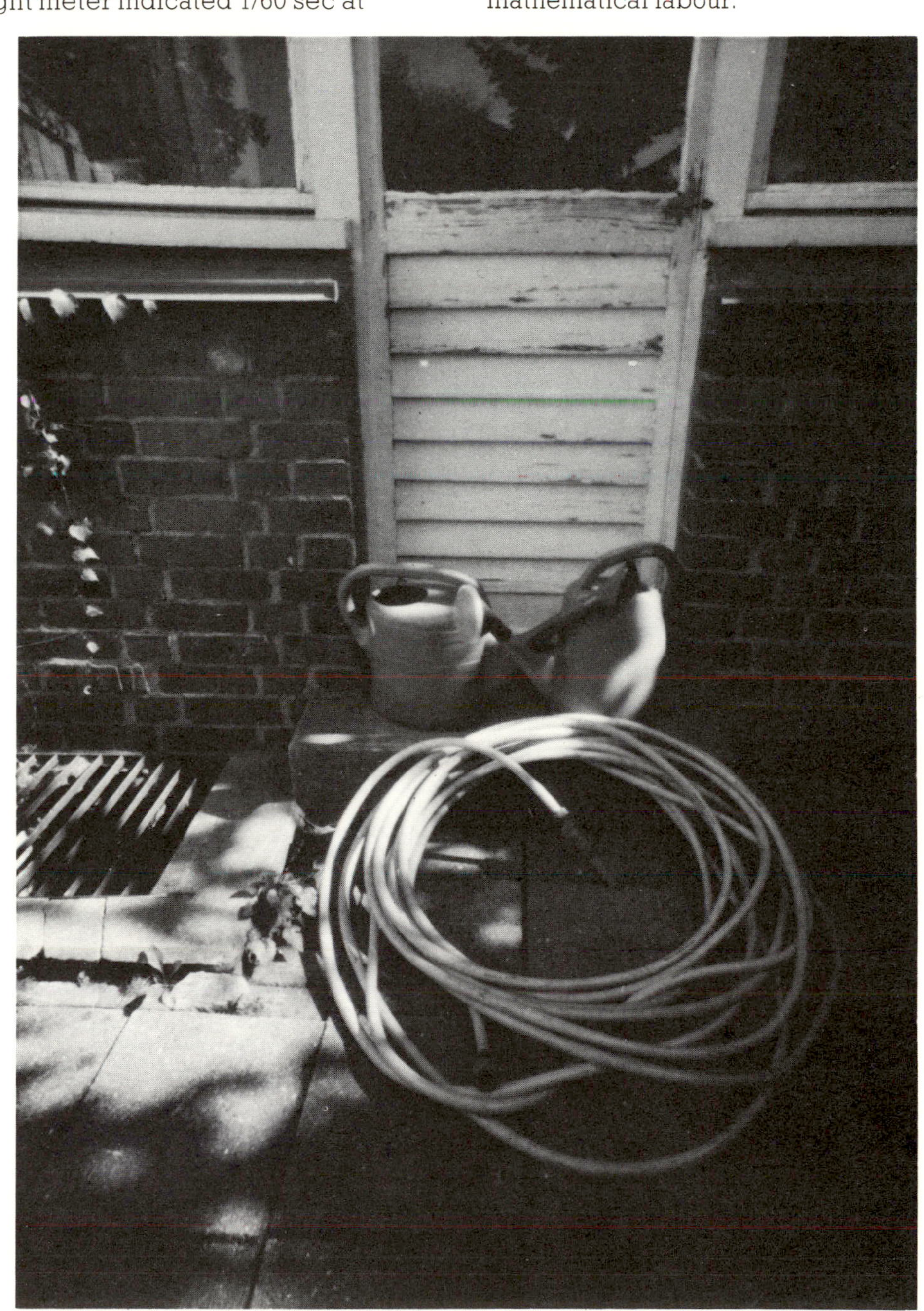

3: PHOTOGRAPHY WITH CONVEX LENSES

As mentioned in the previous chapter, the most serious disadvantage of photography with the pinhole camera is the remarkably long exposure time which is called for. These long periods of time are necessary because of all the light reflected by part of a subject, only a small amount passes through the aperture and can hence be used for the picture. This problem cannot be solved simply by an increase in the diameter of the aperture, which would naturally allow more light to pass through, as this impairs the sharpness of the image. Fortunately, however, there is another way to produce an optical image which avoids this dilemma, namely the formation of an image with a convex lens.

A simplified explanation of how convex lenses work is to say that all the rays of light from one point in a subject which pass through a lens are then brought together again into one point. A comparison of the schematic diagram (*Fig 8*) with the diagram referring to the image in the pinhole camera (*Fig 4*) demonstrates that with this type of image-forming, very much more light is available than with the pinhole camera. In fact, more and more light passes through according to the amount of increase in the diameter of the lens. However, this advantage brings with it a restriction which the pinhole camera does not have.

With the pinhole camera, the image could be made to appear on a screen set at any desired position beyond the aperture (*Fig 5*), and also any alteration in subject distance affected only the size of the image—nothing else. This freedom no longer exists with image-formation using a convex lens. With such a lens there is an exact relationship between subject distance and image size; that is to say, if a subject is placed at a certain distance in front of the lens, a sharp representation of the subject behind the lens will exist only in one plane (*Fig 9*). The consequences of this are significant for the technique of photography, and these can be simply explained.

Generally, because several objects are portrayed in a photograph at the same time which are, inevitably, at various distances from the camera, it should theoretically be possible to reproduce sharply only one of these. In practice, however, this is not so serious as might appear. In the chapter about composition and depth of field, this matter is examined more closely.

With regard to formation of an image with a convex lens, there are some other characteristics—apart from limited depth of field—which are of particular importance at this stage.

As every owner of photographic equipment is well aware, the lens of a camera is not only one of the most important items, but also one of the most expensive. This is to some extent a consequence of the fact that generally the lens consists of a set of differently constructed elements made from various kinds of glass. With these complicated and intricately computed juxtapositions, the manufacturer has tried as far as possible to correct flaws in the capacity of the convex lens to form images. Image-forming with a convex lens does not function nearly so efficiently as might appear from our initial simplified explanation.

The aberrations which occur with the use of a simple convex lens are so significant, in fact, that they render it inadequate for normal photographic purposes. On the other hand they can be used to produce quite unusual effects, which can be deliberately employed in image creation.

It often occurs that, for the achievement of such effects, the performance of costly and optically corrected lenses is 'impaired', by means of special (and by no means inexpensive) accessories. The simple and cheap method, however, in many cases would be to remove the camera lens altogether, and take photographs using a convex lens and various-shaped pieces of glass. In principle, this works quite simply. You require only a single-lens reflex camera, a bellows attachment to fit it, and a simple convex lens. Any mirror reflex camera would be suitable. If integral exposure measurement is available, tedious calculation of exposure times is avoided.

Of course, not every convex lens is suitable for photographic purposes. There is

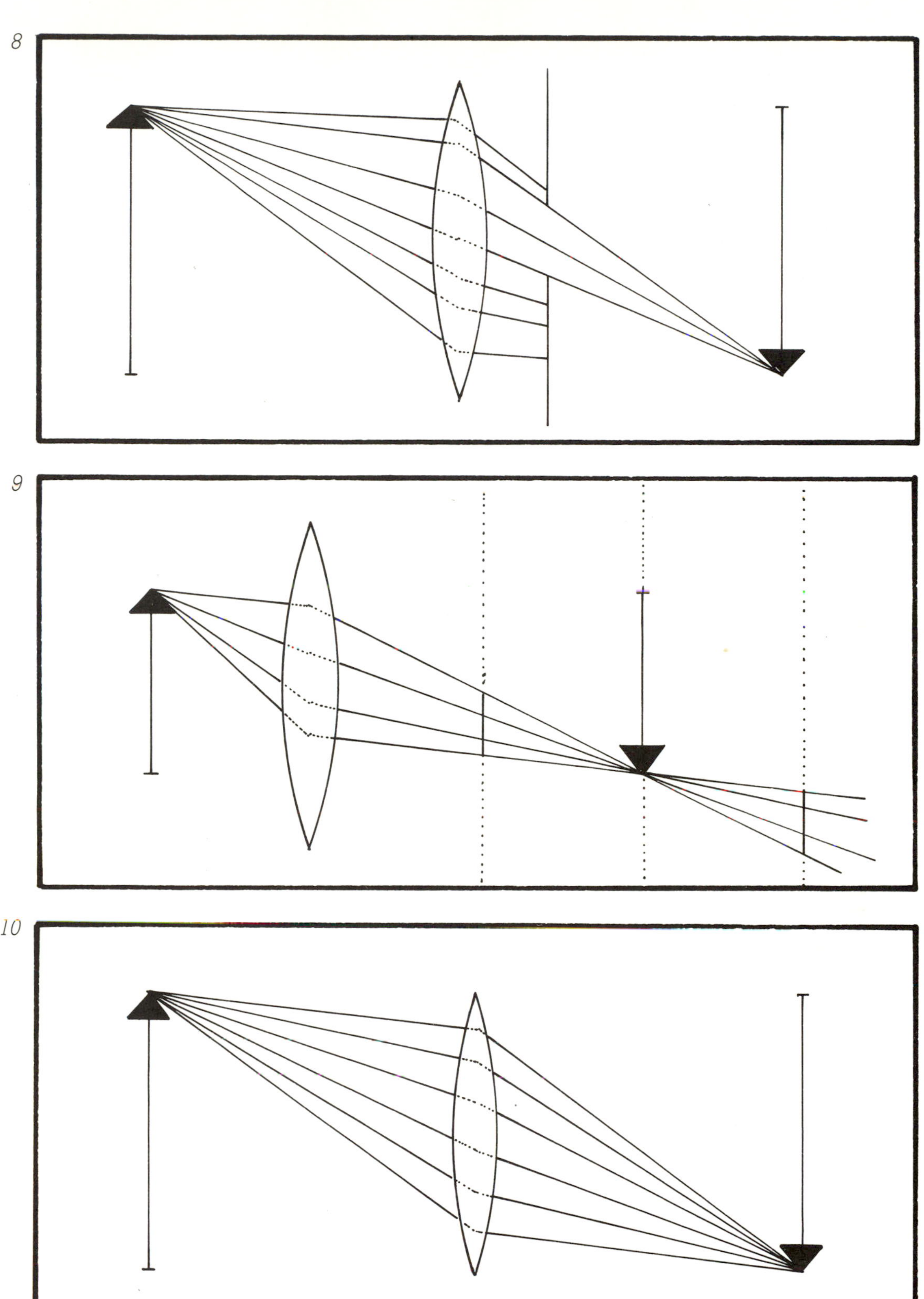
8
9
10

11

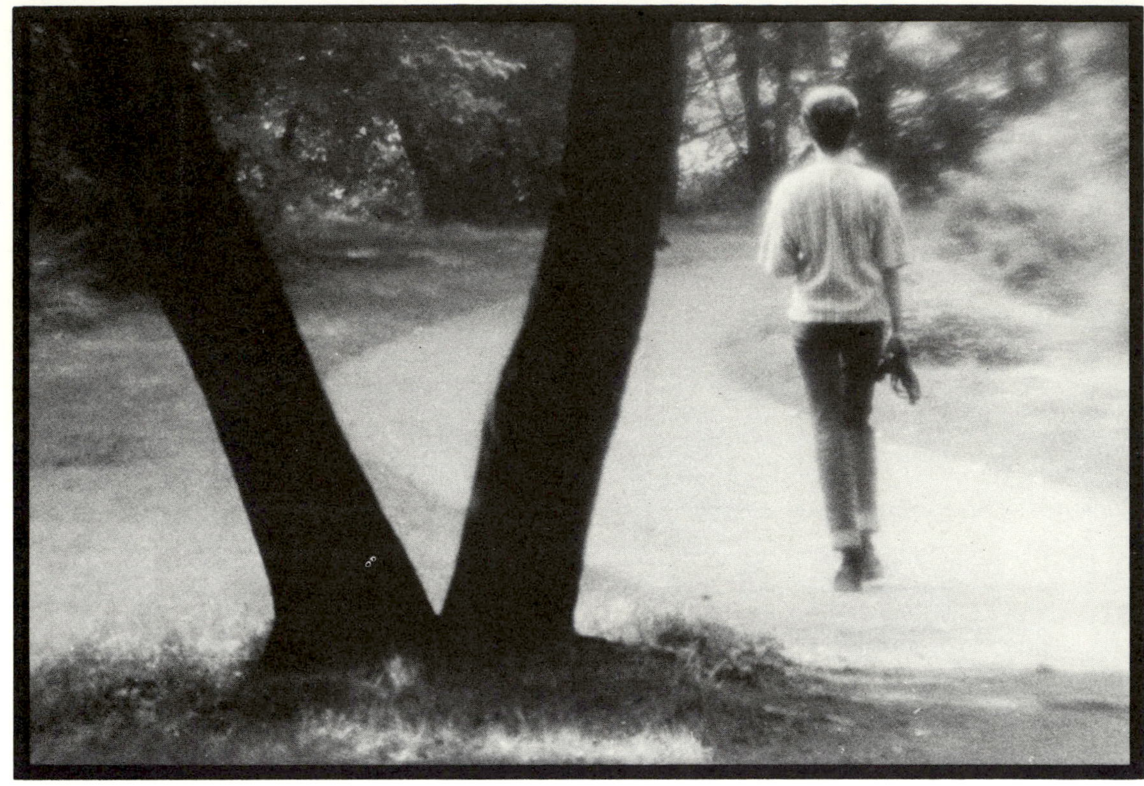

a special relationship, dependent on focal length, between subject distance and image size, and this must be taken into consideration in order to get any picture at all on the film. However, in practice this causes no problems, as many spectacle lenses and reading glasses have focal lengths which are appropriate for photography.

How then can a practicable photographic outfit be assembled for use with a convex lens?

First of all fit the bellows attachment to the camera, and determine the minimum and maximum length of this combination. You can check this simply by means of a ruler (measuring from the film plane symbol on the camera body as far as the front surface of the bellows lens unit). Find the value first with the bellows completely closed and then fully opened.

The focal length of the lens must be less than the maximum extension of the bellows unit, otherwise it will not be possible to render any subjects sharp and there is, of course, no reserve extension for those at close range. If, on the other hand, the focal length of this lens were shorter than the minimum effective bellows extension it may only be possible to use this arrangement for very close-up subjects.

Now ascertain the focal length of the lens. For this purpose, hold the lens in the sunshine above a piece of paper. The distance between lens and paper when the image of the sun is reduced practically to a point is the focal length. If this lies within the extension values you have calculated, then you can use the lens for your experiments. If on the other hand this is larger or smaller, look for another lens.

Of course, the matter could turn out to be much simpler. When I first wanted to experiment with 'spectacle photographs', I just fitted the automatic bellows attachment to the camera, then removed the lens from a reading glass and fixed it to the lens unit of the bellows attachment. Lo and behold, it functioned impeccably, with the automatic system even taking over all exposure worries. (All the photographs in this chapter were produced using the automatic exposure system without manual override.)

However, some cameras do not

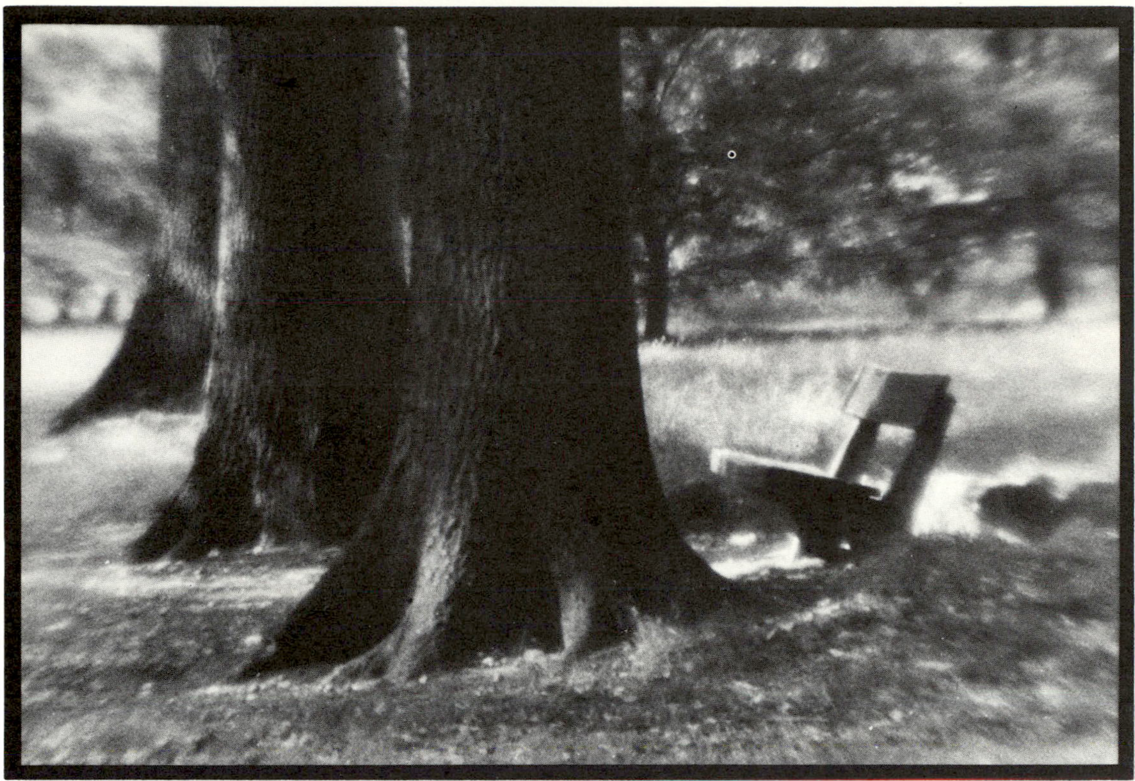

12

incorporate integral exposure measurement, and there are other situations in which it is necessary to determine exposure times separately. To do this measure the light value (the relevant aperture) of your apparatus: the focal length divided by the diameter of the opening = appropriate aperture (*f* value or stop).

The focal length of the lens can be determined in the following way. Set the apparatus at infinity—that is, at a subject which is at least 50 m away. Then measure the length of the extension (from the centre of the lens to the film plane). Now divide this value (ie the focal length) in mm by the front diameter of the bellows attachment, likewise in mm. If this calculation is accurate, the resulting figure indicates the light value of the particular optical system. This is also the aperture figure under which the exposure time may be read as required from the light meter.

(*Note*: If the lens you are using should be larger or smaller than the opening of the bellows attachment, calculate only on a basis of the opening actually being used.)

Let us now turn to the photographs which may be produced by means of this kind of apparatus, as they should prove to be very interesting.

In the monochrome photographs (*Figs 11* and *12*), the pictures are fairly sharp: the images are sharpest in the centre and the sharpness falls away at the edges. (If you intend to compare this with the sharpness of the pinhole camera photograph (*Fig 7*), please note that I used there a contact print from a negative measuring 24 × 18 cm, reduced in size for the book, while *Figs 11* and *12* are enlargements from miniature negatives measuring 36 × 24 mm.) In addition, all outlines—particularly in contrasty parts of the pictures—have minor light-fringing. In the colour photographs (*Figs 13* and *14*), these light fringes can be detected to some extent as rainbow hues, though only with a big enlargement, as for example in slide projection. It is also noticeable that the colour pictures exhibit an appreciably greater proportion of blue (a blue cast) than would be shown in normal photographs taken for comparison in the same circumstances.

The general unsharpness arises from the

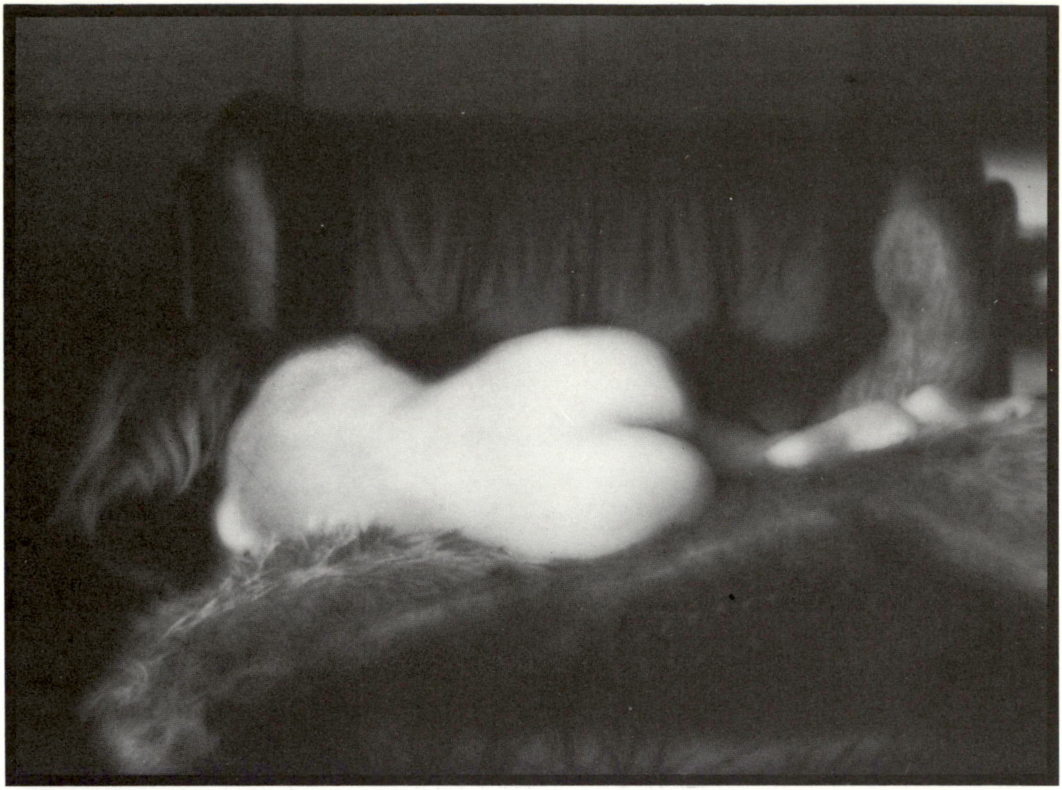

13

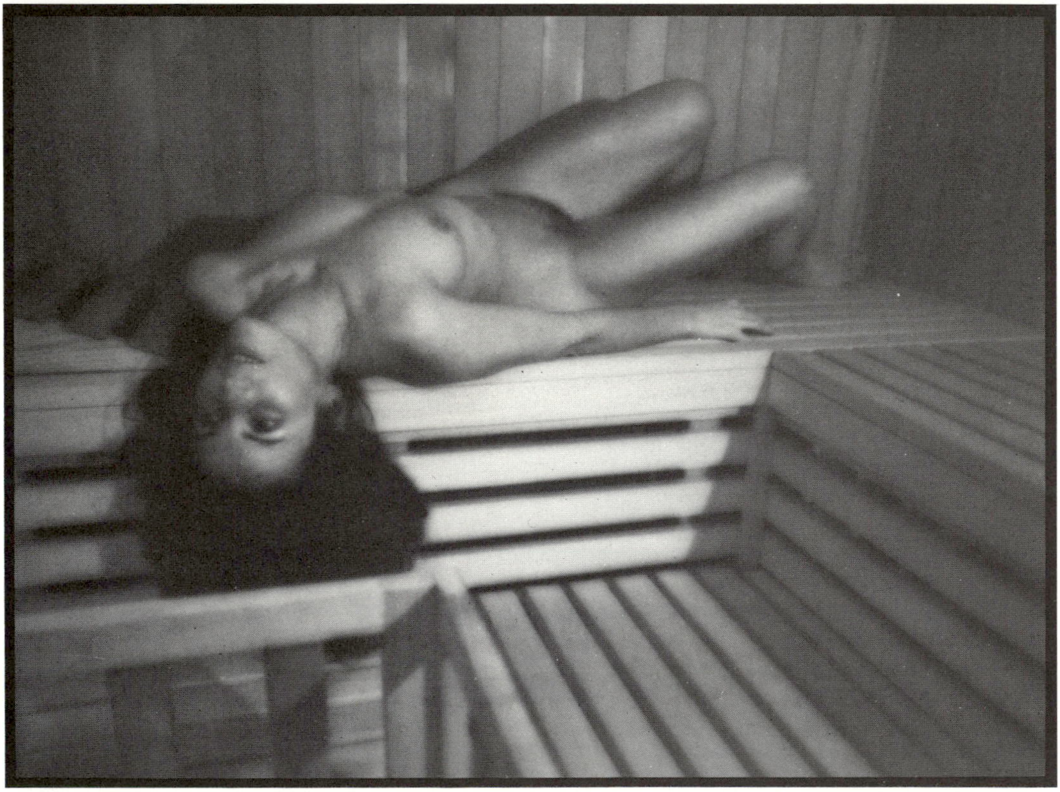

14

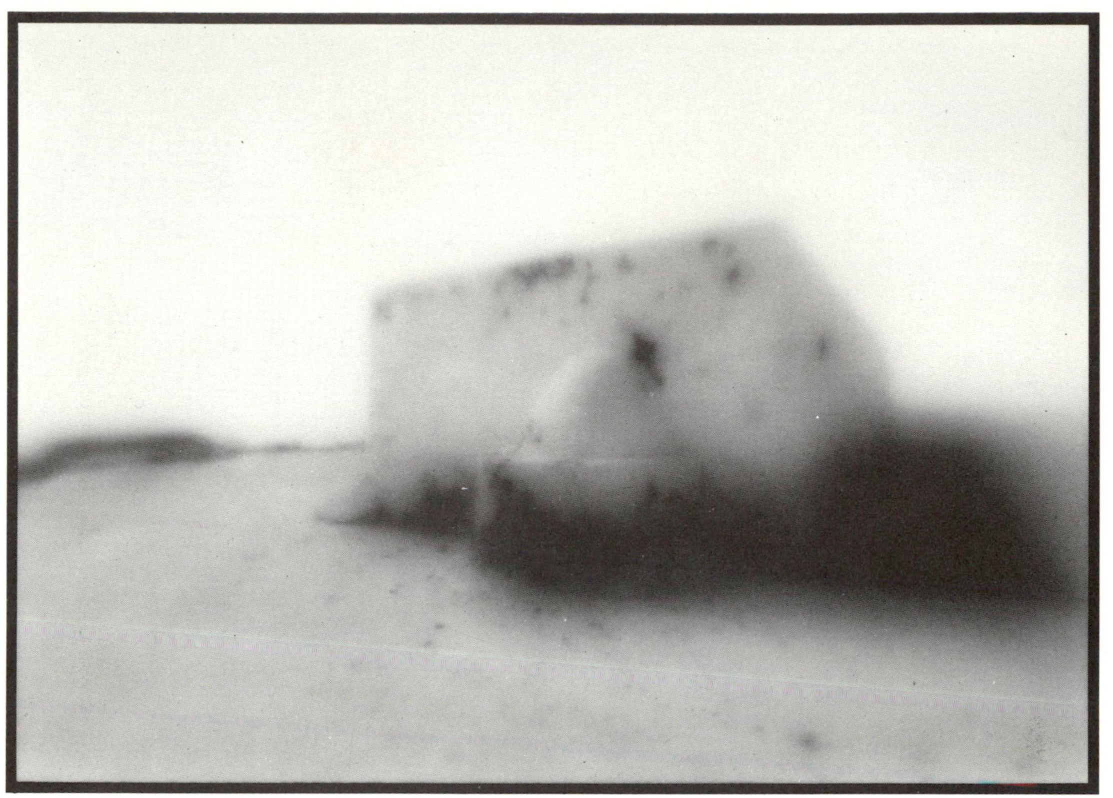
15

fact that light of different wavelengths is broken up to varying extents. The focal point for red light, for instance, lies further from the lens than that for blue. Since the light emanating from the subjects is generally composed of different colours, the picture is formed not on one plane but on several, and thus the picture is unsharp. The occasional multicoloured fringing may be traced to this, and to another lens fault, spherical aberration. The convex lens is also subject to further optical failings (coma, astigmatism and image field curvature), which are responsible among other things for the pronounced falling away of sharpness towards the picture edges.

The blue cast in the pictures stems from another origin. Lenses with many elements absorb appreciably more short wavelength (blue) light than lenses with a few elements only. Pictures produced by means of a simple convex lens, therefore, all incorporate a noticeably greater amount of blue than is seen in normal photographs.

From the standpoint of the lens designer, the emergence of all these image deficiencies must naturally be very much regretted, as the high cost of lens construction is attributed exclusively to attending to these flaws and guaranteeing as far as possible a faultless picture. From the point of view of image construction, however, the matter appears somewhat differently, since these very aberrations can be utilised for specific purposes. To this it must be added that the photographer is not necessarily limited by the characteristics of the convex lens. To some extent it is possible to create effects at will. For this purpose only an iris is required—or several of these, if you wish to experiment more fully. You can easily construct this for yourself.

Cut out of black, lightproof cardboard, a disc of such a size that it can be fixed between lens and bellows. To attach the disc, simply wedge it between lens and bellows.

As accurately as possible, make a round hole in the centre of the cardboard. For only one aperture, make the diameter about half that of the lens.

When you set up this combination of convex lens and iris in front of your camera, it is apparent that the light intensity has been

16

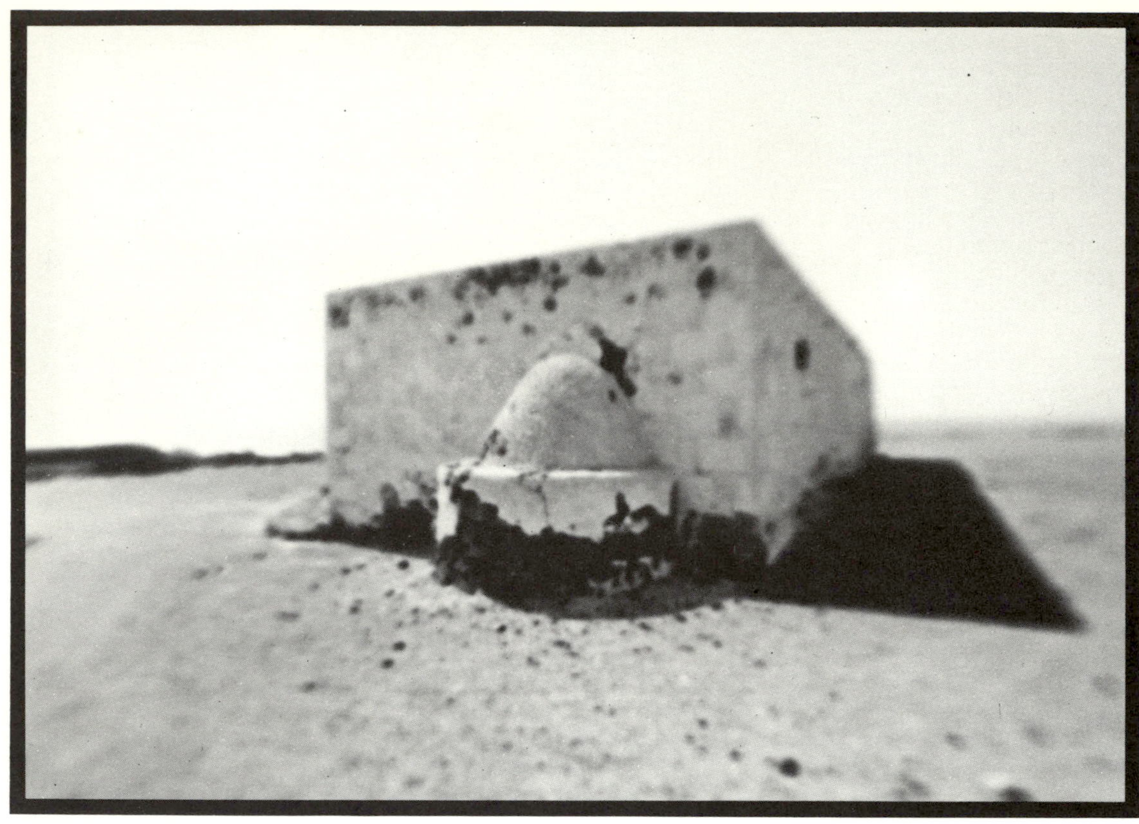

reduced. This must be the case, because if with the same focal length the diameter of the opening is reduced, a correspondingly smaller amount of light falls on the film. At the same time it should be noted that those effects which are created by image aberrations are not so much in evidence. (The only effect which remains unaltered is the blue cast of the pictures, as this is dependent solely on the properties of the glass being used.)

Fig 15 shows a subject photographed with a convex lens. *Fig 16* shows the identical subject, photographed with the same lens, but with the use of an iris of only half the lens diameter. This reduction in image aberration may be simply explained. Through an approximately circular aperture positioned in the centre of the lens, the rays of light at the edges have been obstructed (*Fig 10*)—and towards the centre the lens aberrations become less and less.

With this apparatus (iris and lens) you may now experiment to your heart's content. If you are disinclined to go to this trouble, you can make things easier if you happen to have access to a darkroom. The enlarger lens can naturally be exchanged for convex lens and diaphragm, so that comparable effects can be achieved from normal negatives.

Whether all this represents more than a technical toy, whether the creation of many effects is enhanced by such impairments or alterations, or whether indeed certain effects can be obtained only by the use of such procedures—these are matters for yourself and your 'photographic conscience'. Each technical facility which has been devised makes possible, when used intelligently, a statement and structure which could not be achieved in any other way.

4: INTERCHANGEABLE LENSES AND THEIR EFFECTS

Focal length

Cameras are nowadays equipped not with pinhole apertures or with simple convex glasses, but instead with 'correct' lenses. When you buy a camera, you generally acquire with it a so-called 'standard lens'. At least in the case of the better quality single-lens reflex cameras, this lens may be exchanged for lenses of various focal lengths. However, for the moment let us consider the standard lens.

'The standard lens differs from all other photographic lenses in that it yields a picture which appears to us in Europe as normal, or as "acceptable to the eye", as far as is permitted by the limitations and potentialities of photographic technique.' This sentence is from a previous book written by the author in collaboration with Harald Mante. It is suggested in that book that this statement conceals so many traps and loopholes that it is advisable to turn immediately to practical applications. However, although it is not the intention of this book to explain the physiology of perception, it is useful to give some background information, which is helpful in understanding how special photographic visual effects occur.

The human eye is frequently and aptly compared with the camera. This is justified by the fact that they have some properties in common. Each has a lens, a diaphragm (iris) and a surface on which an image is projected. Here the similarities end, and it cannot be stressed too much that the comparison should not be carried too far, as it produces only false and misleading conceptions about photography.

A camera yields photographic reproductions, if necessary automatically and without human involvement. But the eye alone is unable to 'see' – the brain does the seeing, with the use of the eye. This means that seeing is a process which does not depend exclusively on the eye, but is a consequence of activities of the nervous system, which are highly complicated and scientifically not yet fully explained. It has absolutely nothing to do with photographic creation.

Assembled here is a list of the most important and relevant differences between the photographic process and human sight:

1 The photographic process yields a flat picture. The human brain interprets the environment as a three-dimensional experience.
2 The spatial effect of the photographic image may be altered at will. Human awareness of space is a consequence of binocular vision and of movement; perspective cannot be altered.
3 The distribution of sharp and out-of-focus elements of a photograph are determined at the moment of exposure and cannot be changed. Human perception is a result of a gradual investigation of the field of vision involving alteration of focus, at times influenced by our interest and by the perceived situation.
4 The photographic image may be regarded as 'total', in that everything which is capable of being reproduced in a picture, with the technical means at our disposal and under the prevailing conditions, is in fact reproduced. Human perception, on the other hand, is selective. It operates in a subjective manner, and it cannot be asserted that we comprehend everything that we 'see'.

The conclusion can be drawn that the means which are required and can be employed for the creation of a photographic image are different from the processes which play a role in human perception. Hence the photographic effects produced through the planned use of these procedures may be altered at will within wide limits. To put it briefly, the photographic image is never a representation of 'reality' but only our interpretation of it. If this seems difficult to accept, look at *Figs 17*, *18* and *19*. Which is the genuine representation of what really exists?

A most important facility, that of being able to create a desired spatial effect, is provided by the use of alternative lenses.

Many amateur photographers unfortunately use interchangeable lenses

17 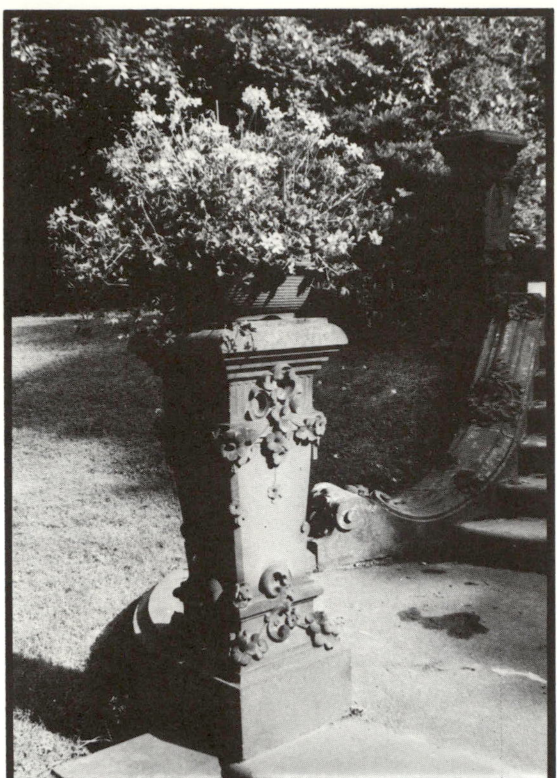

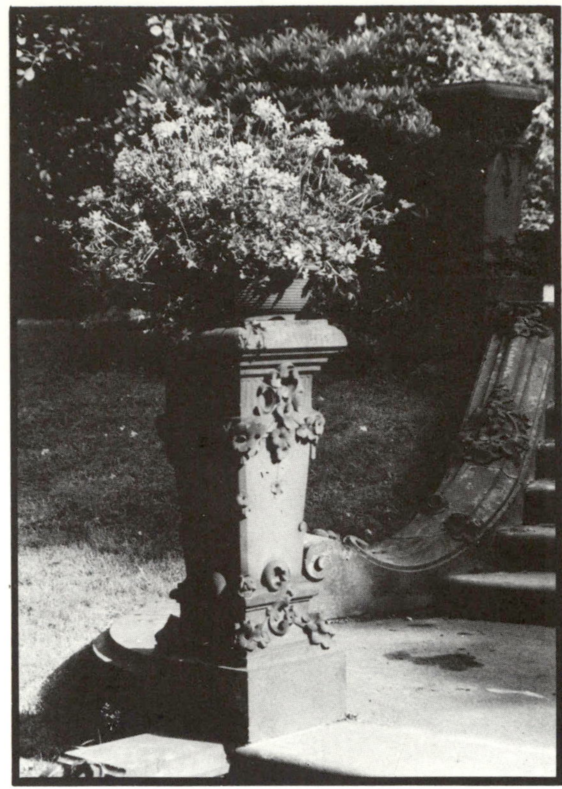 18

19 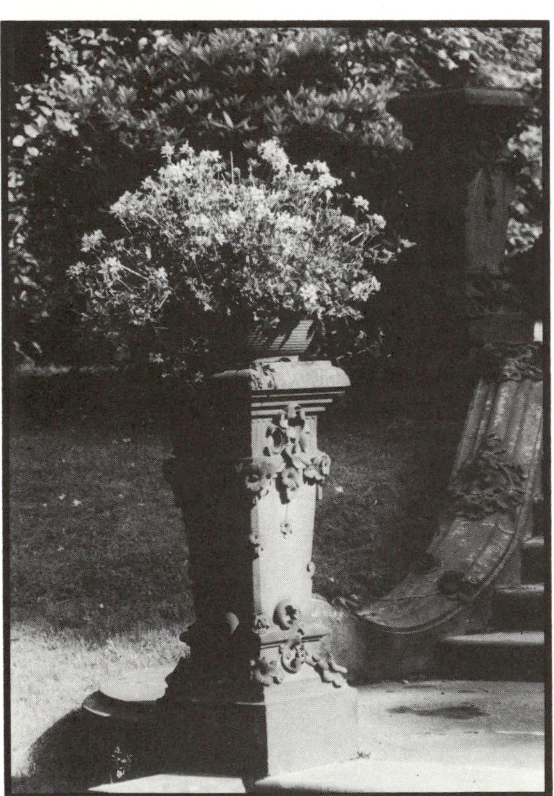

only for very limited purposes. Lenses with a longer focus are employed merely to bring distant objects nearer, while wide-angle lenses are used simply where space is limited. It is true that such uses are extremely important in reportage, scientific and documentary photography. For example, without the telephoto lens much sporting and animal photography would not be possible, and without it many candid photographs of distant film stars would have been missed. In creative photography, however, alternative lenses have an additional purpose to those mentioned above. This is because a certain focal length always produces a quite distinct and (generally) deliberate effect. This applies, for instance, to perspective in a picture. It is admittedly true that geometrical perspective in a photograph of a subject is always the same from a particular viewpoint, no matter what focal length is used (with the exception of a fisheye lens). However, it is equally true that the perspective *effect* when different lenses are used is positively altered.

Examination of *Figs 20–23* furnishes proof

20

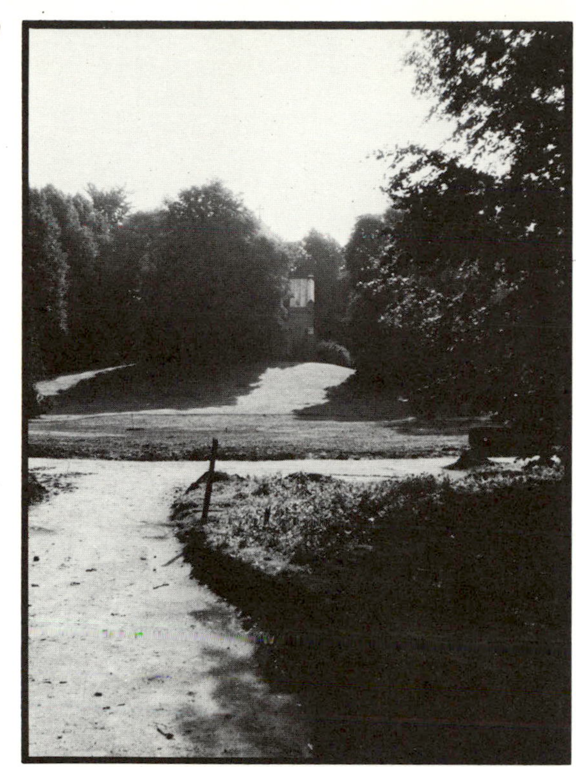

21

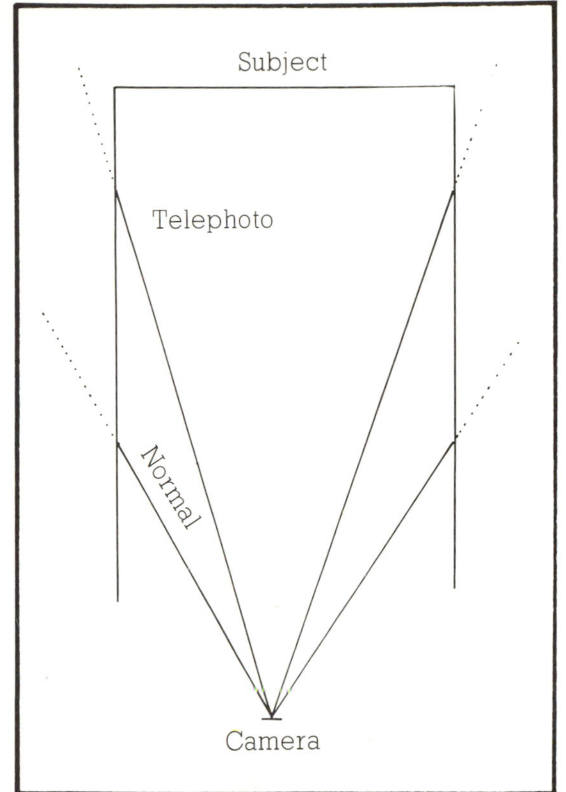

22

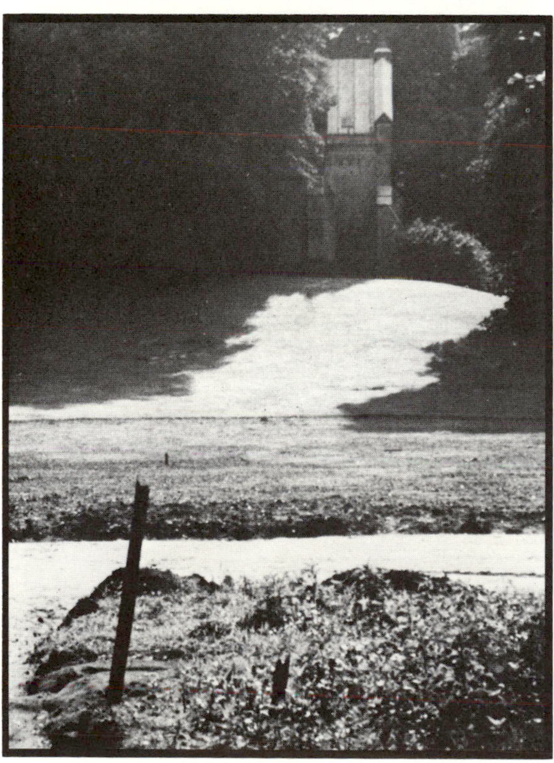

23

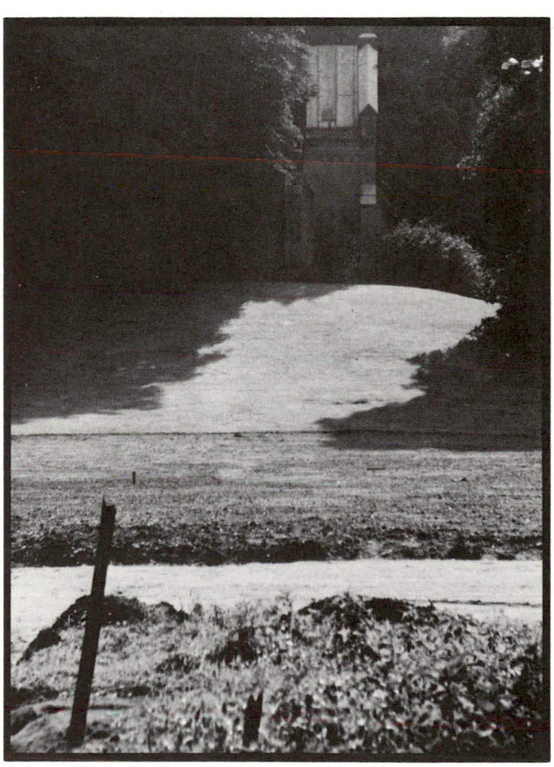

that in photography geometrical perspective with different focal lengths indeed remains unaltered. *Fig 20* shows a subject photographed with a standard lens (*f*1.4/50 mm). *Fig 22* shows the same subject, but this time photographed with an *f*2.5/100 mm lens from the same viewpoint. The diagram (*Fig 21*) demonstrates how the two photographic situations correspond. Final proof is to be seen in *Fig 23*. This is a sectional enlargement from the negative used for *Fig 20*, which was produced by use of a standard lens. The two coincide in perspective construction in all respects. As a consequence, *Figs 20* and *22* should coincide in perspective construction—and yet they actually differ.

The cause of this differing effect can be clarified by an example. Imagine standing on a straight road, at the edge of which at regular distances there are telegraph poles of equal height. The nearest telegraph pole appears to be much higher than the second, and so on until those far in the distance seem to be of practically identical height. This also applies to the distance separating the poles from each other.

If you took a sheet of cardboard with a rectangular shape cut in the centre, and held it in front of you with outstretched arm, only the distant poles could be seen through the cardboard, that is those which appear to be of an almost equal height. The identical effect is achieved by looking through a telephoto lens: in both cases the 'viewing angle' is narrowed (*Fig 21*). There is, however, a major difference. The negative (or transparency) obtained by using a telephoto lens is of exactly the same size as that produced by the standard lens, but with the retention of the distant effect.

Completely different results are obtained by changing not only the focal length but also the viewpoint. *Figs 17*, *18* and *19* illustrate this point. The first photograph was taken with a wide-angle lens (*f*2.8/24 mm), the second with a standard lens (*f*1.4/50 mm), and the third with a telephoto lens (*f*2.5/100 mm). The viewpoint in each was chosen in such a way that the size of the gate in the foreground of each photograph is about the same. It is thus clear to see how the proportionate sizes in foreground and background are radically altered by changes in focal length and subject distance. This means simply that it is possible to alter at will the spatial effect of a subject quite radically, just by changing focal length and viewpoint. The possibilities available in altering the spatial effect of a subject are summarised below:

1 To retain the relative proportions in the picture, but to alter the extent of its borders, change the focal length of the lens but keep the distance between subject and camera the same.
2 To alter the relative proportions in the picture, but to retain the extent of its borders, change proportionally both focal length and distance. For example, if the focal length is doubled the subject distance must be doubled, and so on.

It is certainly not a matter of indifference whether the subject is taken at closer range or the focal length of the lens is changed. Each procedure gives a different and characteristic effect.

Classification of the effects which tend to appear when using wide-angle and telephoto focal lengths can be made by drawing up a comparison. These effects are not due to the actual lenses but only to the working distance.

1 **Proportionate sizes:**
Wide-angle: The proportionate sizes of subjects at various distances from the camera are clearly differentiated—the nearer a subject is to the camera, the bigger it appears. This is often more apparent when using a wide-angle lens only, because the working distance is in many cases quite short.
Telephoto: The proportionate sizes of subjects at various distances from the camera are scarcely altered at all—individual subjects are represented almost in their actual physical relationship to each other. This is because in many cases the camera is distant from the subject.
2 **Spatial separation:**
Wide-angle: The separation between subjects at various distances from the camera appears to be exaggerated, and the nearer the subjects are to the camera, the stronger the effect is.
Telephoto: At extreme focal lengths there

24

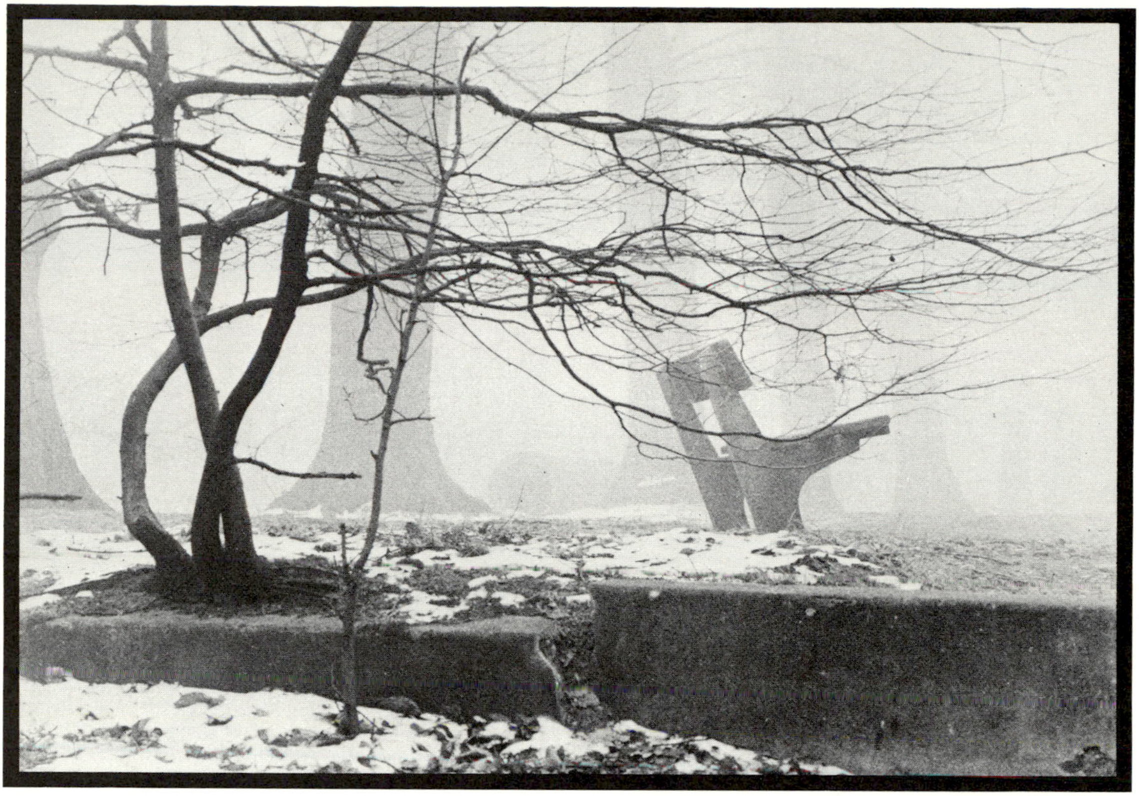

25

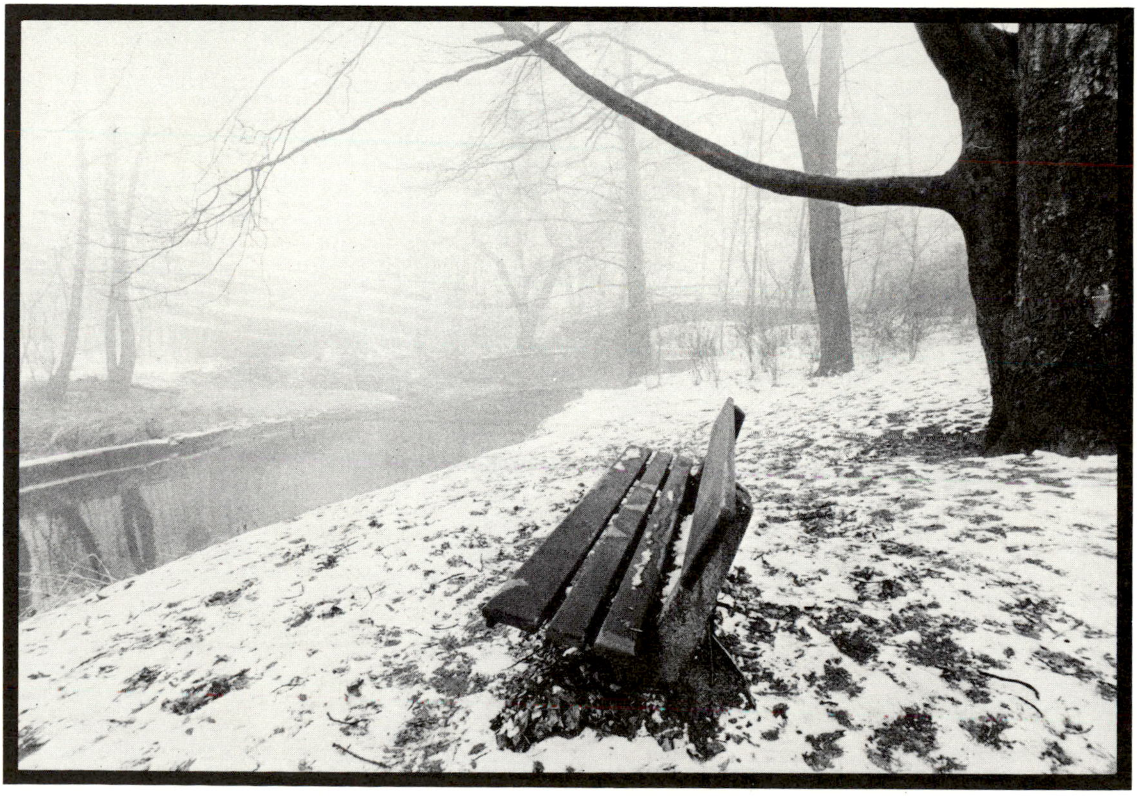

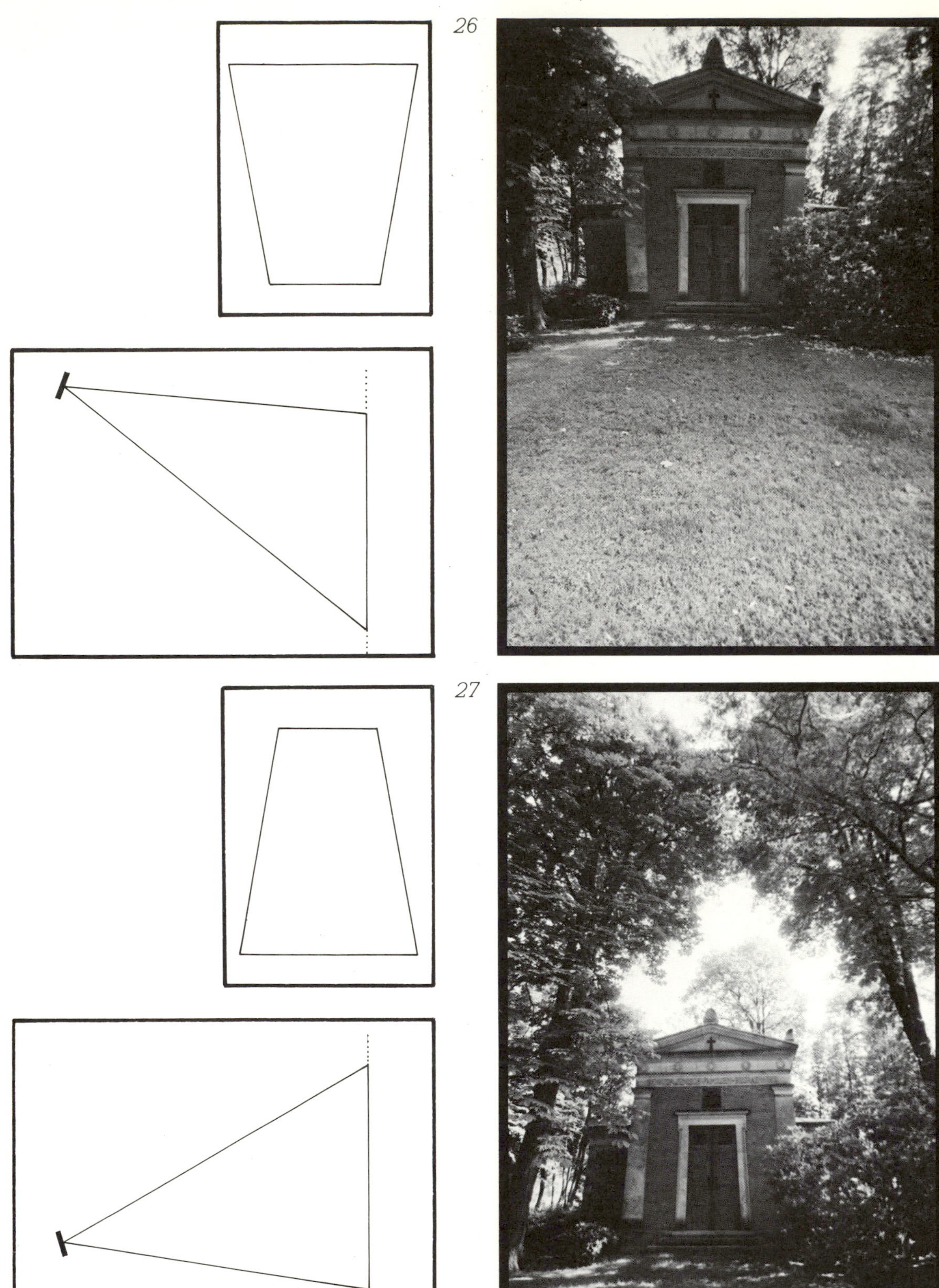
26
27

is no recognisable separation between subjects at various distances from the camera, and in other cases these distances appear to be very small.

3 **Depth of field:**
Wide-angle: At long distances, the depth of field is very great. With an extremely short focal length and small aperture, it may extend from infinity practically to the front lens element.
Telephoto: With a long focal length the depth of field is very limited. With an extreme focal length, even at a long subject distance, it may be reduced to as little as 2 or 3 in.

The spatial effect of a picture depends upon a considerable number of factors, all of which have to be borne in mind in photography. These can be examined more closely, with the aid of photographic examples.

Figs 24 and *25* are extracted from a series taken by the author on the Alster footpath in Hamburg. The first (*Fig 24*) was photographed with a telephoto lens (*f*2.4/100 mm) and the second (*Fig 25*) with a wide-angle lens (*f*4/17 mm). The two photographs are composed of practically the same pictorial elements, and the radically differing effects produced by the two lenses can be seen very clearly.

As the two benches are actually of exactly the same type, the effect of focal length on the proportionate sizes of subjects is particularly clear. In the telephoto picture (*Fig 24*) the nearer and further supports of the bench appear to be of almost equal length, and the bench itself seems to be very short, with the distance between the supports very limited. In contrast, in the wide-angle picture (*Fig 25*) the bench appears to be very long and the horizontal planks more than twice as wide at the front as they are at the rear. Other elements in the picture have the same characteristics—the wide-angle picture is very spacious, while the telephoto picture, with compressed perspective, appears flatter and almost resembles a painting.

The mist, which renders the background of each picture hazy, shows another effect of 'aerial perspective', which in normal weather makes its appearance only in wide landscape photographs (panoramic views). The ubiquitous gloomy and grimy atmosphere in built-up areas produces a dispersion and partial absorption of light, with the result that distant elements of the landscape generally appear vague and indistinct. Since blue light is less strongly affected by this absorption, colour photographs consequently exhibit a 'blue distance'.

In these two pictorial examples (*Figs 24* and *25*) another characteristic may be observed by which telephoto and wide-angle photographs can generally be differentiated from each other. The telephoto lens has a small viewing angle which severely limits choice in the height of viewpoint. If it is impossible to climb to a higher level, slight changes in camera position (up or down) have scarcely any effect. On the other hand, the large viewing angle of the wide-angle lens permits an effective bird's-eye view to be taken from normal eye level (*Fig 25*) and likewise an impressive worm's-eye view from stomach level.

Bird's-eye and worm's-eye views, which both make possible the representation of the full extent of a subject, have a noticeably more spacious effect than the frontal picture generally associated with the telephoto lens. However, if, for this kind of low- or high-angle picture, or for full use of the format, the camera is held not vertically but obliquely upwards or downwards, another effect is produced. This consists of so-called 'converging lines', and these naturally occur particularly strongly with straight-sided architectural subjects.

Normally, when photographing buildings the camera is either held exactly vertically, or directed obliquely upwards so that converging lines appear. However, in the photographic examples (*Figs 26* and *27*) it can be seen that this is not necessarily the case. For both pictures the same subject was photographed from practically the identical viewpoint. In the first instance (*Fig 26*) the camera was merely held at eye level and directed downwards, while in the second case (*Fig 27*) the photograph was taken from ground level with the camera inclined upwards. It can clearly be seen that the lines converge towards the lower and upper margin respectively.

The fact that converging lines can be seen

chiefly in wide-angle photographs leads many people to suppose that this is a unique characteristic of the wide-angle lens. However, this does not apply. Every lens of every possible focal length can produce converging lines, provided that it is not set up vertically. With wide-angle photographs the effect is stronger and this may be readily demonstrated. For example, to photograph a tower to fill the frame, when using a 100 mm lens the camera has to be at a considerable distance from the building, and consequently the camera only needs to be tilted very slightly or not at all. However, to fill the frame with the same tower using a wide-angle lens (eg 24 mm), the camera has to be very much closer and must be inclined correspondingly further upwards. The result is that in wide-angle photographs more extreme convergence appears than in telephoto pictures.

Depending on the desired effect, then, it is possible to minimise or exaggerate converging lines at will, simply by selection of appropriate viewpoint, focal length and inclination of the camera.

The only practical difficulty in the production of an undistorted image is that frequently it is not possible to move far enough away from the subject for a long-focus picture, while with shorter focal lengths the camera has to be tilted in order to include the entire subject in the frame.

A remedy here is supplied by the very interesting 'shift lens'. Adjusting it allows for success in difficult cases. The two drawings (*Fig 28*) give a simple explanation of how the use of this lens obviates converging lines. Since the shift lens is designed principally to rectify distortion in photographs, there is a tendency to overlook the fact that it can also result in the precise opposite, namely deliberate distortion for the sake of achieving a particular visual effect.

The exceptional possibilities of this are instanced in *Fig 29*. Adjustment of this lens has here permitted a much stronger distortion of the subject than would normally have been possible at this focal length. The alteration in the curvature of the image field which can be produced by the use of this lens ensures a further strengthening of the effect, so that the depth of field in this picture is altered to a most unusual extent. The drawing alongside *Fig 29* indicates the inclination of the camera, the alteration of subject position and the change in image-field curvature.

(*Note on image-field curvature:* Normally the region of sharpness runs parallel to the image-field plane. With the shift lens, however, the region of sharpness can be adjusted towards or away from the camera, so that by a simultaneous adjustment of the lens, as in *Fig 29*, the region of sharpness is at an angle to the image-field plane.)

The effect will not necessarily please everyone, and anyhow it should be used only on infrequent occasions; it is simply one of the methods of influencing the representation of situations in a photograph.

There remains only one more subject to be dealt with on the theme of interchangeable lenses at various focal lengths: depth of field as an element in visual creativity. The first task is to define precisely what depth of field really is.

It has already been established that when using a convex lens within a three-dimensional situation, theoretically only one plane can be sharply represented. Although this indeed applies, it is not quite the same as saying that everything else must appear unsharp; for the borderline between sharpness and unsharpness is a vague one. That is to say, objects which are situated within the region of the depth of field still appear sharp.

This may be explained as follows. Theoretically, a point on the plane in focus is also represented photographically as a point. However, because of image aberrations, which even the best and most expensive of lenses cannot eliminate completely, and because of certain dispersion phenomena which appear on the negative or transparency, this ideal situation is not achieved. A point is represented not as a point but always as a small circle. The farther a point emerges outside the actual plane in focus the greater the diameter of its 'circle of confusion'. This image nevertheless appears sharp, because with the naked eye (that is without a magnifying glass) individual features below a certain size cannot be distinguished from each other.

Accordingly, all objects within a zone in front of and behind the plane of sharpness likewise appear sharp. For this there are numerical values. From a normal viewing

A

B

28

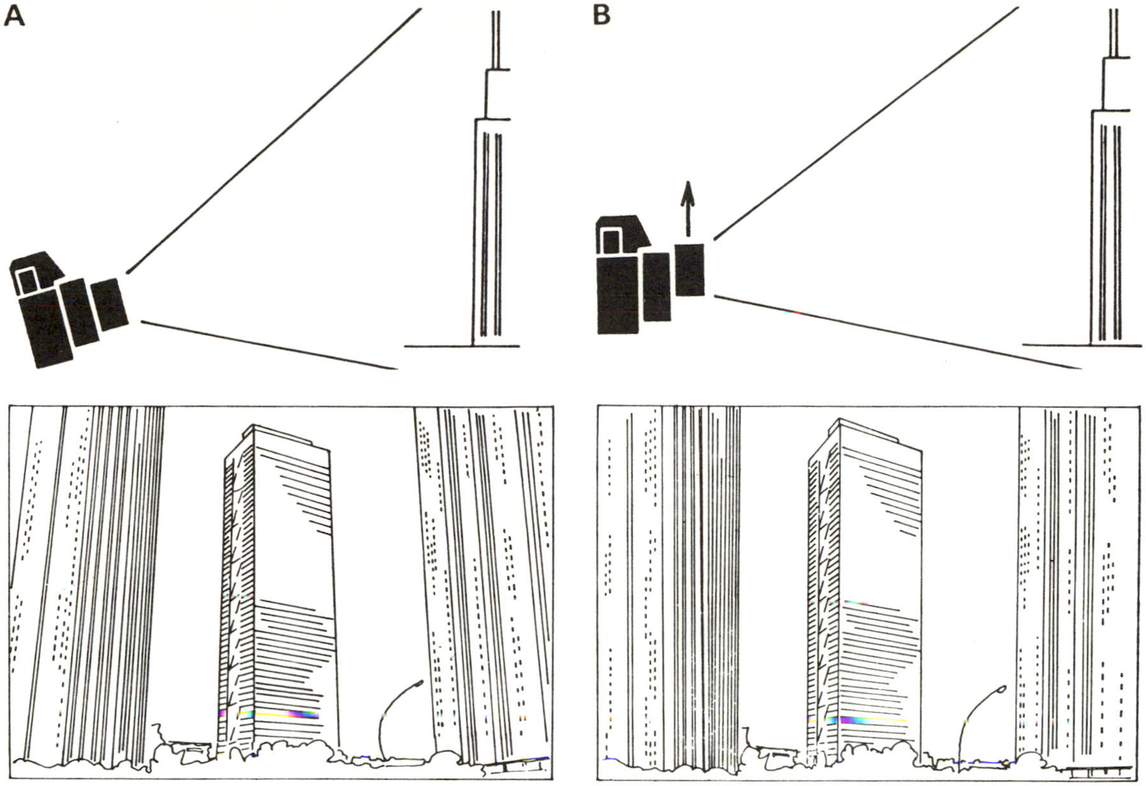

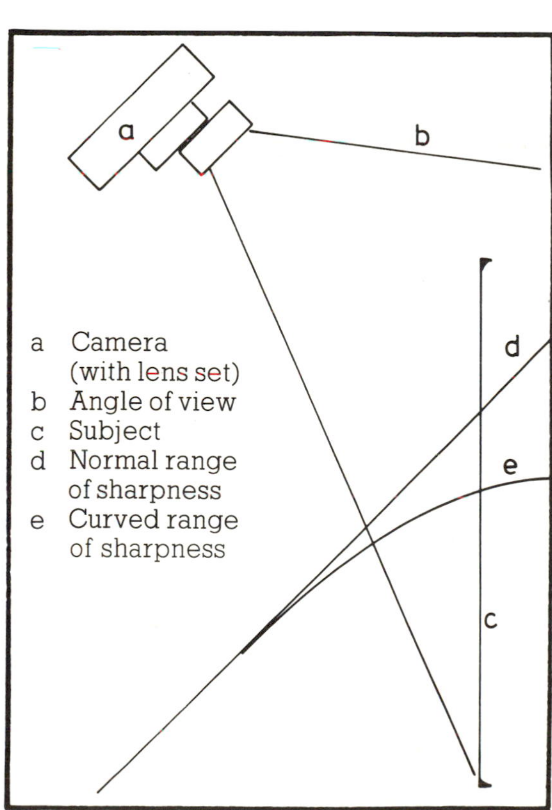
a
b
d
e
c
a Camera (with lens set)
b Angle of view
c Subject
d Normal range of sharpness
e Curved range of sharpness

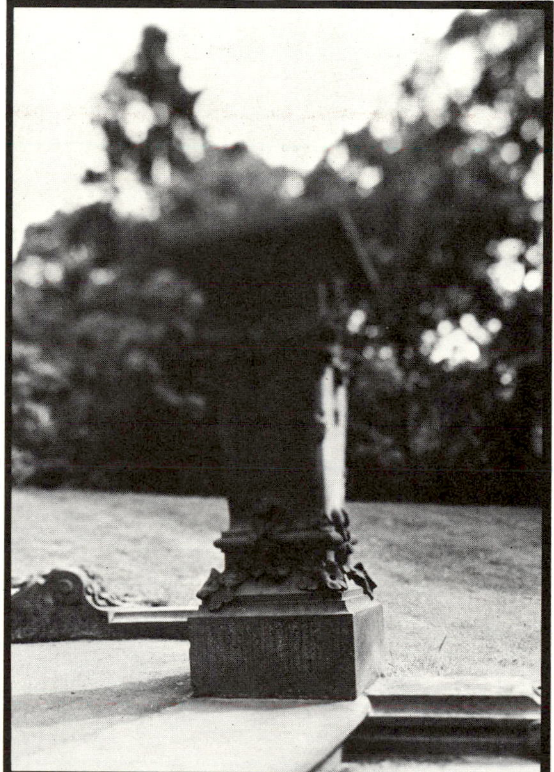

30

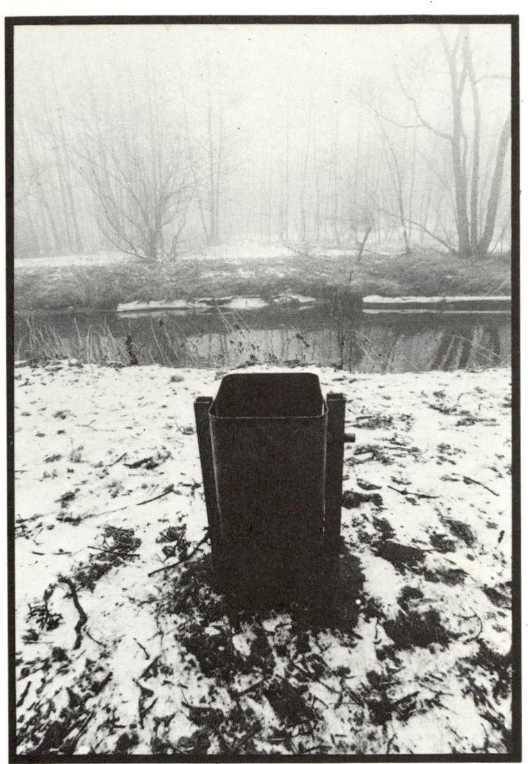

distance it is possible to distinguish objects from one another which are separated by about 1 mm. The diameter of the circle of confusion on a miniature negative, therefore, should not be greater than 1/30 mm if the image is to appear sharply in an enlargement. From this it follows that the normal viewing distance for an enlargement corresponds to the diagonal of the negative times the degree of enlargement. (For an enlargement to 12 × 9 cm, this would be about 25 cm, and for larger formats correspondingly more.) The impression of sharpness of an enlargement depends on the diameter of the circle of confusion, the scale of enlargement and the viewing distance.

The extent of the depth of the zone within which these conditions are fulfilled can be influenced by two factors: the size of the aperture and the choice of focal length. The smaller the aperture, the greater the depth of field and the larger the aperture, the smaller the depth of field.

More exact information about the extent of the depth of field in a given situation can be obtained in three ways:

31

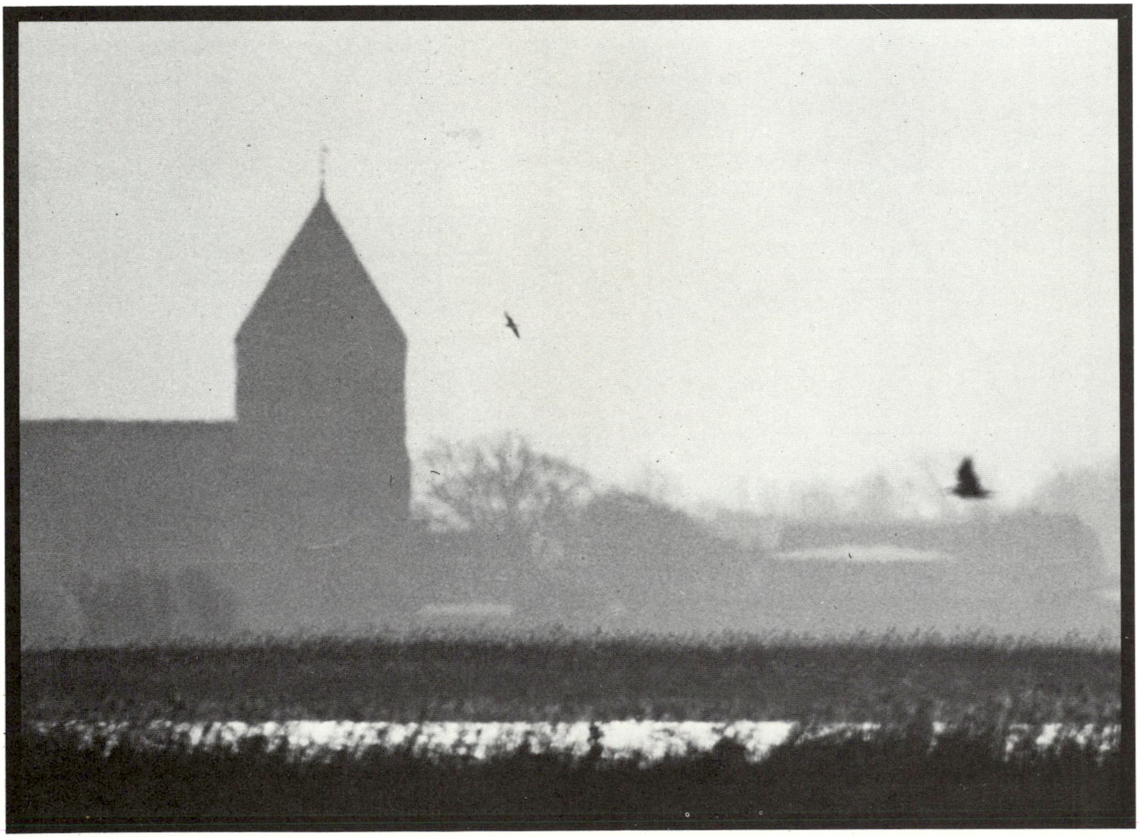

ALTERING SPATIAL EFFECT

Spatial effect caused by	Spatial effect diminished	Spatial effect increased
height of viewpoint	eye level (normal)	higher or lower
tilt (of camera)	parallel (vertical) lines	converging vertical lines
depth of field*	more limited	more extensive
subject distance	further	nearer
perspective magnification†	long focal length	short focal length

Effects of longer focal lengths	Effects of shorter focal lengths
more limited depth of field	more extensive depth of field
greater subject distance implied	smaller subject distance implied
less tilt required	more tilt required
more limited variations in height of viewpoint	greater variations in height of viewpoint
stronger aerial perspective	weaker aerial perspective
greater dominance of individual colours	more generalised colour scheme
In general therefore: more limited spatial effect	In general therefore: stronger spatial effect

* This varies in effect according to individual cases. A slight separation in sharpness between subjects at different distances can actually increase the impression of depth. In general, however, a scene with many other indicators of depth—lines converging to a distant point, aerial haze etc—suffers in the impression these give when they are not rendered with sufficient sharpness.

† Perspective is not dependent upon focal length, but on subject distance. Changes of focal length affect the rendering by different magnifications and angles of view, causing apparent compression, or deepening, by inclusion of a lesser or greater area of the scene respectively.

1 **Tables:** With every lens a leaflet is enclosed with tables giving information about depth of field for every focal length at various distances.

2 **Lens engraving:** On every lens a depth-of-field scale is engraved from which the appropriate value can simply be read (see the manufacturer's instruction booklet).

3 **Aperture control:** Generally a single-lens reflex camera is fitted with an aperture-control button. By pressing this, the working aperture is engaged, and it is possible to see in the viewfinder the actual range of sharpness.

Before every exposure in any circumstance it is advisable to assess conditions of sharpness in the picture. This is the only way to avoid image errors, whose frequent appearance proves that many amateur photographers do not take the trouble to do this. It is not otherwise possible to ensure clarity of impact in the finished picture.

If the photographic situation is appropriate, it is generally preferable to have visual control of image sharpness by stopping down the aperture. In certain tricky situations and with very small apertures, however, use the scale engraved on the lens mount. The second method is more reliable with a small aperture, because when it is stopped down, the viewfinder often becomes so dark that it is impossible to judge the sharpness. After a few experiments you can decide which method gives the best results.

Depth of field can be controlled and altered at will as described above. There are, however, situations where this is not applicable. There are 'detail enthusiasts', who find a picture acceptable only if all objects in it, near and far, appear pin-sharp. These people, however, have never heard of the structure of a picture. The allocation of differential sharpness within a picture has a very strong effect on the observer, and should therefore be determined according to theme and with due regard to the statement to be made in any particular case.

Figs 30 and *31* provide some insight into the possibilities in this respect. In the first photograph (*Fig 30*) complete sharpness is evident (taken with an *f*4/17 mm lens); while the second (*Fig 31*) depends for its effect on a depth of field of only a few metres and a simple back-drop effect (taken with an *f*11/1600 mm lens). It is clear that this particular visual effect can only be achieved by using limited depth of field.

(*Note:* These remarks on the subject of depth of field do not apply in the cases of close-up and macro photography. These subjects are discussed in Chapter 24.)

The table (*Fig 32*) indicates the various factors which may be influenced through choice of aperture, or which are related to it.

5: CIRCULAR IMAGES

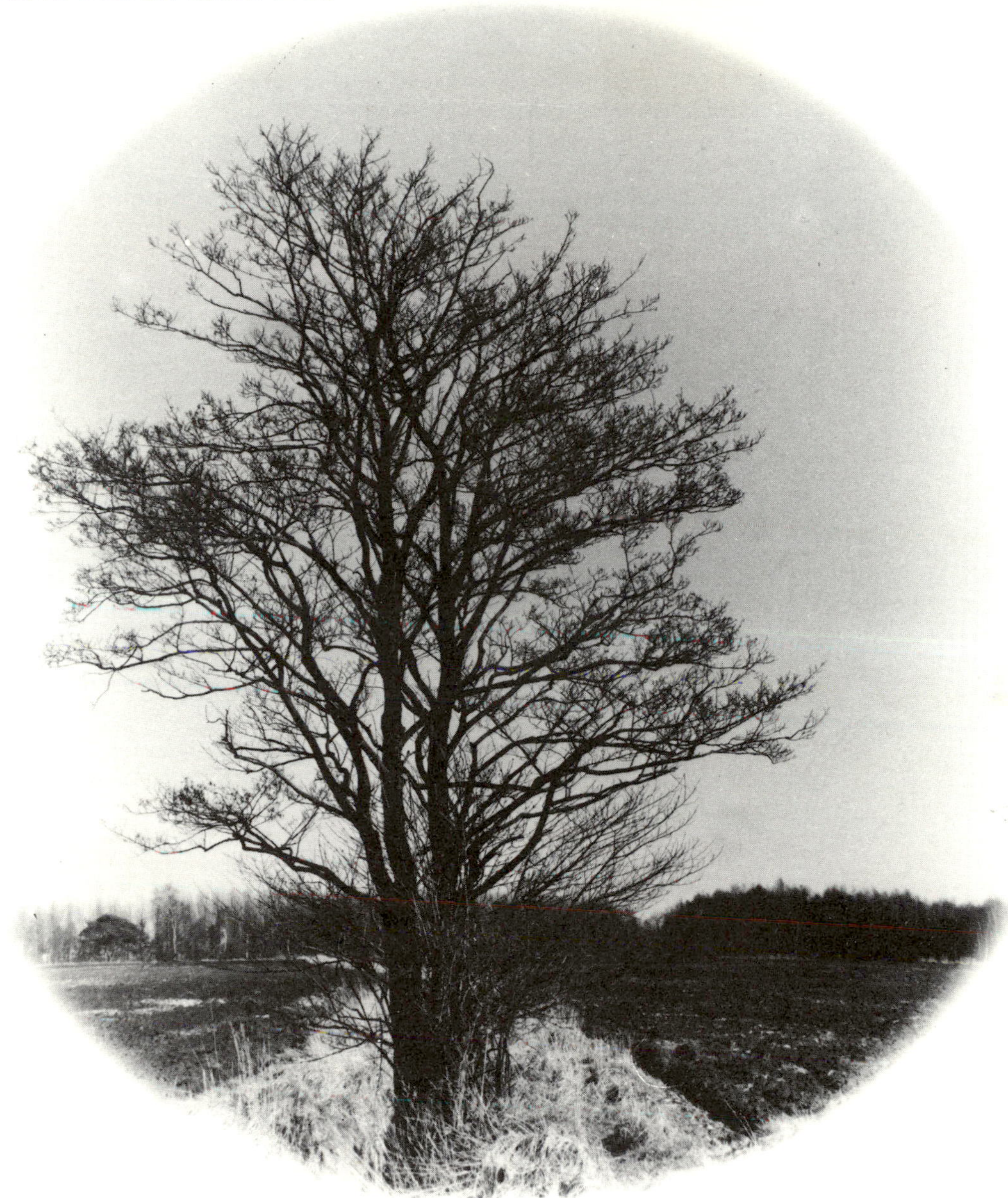

The circular image

According to the type of lens, the iris is more or less round. That is to say, it is a polygon approaching a circular shape, and the glass-elements of which the lens is composed are round as well.

From this it follows that the picture itself which is created by the lens is inherently circular. At one time indeed a few commercially built cameras existed which gave not a rectangular or square picture but a round one. Nowadays this format has receded into the realms of oblivion, as all cameras, by means of margins (field apertures), produce rectangular or square negatives or transparencies. We have become so accustomed to this that the round pictures produced by extreme fisheye lenses seem most bizarre. As far as format is concerned, the fisheyes differ from all other lenses in that their entire image field is reproduced on the negative, and not just a rectangular or square section of it.

The interchangeable lens of any camera may theoretically be used to produce images of any rectangular or square format, as long as its diagonal is not greater than the diameter of the image circle. In addition, circular photographs may be produced if required.

If a circular image is wanted for a specific theme it is of course possible to just go ahead and, using compasses and scissors, remove the appropriate outer section. There are, however, two other possibilities, which allow the use of the entire image circle of the lens:

1 A miniature lens fitted to a medium-format camera, using a special attachment.
2 With a 50 mm enlarging lens, enlargements can be made from medium-format negatives, which turn out to be circular.

The first procedure involves considerable technical and financial expenditure. The second method, using the enlarger, is much easier, provided that the eventual circular portion of the picture is taken into account when shooting.

Fig 33 was produced by using an enlarger. It is easy to tell at once which method has been used for the production of a circular picture: method 1 provides a black surround, while method 2 gives a white one.

It might well be asked at this point why anyone should go to all this trouble when a pair of scissors would do. The fact is that the result with scissors is not so satisfactory, since particularly with big enlargements made with large apertures, a slight falling-off of brightness and sharpness may be detected at the edges of the picture, which normally would lie outside the selected picture section. In this way the circular image is given a sort of 'natural' finish at the margin, whereas a section simply cut out appears so and hence looks 'unnatural'.

6: LENS REFLECTIONS

Reflections

In any discussion about images and reflections, two difficulties arise. The first lies in the fact that no manufacturer admits readily that his lenses can cause reflections at all. However, this is not the case, as even the best of lenses with the most superb corrections are, in certain lighting conditions, liable to create reflections. The second difficulty becomes apparent when you attempt quite consciously to work with reflections and to incorporate them in a composition. As a result of specially thorough preventive measures (particularly multiple-coating treatment), high-quality lenses have become so good that it is no longer simple to create lens reflections deliberately if desired.

What are lens reflections, and how are they caused?

Lens reflections are patches of light on negative or transparency, which are caused by the refraction of rays of light on the outer surfaces of the individual lens elements. They arise in photography against the light, created by strong light sources in the image area or close to the border (sun, highlight, specular reflections et al). The more elements a lens has and the greater its angle of view, the more likely it is for lens reflections to appear. The size and shape of the reflections depends on the size and shape of the aperture.

Normally such reflections are to be avoided. This can be achieved to a considerable extent by making use of the lens hood appropriate to the camera and lens. Avoid the use of a so-called 'universal rubber lens hood'; and do not use a filter in front of the lens in contrejour lighting situations, as its glass surfaces are particularly susceptible to reflections.

On the other hand, if for the purpose of pictorial composition lens reflections are desired, merely follow the reverse procedure: use a wide-angle lens, do without a lens hood, and even fit an external filter. It is then easy to capture reflections.

34

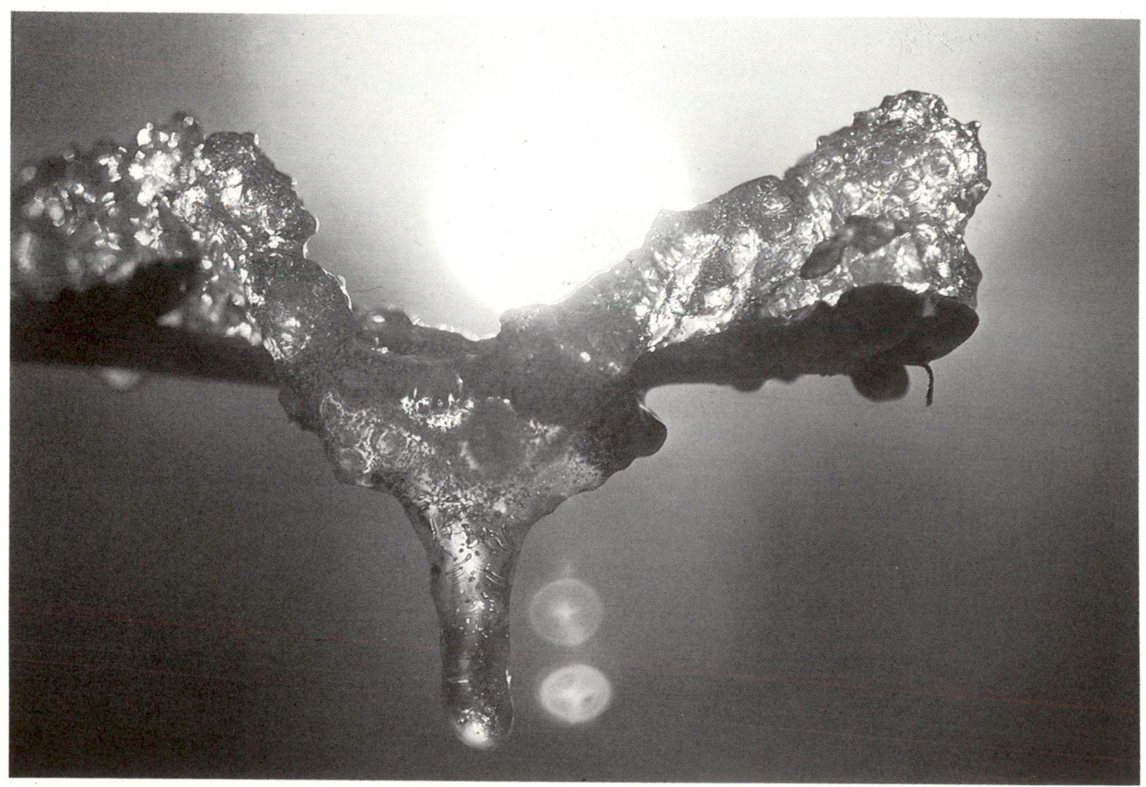

35

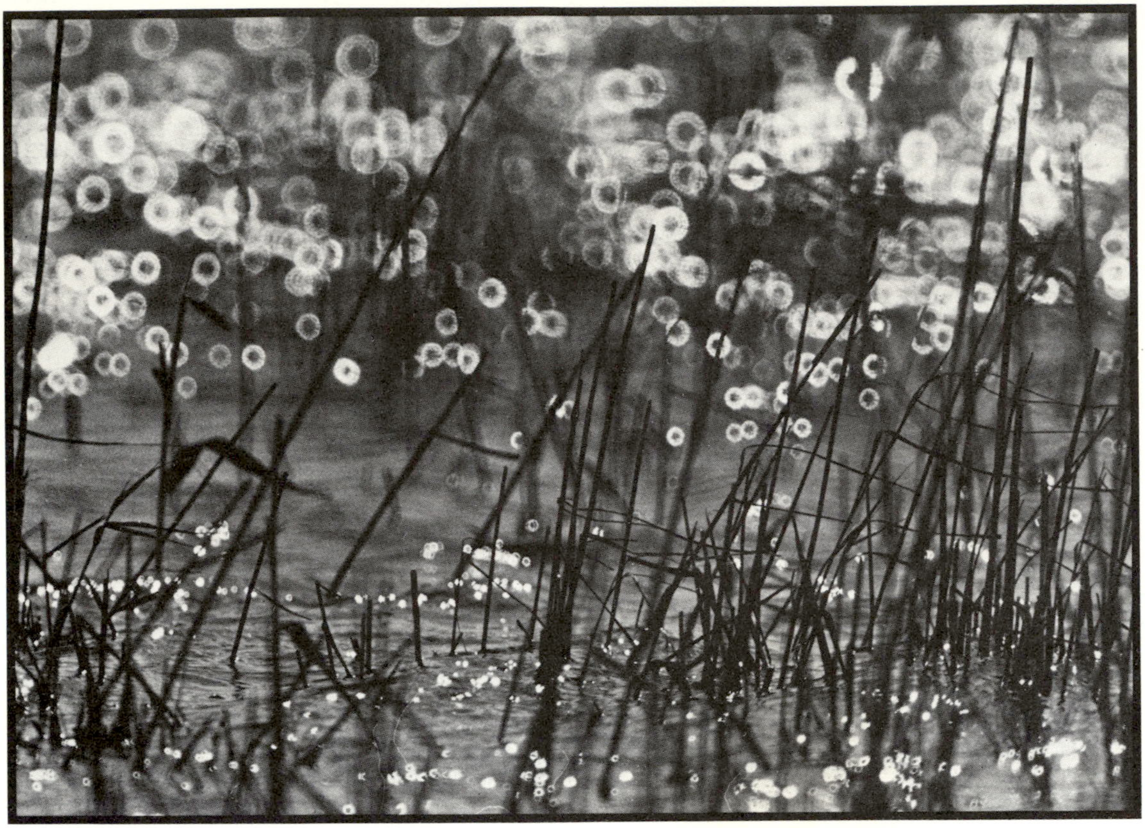

The only difficulty occurs in trying to control the effect.

This kind of lens reflection is produced only by the light sources; it originates from within the lens itself. Thus it cannot be avoided by the use of a polarising screen. It is quite a different matter, however, with the direct creation of light sources or points of light within the picture area. If these are to be found within the picture area, but outside the sharpness zone, they may be described as 'theoretical circles of confusion', as mentioned in the previous chapter. Their shape and size depend on the shape and size of the aperture.

In *Fig 35* there is a whole series of reflections. However, these are not in the shape of a disc or a solid polygon, as might be expected, but ring-shaped. This is a consequence of a lens characteristic; the photograph was taken with a mirror lens (*f*1 1/1600 mm), which has no iris diaphragm in the normal sense of the word. The shape and size of the aperture are determined rather by the main mirror and the central mirror (see *Fig 35a*) and this is why the

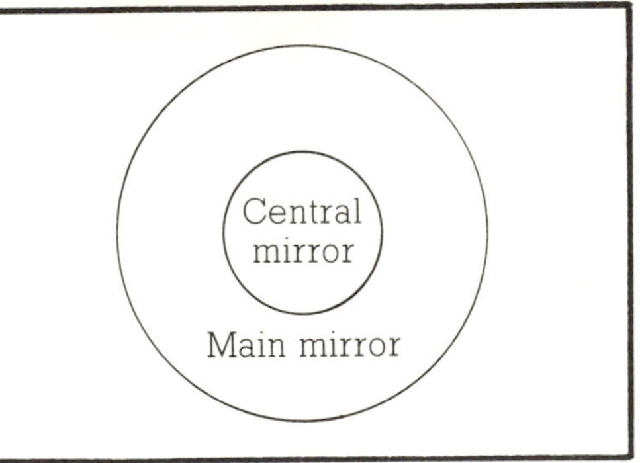

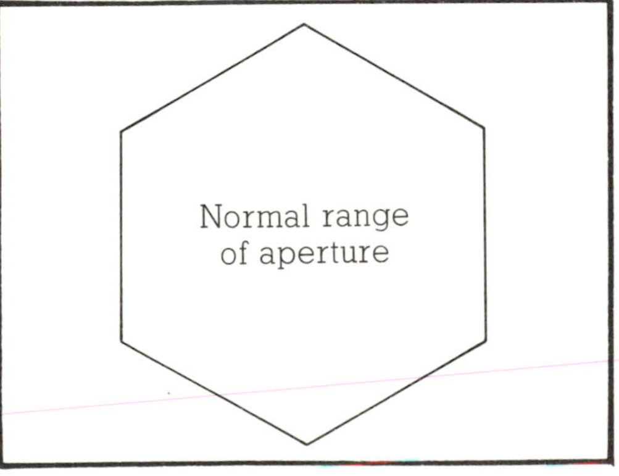

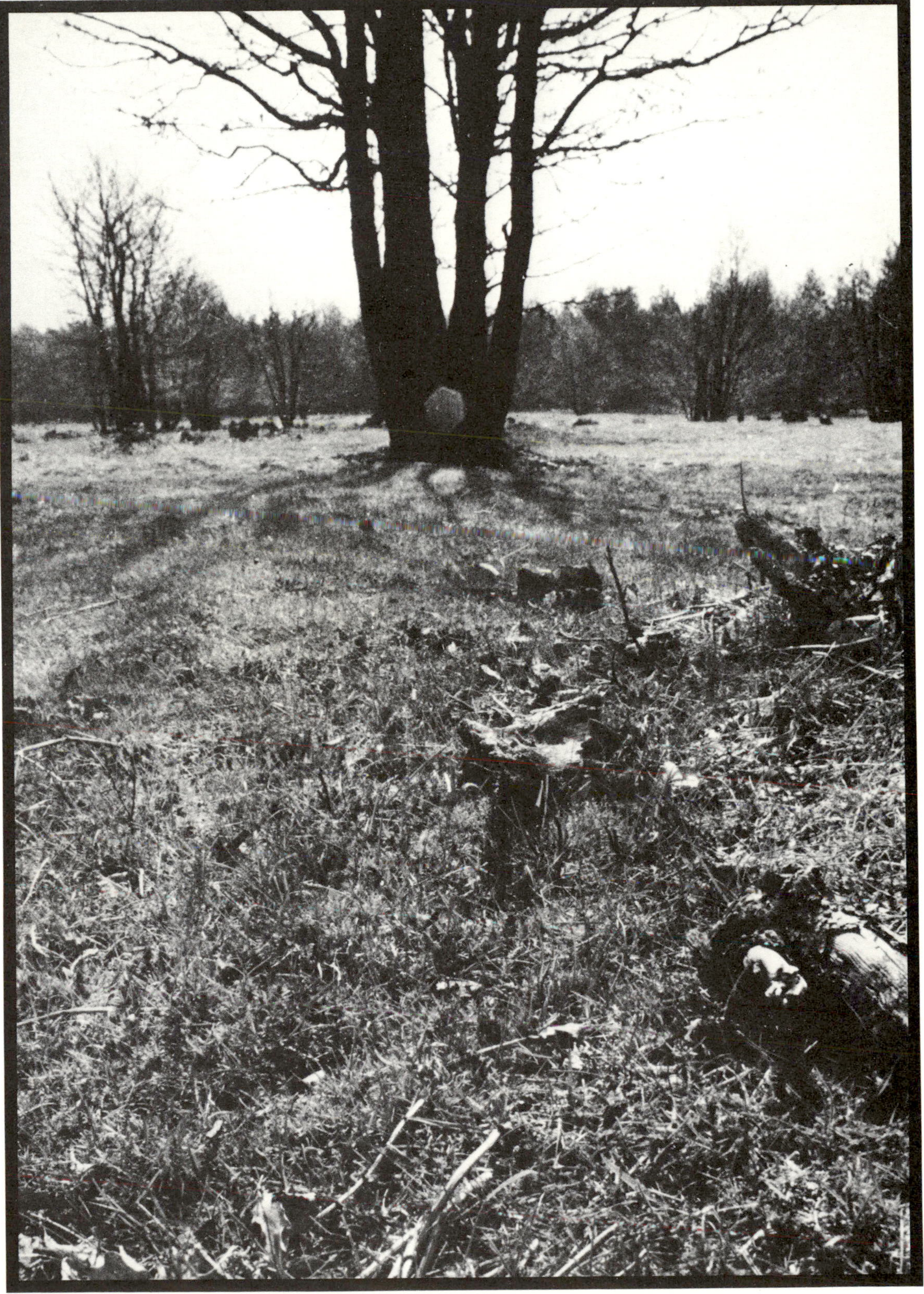

reflections are shaped like rings. It should be added that it is not essential to have a lens of such a long focal length as 1600 mm to create ring-shaped iris reflections. Mirror lenses are available in long, and some medium focal lengths, and are much more compact than equivalent types using conventional glass elements.

Fig 36 shows a reflection of another kind. This photograph was taken with a *f*2.8/21 mm lens at aperture *f*16. Hence the only discernible reflection in the picture is very small, and takes the shape of the closed iris of this lens.

In *Fig 34* two possibilities are combined in one photograph. The setting sun appears as a white disc (the iris of the *f*3.5/50 mm lens was wide open, and thus the shape is that of a full circle) while in the foreground three reflections of another kind add some confusion. The reflections were meant to appear directly under the ice-structure, but they were so difficult to see when the lens was stopped down that the effect did not succeed completely.

Fortunately it is possible to see reflections in the viewfinder of a single-lens reflex camera. It has been pointed out already that the size and shape of the reflections depend on the aperture, and thus the effect can be judged in advance only by using a normal working aperture. So use the aperture control.

It often occurs that the reflections appear so faintly that they can hardly be seen. In these cases, move the camera slightly to and fro to make them more readily discernible. By opening the iris wider, the reflections become larger and fainter—and vice versa.

Reflections of the kind appearing in *Fig 35* may be influenced by increasing and decreasing the aperture. In addition, it is possible to diminish their brightness by means of a polarising screen—or indeed to make them disappear altogether. This of course applies only to reflected lights, and not to light sources themselves. (Further information about polarising screens is given in the chapters on photography with lens attachments.)

It should be mentioned once again that every change in position of the camera—be it quite minute—can alter lens reflections radically. To give an example, for *Fig 36* I had to wriggle around on my stomach for a considerable period in a damp meadow in order to discover the exact position which would give the desired effect.

7: ZOOM LENSES

Although a review of individual lenses is not part of the plan of this book, it is essential, in order to round off the subject of interchangeable lenses, to consider one other group of lenses which, on account of their special design, have unique creative potential: zoom lenses.

In the first place, these offer everything that can be achieved with appropriate fixed-aperture lenses. In addition, they facilitate, within their aperture range, the selection of any desired focal length, and hence of precisely accurate composition.

It is not the intention to cover here animal and sporting photographs, reportage or adventurous areas. This is simply because the advantages of the zoom lens in these regions are so self-evident that discussion is superfluous. The case is different, however, in the type of photography which was once designated by the unsatisfactory and meaningless name of 'pictorial photography'. Here the potential of a 'spot-on' choice of focal length has not been so fully appreciated.

The 'conventional' use of the zoom lens does not concern us here, since the same possibilities and conditions apply as with the fixed-aperture lens. However, it is possible to adjust the focal length in a different way from that hitherto considered—namely, during the exposure of the film. This results in pictures showing explosive streaks of light, examples of which are commonly seen. This effect is easily achieved. Only sufficient duration of exposure is required to permit time for a suitable adjustment of the zoom ring to be made. With regard to the brief periods of time applying to sporting photographs and the like (between about ½ and 1/30 sec) with handheld shooting, it is best to start moving the focal length control before releasing the shutter, to ensure it is done quickly enough.

To distort striking 'action shots' in this way, in general it is not possible to rely on taking a direct photograph during the event. To ensure a good result, illuminate a conventional photograph of it (by enlargement or projection) and then adjust the zoom setting.

An example of the unusual kind of impression, which may also be achieved if you have grasped the technique of zooming during exposure, is shown in the dramatic photograph of the statue (*Fig 37*). In this instance the streak effect created by the zooming enhances the picture, in that it adds movement to an otherwise static subject.

There are, of course, many ways in which you can experiment and practise using static subjects. For example, *Fig 38* depicts another small sculpture, photographed with a 100—500 mm zoom lens. The total exposure time amounted to 28 sec: 8 sec at 100 mm focal length, then a change to 250 mm during the next 8 sec exposure, then a further exposure of 8 sec, and finally a zoom to 500 mm during the last 4 sec.

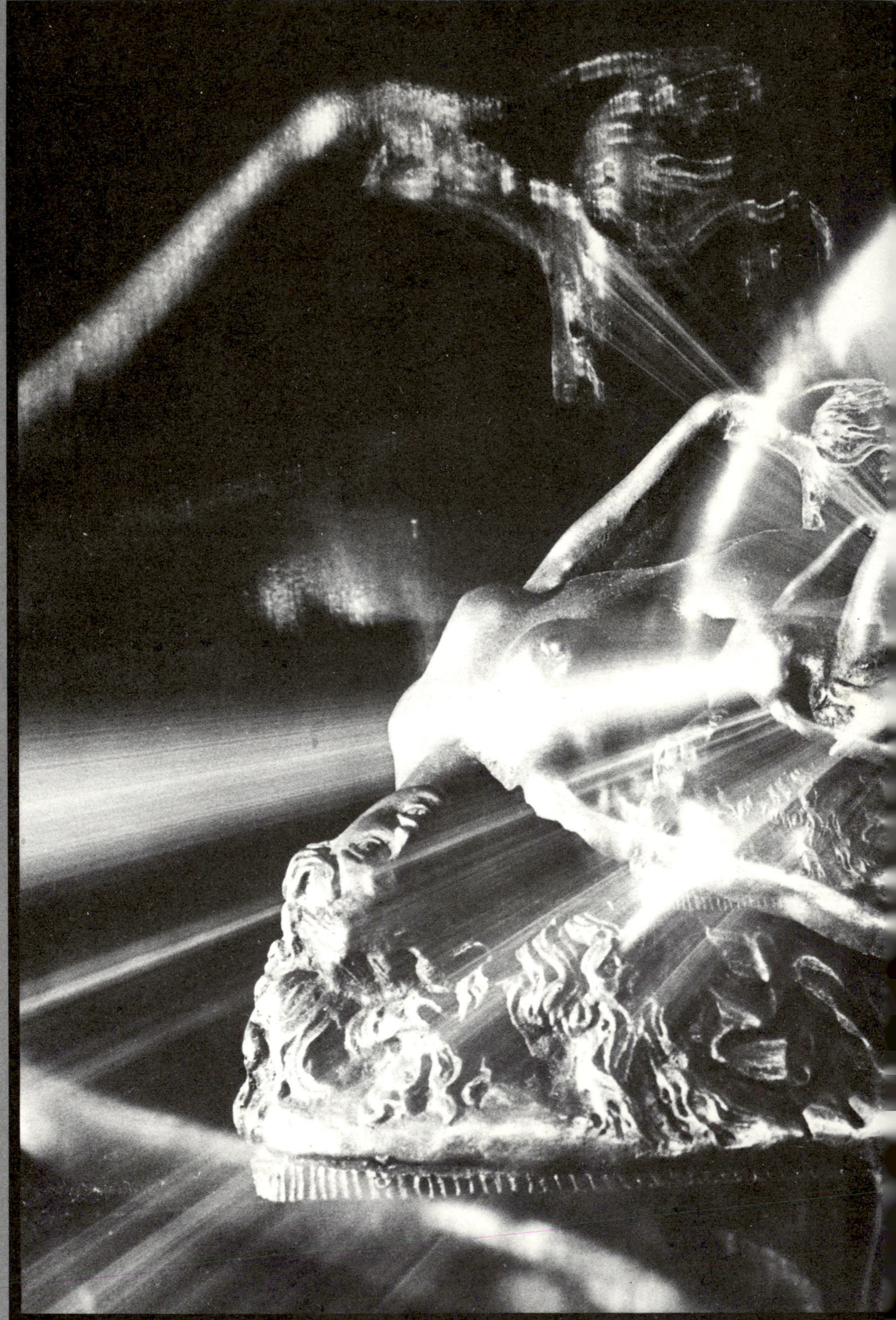

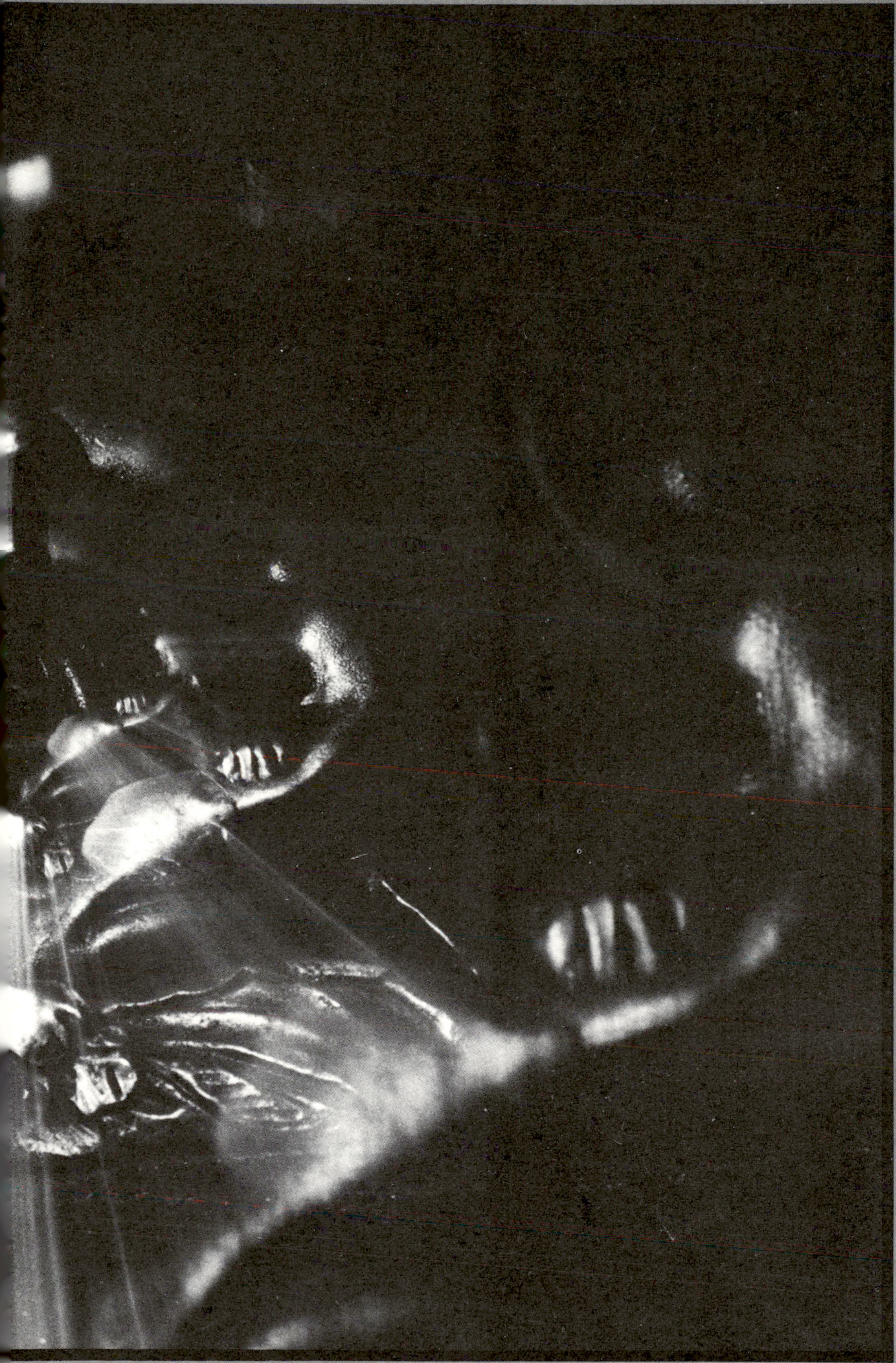

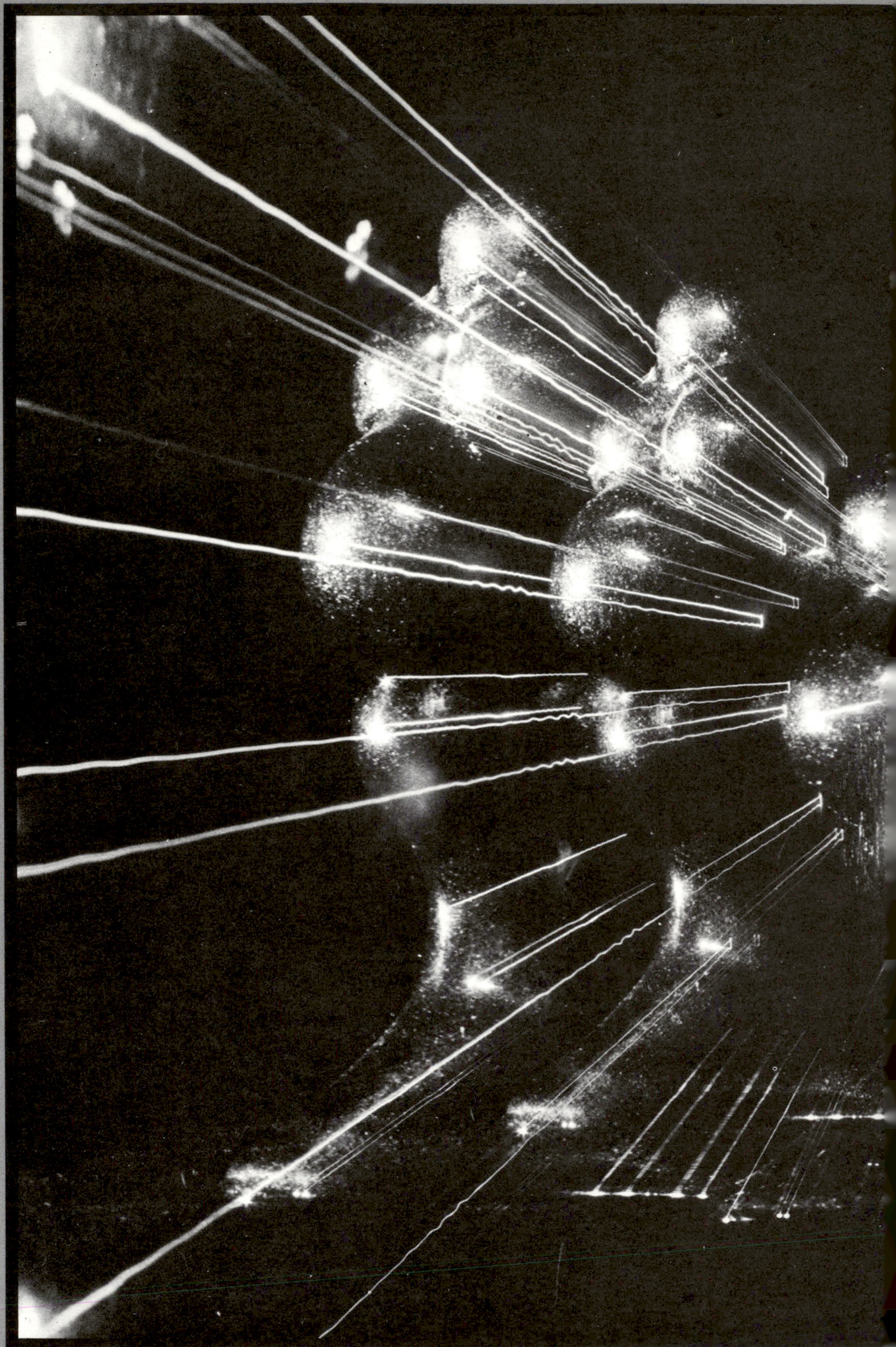

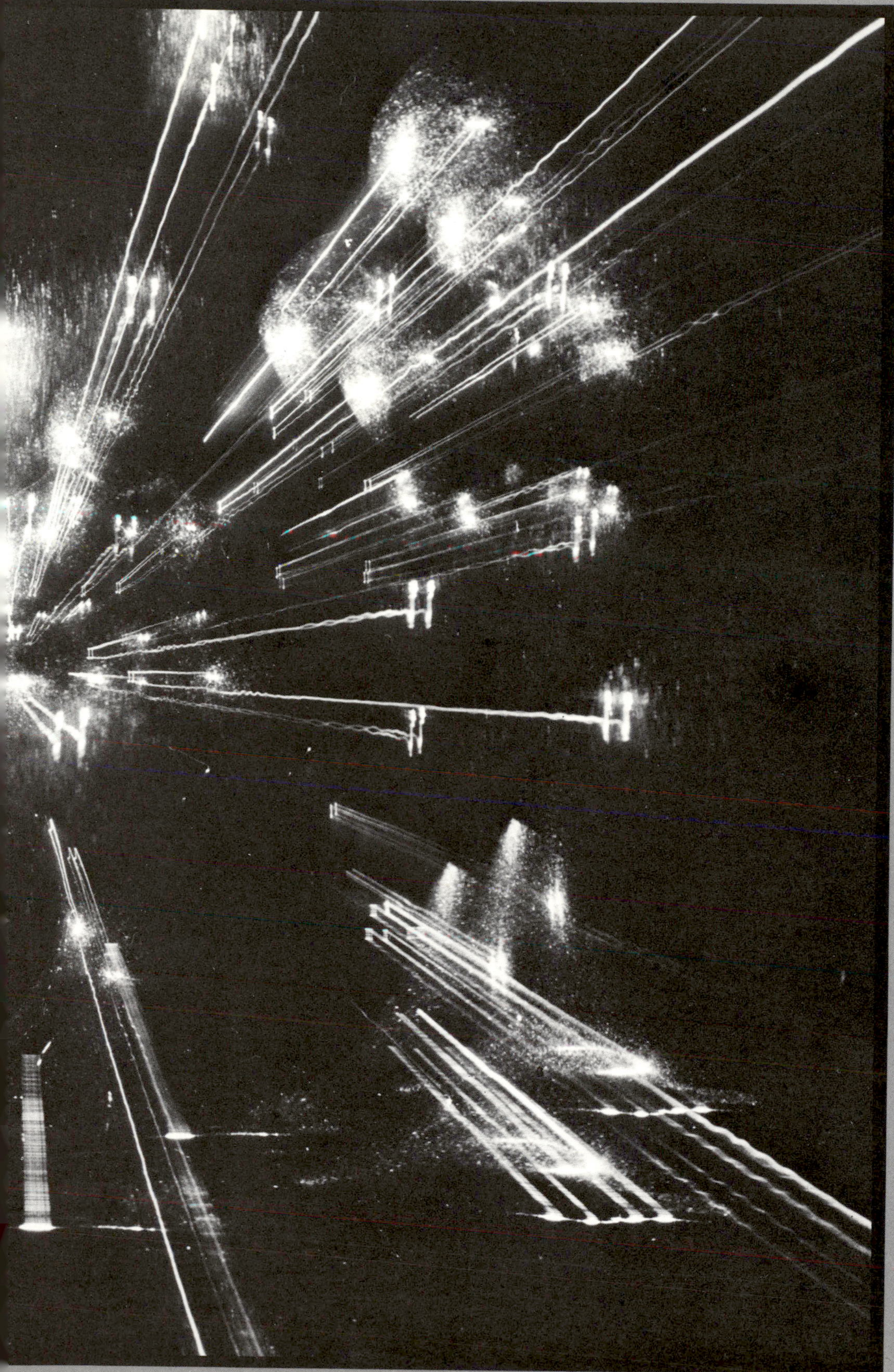

8: MONOCHROME FILTERS

There is a wide range of lens attachments available. First of all let us consider conventional photographic filters, which, at least in monochrome photography, seem to be used far too infrequently. There are many possibilities for the use of filters, which the amateur photographer may not be aware of.

In general, filters may be divided into three groups:

1 Filters for monochrome photography.
2 Filters for colour photography.
3 Universal filters for monochrome and colour photography.

Although later in this book uses which, under this classification, might be regarded as 'erroneous' are discussed, for the sake of simplicity it is best to initially adhere to the three categories.

Monochrome filters

Without delving too deeply into scientific processes, a brief look at the technical factors is useful. Normal panchromatic monochrome film is so sensitised (ie made to accept the various colours of the spectrum) that under conventional photographic conditions it transforms all the various subject colours into shades of grey. This is achieved in such a way that the monochrome picture goes a long way towards providing a similar impression of brightness to that given by observation of the coloured subjects themselves.

Now it might quite possibly occur that two different colours within one subject possess the same brightness, and consequently are reproduced in the photograph with the same degree of greyness. On the other hand, it might also occur that because of the way the film is sensitised, the grey values in the picture are for some reason not pleasing.

In both instances a filter can come to the rescue. This is because coloured filters possess the property of allowing light of their own colour to pass through, while absorbing light of other colour values—excluding them, so to speak. This simply means that in the eventual monochrome enlargement, all parts of the subject that match the filter colour appear brighter, while all other portions of the subject appear darker.

In theory, this sounds fine, and in fact it generally works well. There is one practical difficulty: most colours which in a subject are mixtures—that is to say, light of contrasting colours (eg blue and yellow) mix to form a third colour (in this case green). Thus the effect of a filter cannot be predicted with accuracy and —as almost invariably in photographic practice—the effect has to be estimated. This can be done by setting it up in front of the lens and viewing the subject through it.

Figs 39—42 illustrate the effect of various colour filters on a monochrome picture. *Fig 39* shows the 'normal' scene taken on panchromatic monochrome film without a filter. The colours are distributed in the following way: background—a blue cloth; base—a dark grey cloth, almost black; the (artificial) rose—yellow; the leaves—green; the vase—dark red.

Fig 40 shows the same subject taken using a red filter. It can be clearly seen that the originally dark red vase appears almost white, and that both the leaves and the petals have become brighter.

A more bewildering effect is shown in *Fig 41*, which was photographed with a green filter. In contrast with the previous pictures, the vase looks almost black, while very little has changed in the other parts of the scene.

The most radical departure from the 'normal' scene is to be found in *Fig 42*, which was taken using a blue filter. Here the vase is once again almost black, and petals and leaves are somewhat darker, while the formerly dark background has been transformed into light grey.

When you consider that all these photographs were produced under otherwise identical conditions and with the same lighting, it is possible to get a true impression of the extent to which the effect of monochrome photographs can be influenced by the planned use of filters.

It must be admitted that to show the effect of filters as impressively as possible, conventional photographic filters were not

39

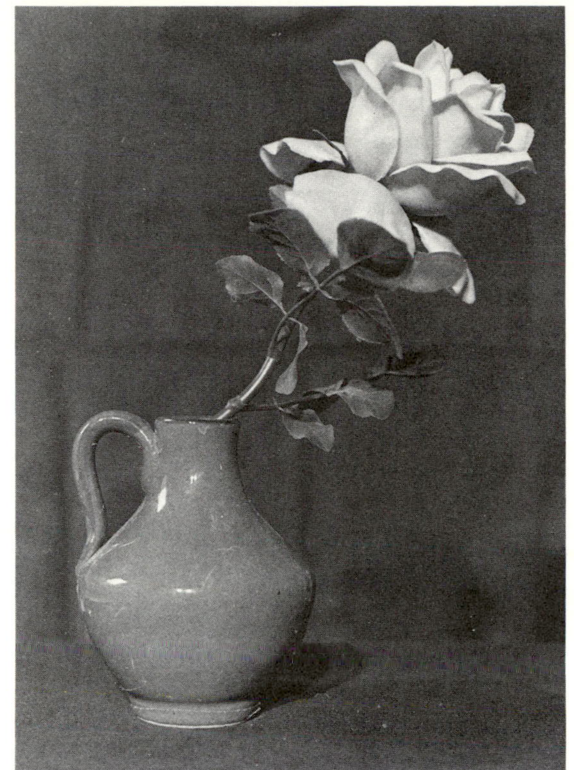

40

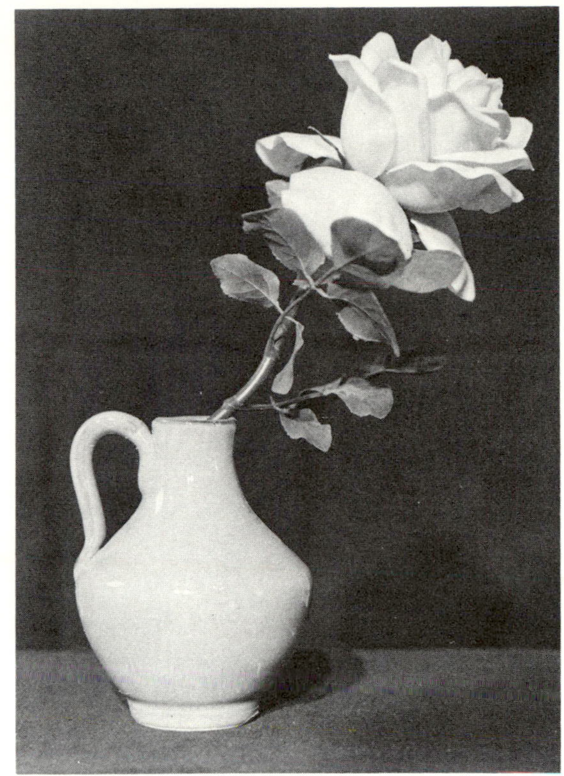

41

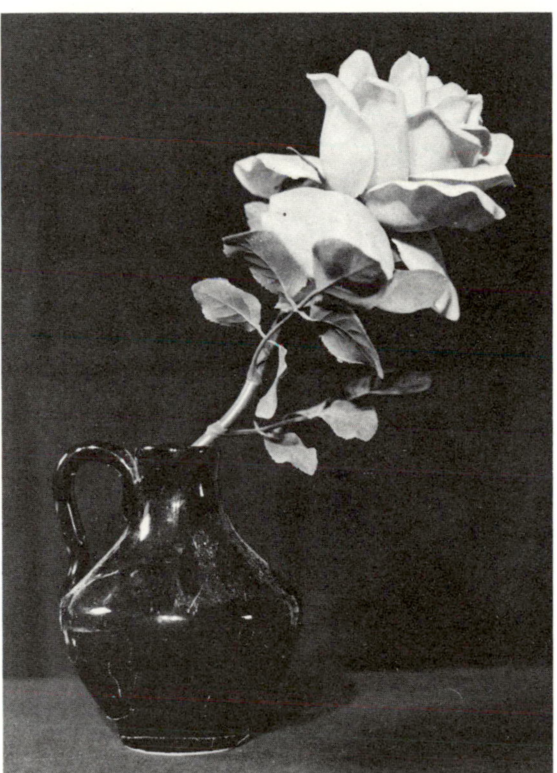

used for this sequence. Instead gelatin 'repro-filters'. were used, which are very much stronger in their effect than normal photographic filters. It is useful, besides the usual photographic filters, to have available a set of repro-filters. They are not expensive (the three together cost roughly the same as a first-class photographic glass filter with screw fitting) and they can be used in many ways. In colour photography too there are interesting possibilities, which are discussed in the chapter on multiple exposures.

The table (*Fig 43*) lists the most important kinds of filter available, with brief information about their use. Filters for colour photography and for universal use are dealt with in the next chapter.

42

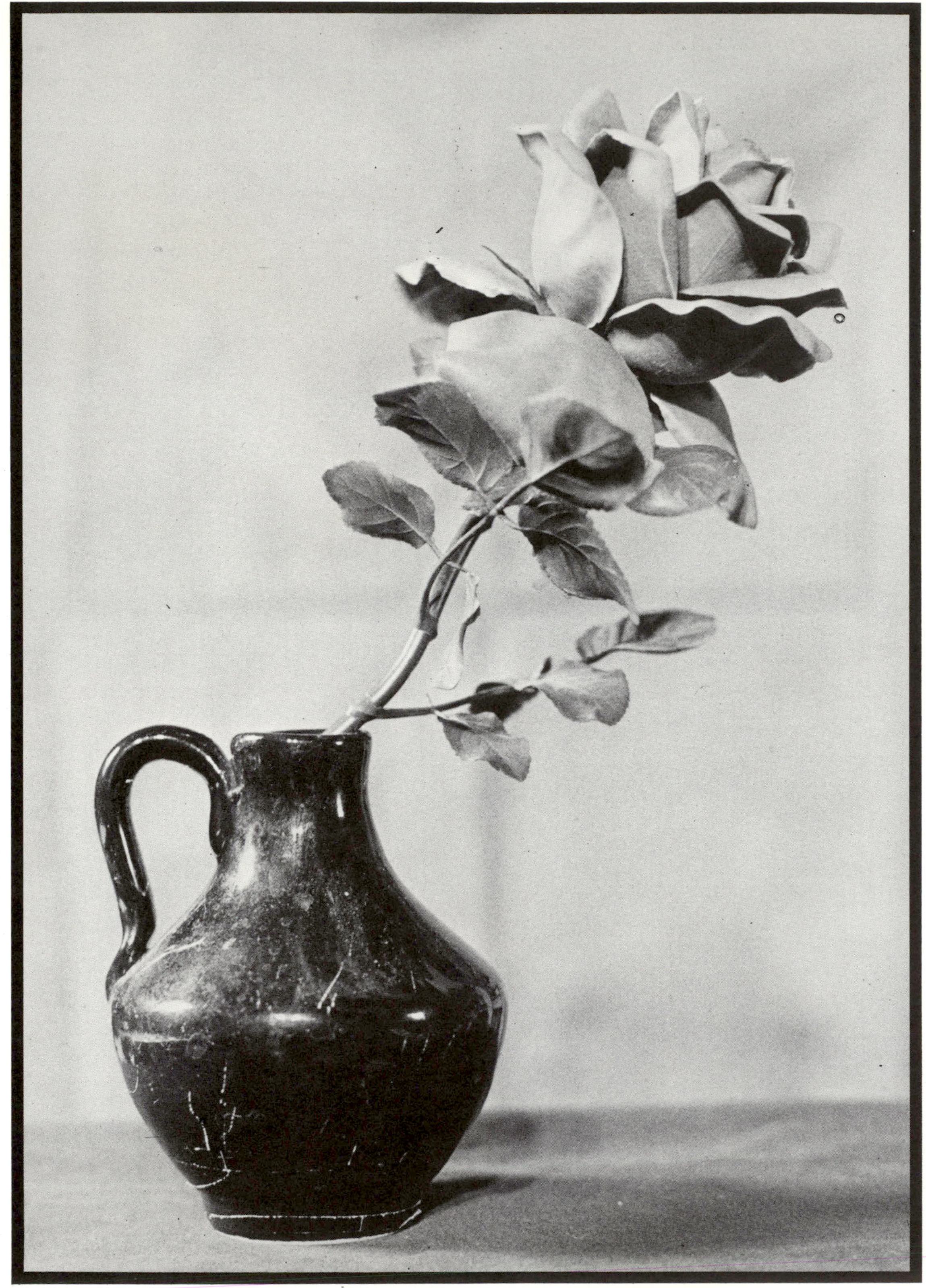

FILTERS AND THEIR EFFECTS

1 Yellow filter Blue sky becomes darker, clouds whiter, shadows become stronger.
2 Orange filter Stronger effect than the yellow, gives dramatic cloud effects against blue skies, excellent haze penetration.
3 Red filter Almost black rending of blue areas of sky, good haze penetration for distant scenes, brightens warm colours in relation to others.
4 Green filter Darkens skies, absorbs UV, improves contrast between different shades of green. Very good for landscapes.
5 Blue filter Makes the sky lighter, clouds disappear, water under clear skies becomes brighter, increases contrast between different types of vegetation increases effect of aerial perspective in distant scenes.
6 80A (B13) (D-A) Dark blue filter for using daylight film with artificial light.
7 85 (R11) (A-D) Orange filter for using type A (tungsten) film in daylight. 85B (R13) For using type B (artificial light film in daylight.
8 Skylight filter (1A) Decreases blue haze. Very useful in shadow, or cloudy weather.
9 UV absorbing filter Reduces UV haze especially apparent at high altitude or by the sea.
10 Neutral density filter (ND) Reduces light reaching the film without changing the colour.
11 Polarising screen For reducing reflections and improving colour saturation.

9: COLOUR AND FILTERS

Universal filters

Up till now it has been assumed here that the subjects to be photographed with the aid of filters have been lit by 'neutral' lighting. This is, of course, only a hypothetical ideal situation. In reality, light has a varying colour quality, according to external circumstances. For example, morning and evening light is appreciably redder than midday light; artificial light is yellower and neon lighting is bluer than daylight; and with a blue sky, daylight takes on a different colour from that which it has in dull weather.

The human eye subconsciously takes into account the hues of various kinds of lighting (these are referred to as colour temperatures, which are measured in Kelvins [K]) so that, for example, a sheet of white paper seems white, no matter what the lighting colour is. Colour film, however, is not capable of such adaptability. According to the prevailing colour temperature, the white piece of paper may be reproduced sometimes as reddish and sometimes as bluish, but seldom as pure white—simply because the physical circumstances dictate it.

In order to overcome this drawback, two different kinds of colour film are available: daylight colour film, set at about 5500 to 6000 K, and artificial light colour film, set at about 3100 to 3400 K. However, since these colour temperatures can represent only averages, which may differ from the actual lighting, theoretically almost every photographic exposure should be corrected with an accurately tinted colour filter, in order to achieve a 'natural' colour effect. However, this is not generally practicable and even if it were feasible, in order to determine which correction filter is appropriate, a colour temperature meter would be necessary, which is not only costly but is of real use only in studio conditions or in certain areas of scientific photography.

Accordingly, for all practical amateur photographic purposes, only three colour correction filters are of significance:

1 The blue tinted D-A conversion filter allows the use of normal daylight film for artificial-light photography. Artificial-light photographs on daylight film without this kind of filter have a yellowish red cast.
2 The reddish tinted conversion filter serves the opposite purpose, and allows the use of artificial-light film in daylight.
3 The skylight filter is of a pale rose colour. This is used in cases where a very light blue cast is to be cancelled—for example, where a subject is in the shade but brightened by the blue sky. Another sort of bluish-violet cast is caused by excessive ultraviolet rays, such as occur in mountains at an altitude of over 2000 metres, or on the sea. In such cases a UV protective filter should be used, which shields the film from ultraviolet light. (A good rule of thumb is that you should always use a UV filter when you yourself are in danger of a sunburn.)

The 'erroneous' use of these filters may on occasion prove satisfactory, as may be seen in *Fig 44*. This photograph was taken using daylight colour transparency film, and was taken in daylight, but with the use of the blue conversion filter. This produces the unnatural blue cast of the picture, which in my opinion is particularly suitable for the cool and moist autumnal atmosphere of the subject. For such experiments, subjects which include a strong red or orange are particularly suitable, such as the leaves in *Fig 44*. The warm-coloured parts of the picture still have a warm effect, so that the blue cast does not appear to swamp the whole scene. Thus, despite the colour cast, the general impression is a natural one.

There is, however, a very widespread bad habit among photographers of permanently retaining one of the three filters, as protection, in front of the camera lens. This is not a good habit to fall into—remember the advice in the chapter about lens reflections.

Polarising screens

The polarising screen is suitable for use as a truly universal filter for monochrome and colour alike, and for the production of a whole series of effects.

44

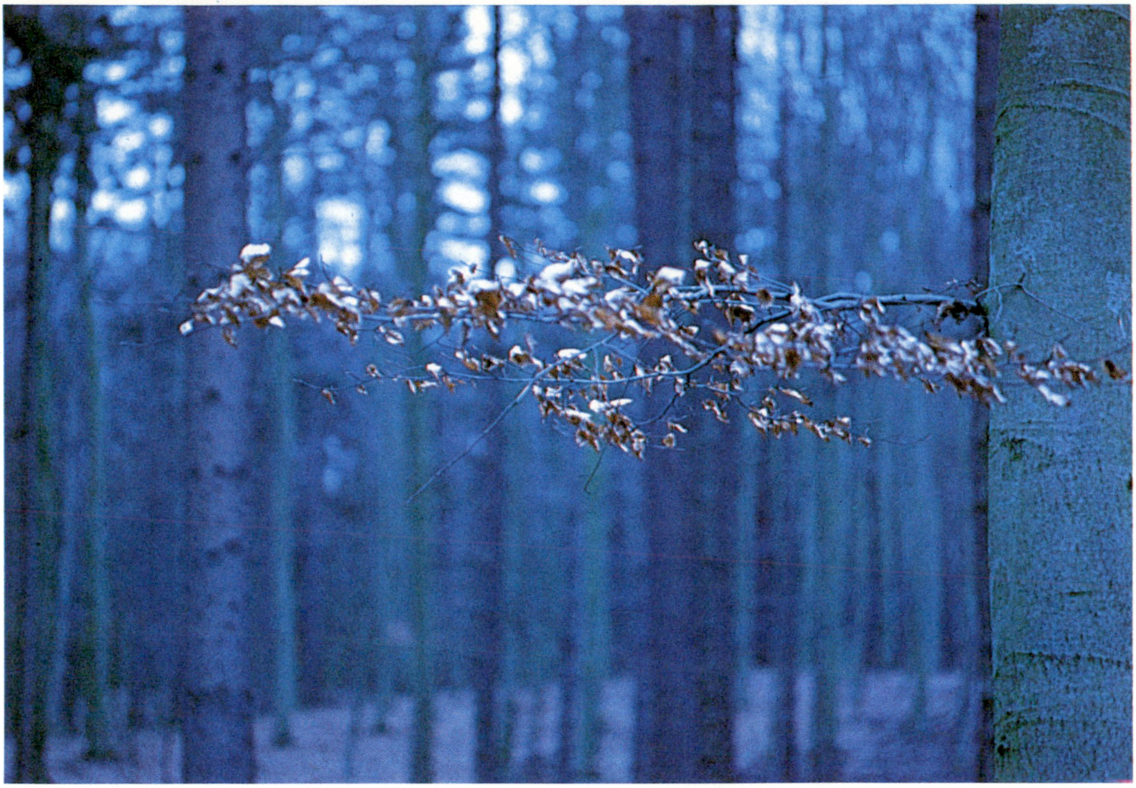

45

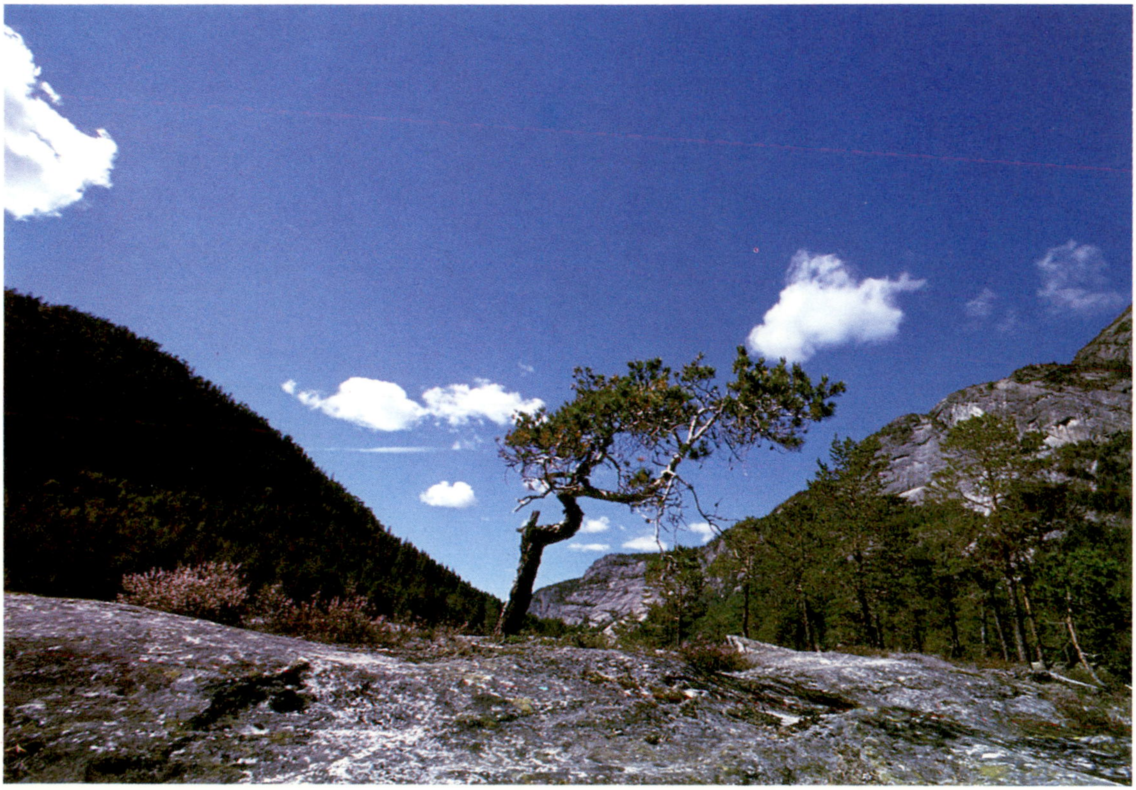

Firstly, it must be made clear that the polarising screen is designed to remove reflections from gleaming objects in the scene. When making practical tests, however, it is soon noticeable that the polarising screen has its limitations. Reflections from metallic objects are not removed at all and reflections from other materials vanish completely only if the reflecting surface is at an angle of between 30° and 40° to the camera direction.

With colour photography, the reflection-cancelling effect of the polarising screen is brought into play for strong colour saturation and for an increase of contrast. This is because in direct sunlight, broad reflecting surfaces often exist which are difficult to detect and which can impair the brilliance of colour. In both these cases, make sure that a maximum cancellation of reflections is really desired; many subjects become lifeless and unnatural without reflections. This applies particularly to windows and water surfaces, which with total elimination of reflections may disappear altogether!

Polarising screens may also be employed to darken the blue of the sky, and thus make clouds appear more distinct. However, since this effect depends on the angle between the camera and the sun (the strongest effect is at an angle of 90°, that is to say when the sun is practically directly to the left or the right of the camera), it might occur that the sky in part of the picture appears extremely intense in colour, especially in photographs taken with a wide-angle lens. This effect is shown very clearly in *Fig 45.* The sky at the left side looks much lighter than at the right.

A further property of the polarising screen, namely that of creating coloured pictures from doubly refracted objects, is dealt with in the section on macro photography.

10: LENS ATTACHMENTS FOR SPECIAL EFFECTS

In addition to actual filters, there is an extraordinary proliferation of so-called trick or effects attachments, which can often be purchased, but sometimes have to be home-made. At least a few of these are examined here, to give some idea of what is possible in this area. Do not, however, lose sight of the general principle that every sort of special effect must be regarded as a mere triviality if it cannot be employed in the achievement of a specific purpose. Only the technical possibilities are discussed here. How they are to be used in creative photography, if at all, has to be left to the individual.

Nevertheless, it is useful to try and sum up the most important and popular purposes in the five groups listed below. (For special lenses which are not included in this list, please refer to dealers' publicity material; as to the possibilities for home-made devices and personal experiment, there are no limits and no restrictions.)

1 Diffusing discs or screens, including those with clear centre areas.
2 Multi-image prisms.
3 Split-field lenses and split or graduated filters.
4 Distortion lenses.
5 Mattes.

The first group, diffusing discs, are chiefly popular with followers of a particular fashion in portrait photography, since they are generally used to subdue certain visual details without making the whole picture unsharp. This is achieved by allowing part of the illumination to fall unhindered on the film, while the rest is scattered so that it is noticeable as irradiation. The simplest way of achieving a diffused effect is to stretch a piece of spun nylon (eg a stocking) in front of the lens. This method produces a picture with general 'misty' irradiation. In principle this procedure can be carried out in the darkroom, but in this case the irradiation appears dark.

Similar effects are achieved with a diffusing disc with a clear spot in the centre. The difference in the effect is that the centre of the picture appears normal and sharp, while an unsharp zone extends to the edge of the picture, its width varying according to the extent of the aperture used. *Fig 46* depicts the standard subject, a vase with roses, already familiar to you from Chapter 8, but this time photographed with a centre lens element. *Fig 47* shows the same subject again, this time taken with the aid of a 4× multi-image prism with a centre field. The subject is dispersed into several individual images, which are reproduced on the same portion of film, partly overlapping and combining with each other.

These effects can be varied either by the number, shape and size of the facets incorporated in the trick lens or by choice of focal length and aperture. There is, therefore, great scope for personal experiment.

In addition, these trick lenses may be combined with other effects attachments, so that the field of possibilities can be extended at will. *Fig 48* was produced by means of a 4× multi-image prism with a centre field, in combination with the centre lens element used in *Fig 46*. Only the centre field of the prismatic lens remains free from irradiation, while the other parts of the picture are held back.

The third group, split-field lenses and split or graduated filters, comprise a whole series of different effects attachments. For example, this group includes filters which are tinted in a distinct colour on one half. These filters alter the colour of half of the image, while the other half remains unaltered. Also in this category is the split-field close-up lens, with which, for example, half the picture may be in the close-up region, while the other half, depending on the distance setting, may be sharp at any position.

Together with these effects there are numerous other special devices. For example, *Fig 49* shows a simple glass marble which is held in the hand about 60 cm in front of the lens (*f*3.5/50 mm macro). This picture is composed of an image of the subject within the glass marble as well as the image of the surroundings (hand, etc). The marble is acting here as a split-field lens.

46

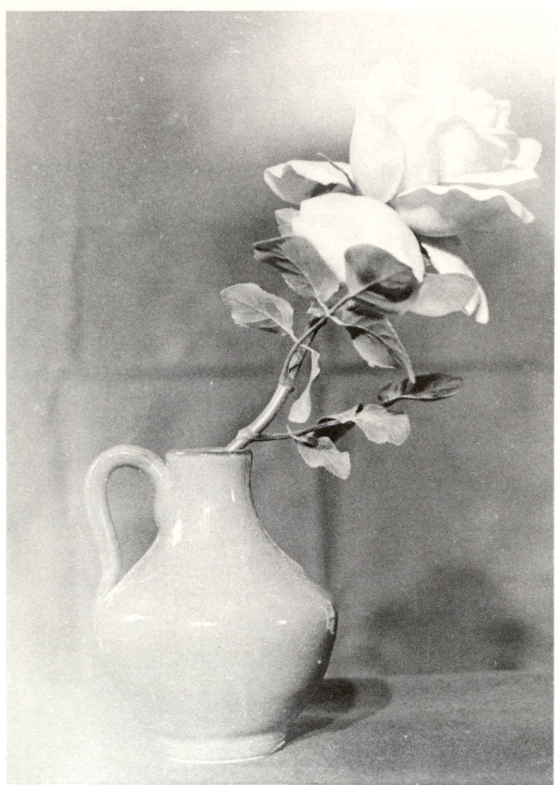

47

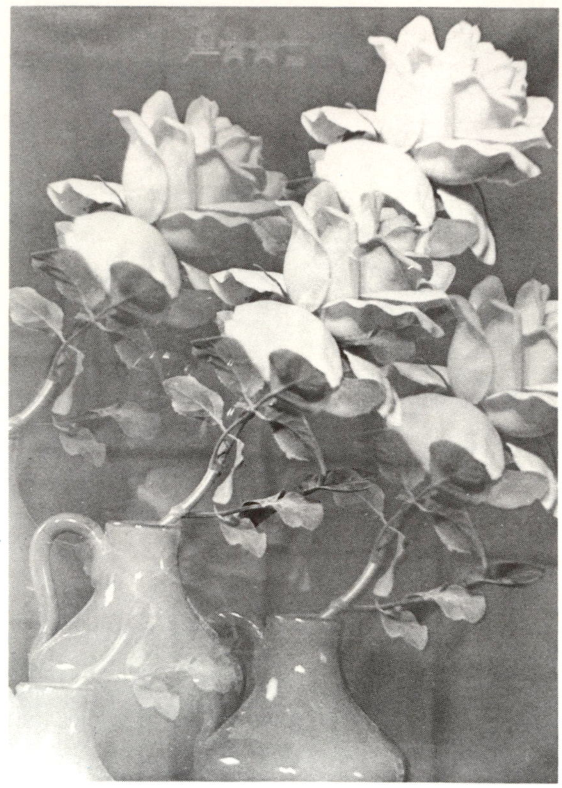

With this group of effects attachments and the fourth group (distortion lenses) experiment for yourself with anything that is partly or wholly transparent: with tumblers, bottles, glass ornaments, stained glass, gauze, lattice, pieces of polyester, and so on. Although it is not feasible to show practical examples of all these possibilities, *Figs 50* and *51* show how interesting effects may be accomplished with the simplest of materials. Both pictures were produced with the aid of a simple glass prism, about 3 cm wide. The prism was fixed with one flat side to a specially cut aperture in a piece of black paper. Having been cut into a circular shape, this was then attached by means of black adhesive strip to the mount of a 50 mm macro lens, in such a way that the 'dome' of the prism faced the lens. (With other lenses this may also be done, but the lens mount would have to be lengthened a little with a black cardboard tube, so that the 'dome' of the prism would not come up against the front lens element. With a 50 mm macro lens this is not necessary, as the front lens element is set deep in the mount.)

With this device you can carry out distortions and colour separations similar to those shown in the two other illustrations.

Furthermore, if the prism is simply turned around and set in front of the lens with the 'dome' outwards, two partial images of the same size are produced on the film, and each of these portrays a different section of the picture.

The last group of effects attachments, mattes, can be set at varying distances in front of the lens, in order to hold back part of the image field. To this category of course belongs those awful keyhole and heart shapes, the use of which can easily ruin the best of pictures. In the same group are mattes which are used for twin photographs and comparable multiple exposure tricks. These are discussed in detail in the section about multiple exposure.

Experimentation with technical devices and especially the discovery of new forms of image is not only instructive, it can also be great fun. A successful effect, however, be it ever so fine and new, does not necessarily imply a good picture. Quite on the contrary. For example, again and again in photographic journals new techniques

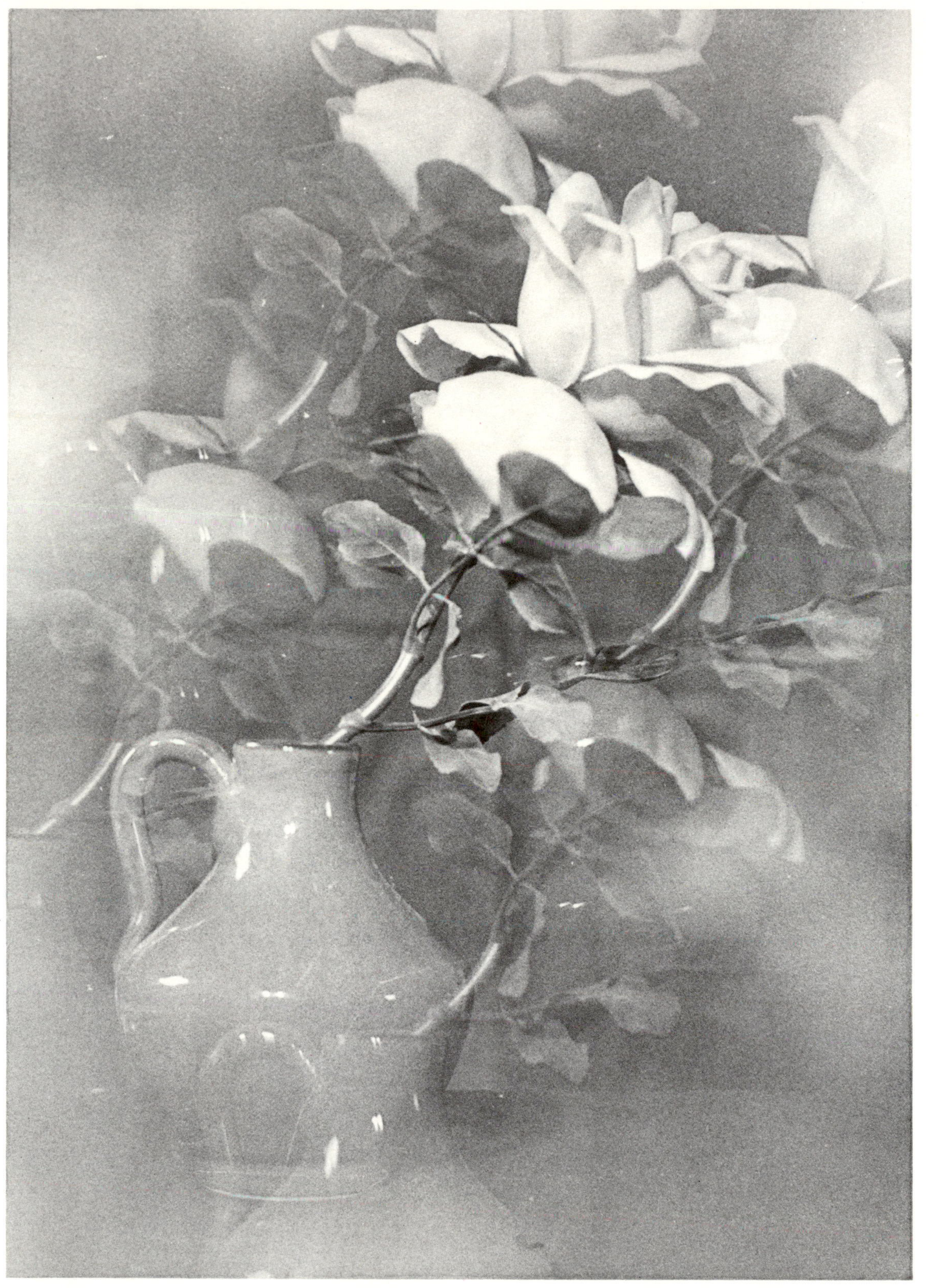

48

49

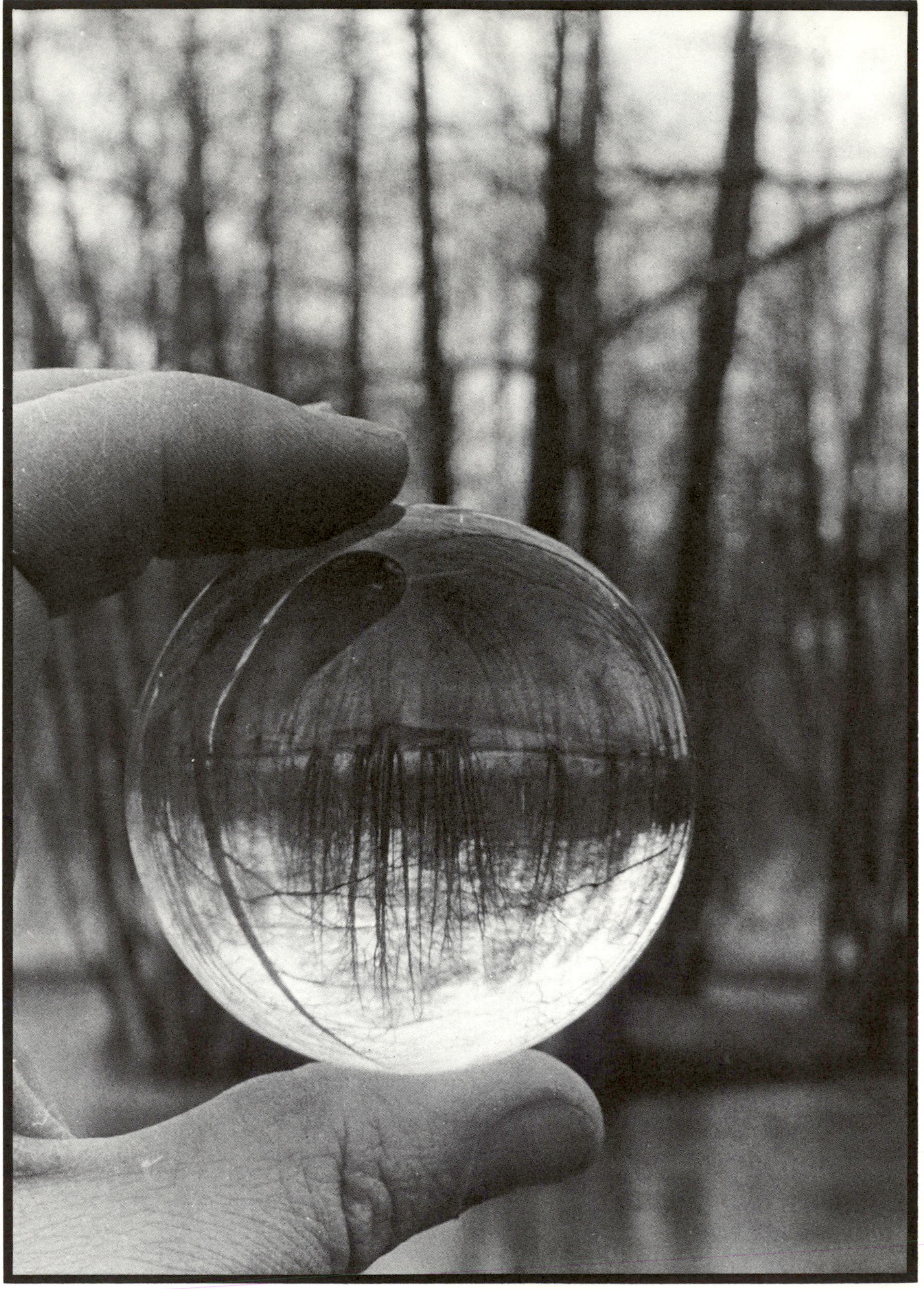

appear which achieve nothing more than to raise the expression 'Ooh—ah!' from the observer. They achieve nothing more simply because, apart from the technical effect, they say nothing. A good picture must offer considerably more than this. It must say something to the viewer: it must make a statement to him and/or provide a positive piece of information.

Whether a particular effect is designed to help the statement of a picture or not has to be decided according to the case in point. This requires some care in planning the picture in advance, as it can easily happen that elaborate techniques obscure the other facets of a picture's statement.

On the other hand, do experiment enthusiastically; for apart from the fact that experiments themselves provide pleasure, it is certainly important to be aware of all possibilities before deciding whether to use them or not.

This concludes our discussion of the creative possibilities of apertures and lenses—from the simple pinhole camera to the highly sophisticated single-lens reflex camera with interchangeable lenses and effects attachments.

50

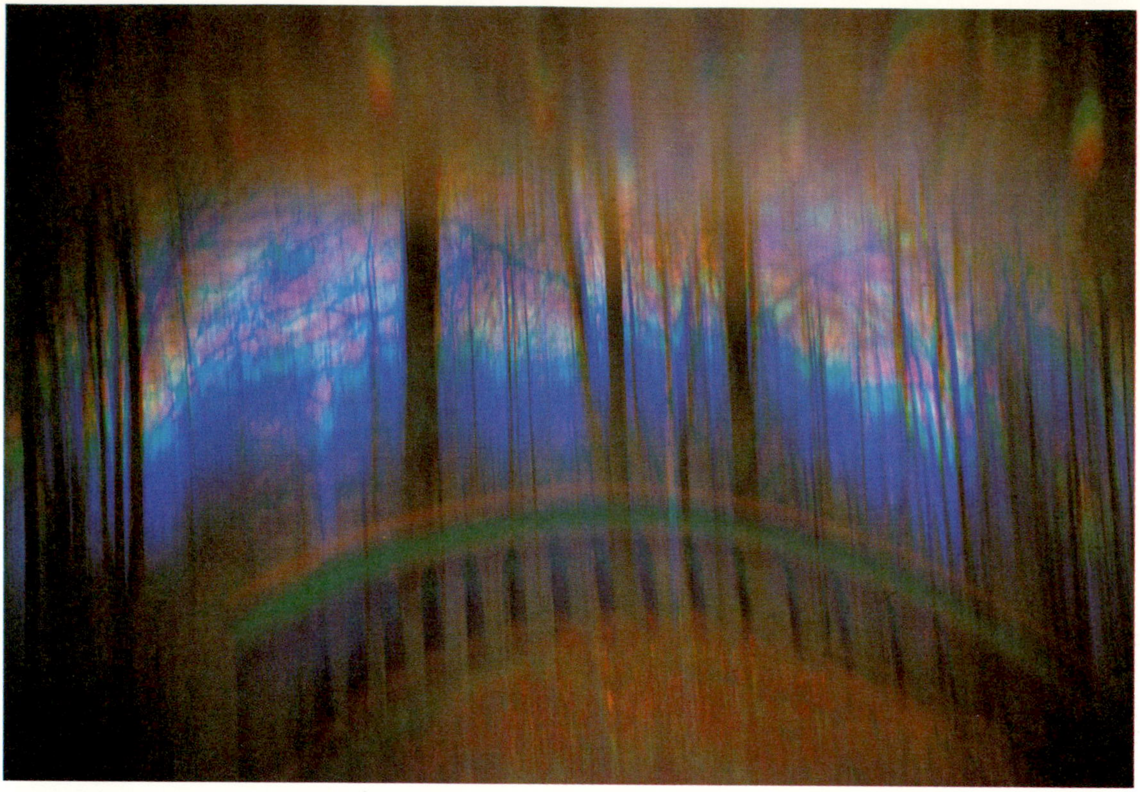

51

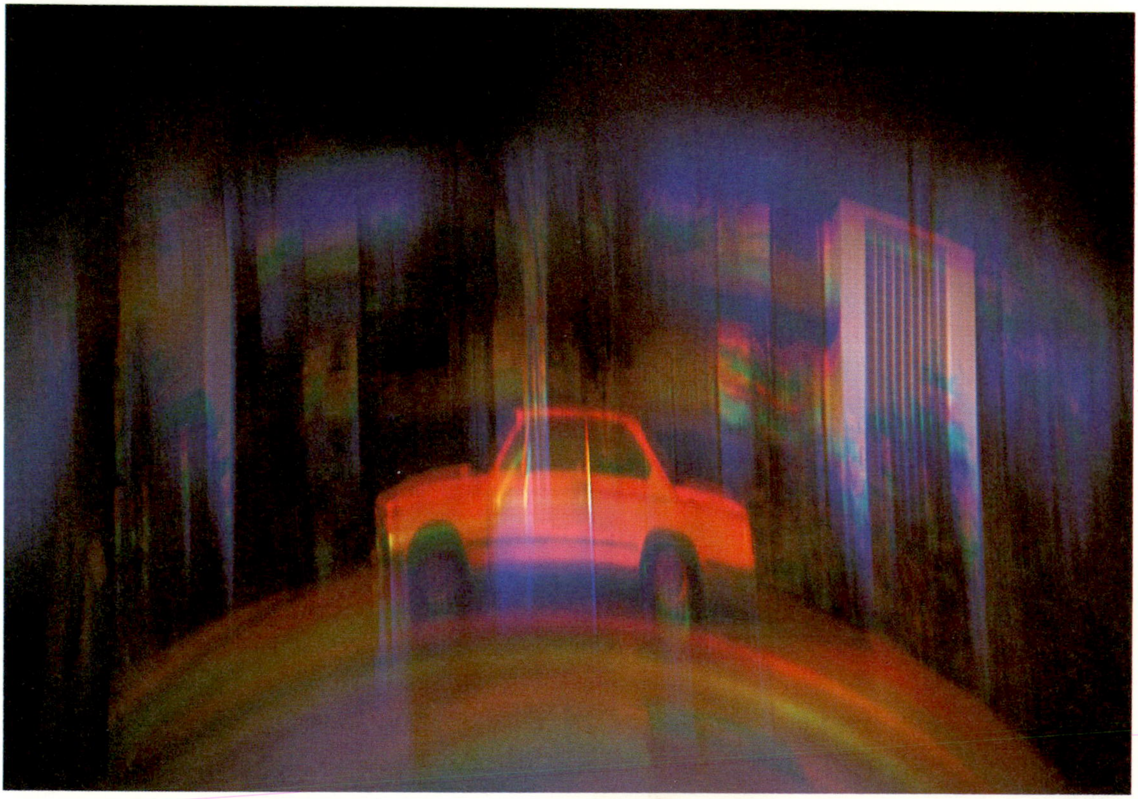

11: PHOTOGRAPHY WITH THE SHUTTER

The shutter serves as a means of allocating exposure time; that is to say, it exposes the film for a definite, predetermined period, during which light falls on the film.

The exposure times usual today have been selected so that the step between one shutter speed and the next involves exactly a halving or a doubling of the amount of light falling on the film. Similarly, the values for iris opening have been determined so that a move from one aperture number to the next (eg from *f*8 to *f*5.6, or from *f*8 to *f*11) brings about precisely the same gain or loss of light as does a doubling or halving of the exposure time.

If the exposure meter gives as a correct figure, for example, *f*8 at 1/30 sec, the following time/aperture combinations will result in the same amount of light falling on the film, and hence a correct setting:

1/4	1/8	1/15	1/30	1/60	1/125	1/250	1/500	1/1000
22	16	11	8	5.6	4	2.8	2	1.4

As described in the chapter on depth of field, choice of aperture has an important pictorial effect. In addition, the duration of shutter opening can play a significant part in visual effect. Thus a compromise between the alternative values must be found.

Firstly, there is a curiosity which lends itself to a highly interesting creative effect; that is, it is possible to produce photographs using shutter alone, without lens or iris.

Figs 52, *53*, *54* and *55* were produced in this way. The body of a single-lens reflex camera was fitted with an angled viewfinder, and was placed in the light cone of an enlarger, with the lens bayonet mount pointing upwards. (Propped up by two cigar boxes placed edgewise, so that the angled viewfinder could be used with a minimum of neck dislocation!)

All four photographs show different 'aspects' of a wine glass, which was placed at the edge of the lens bayonet mount and photographed in various positions. The

52

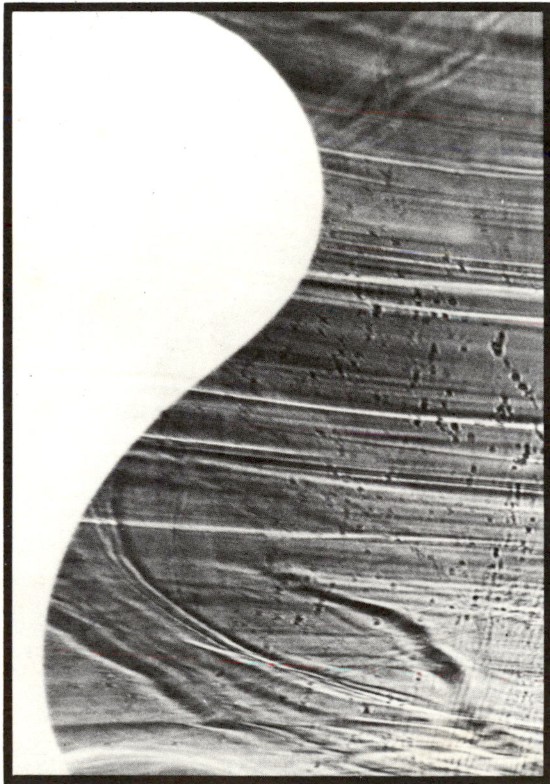

53

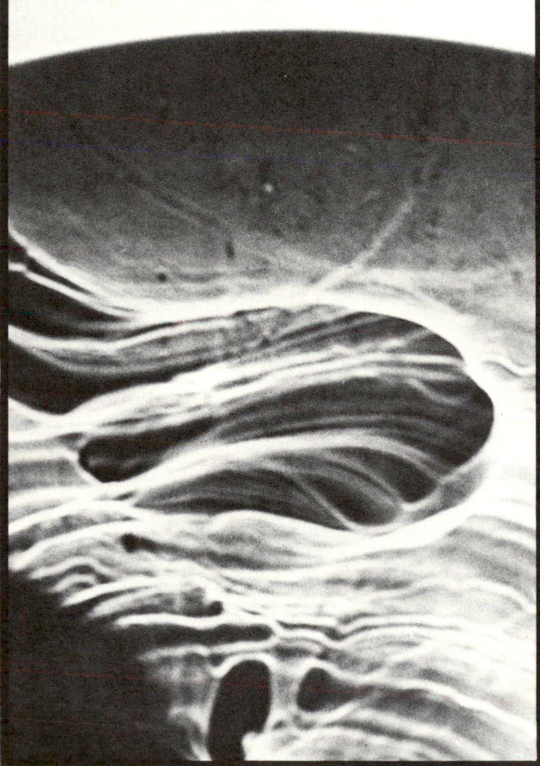

54

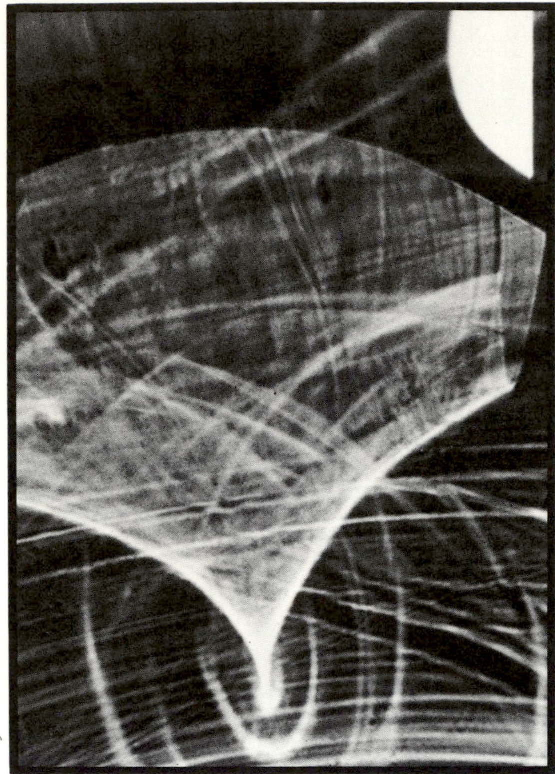

55

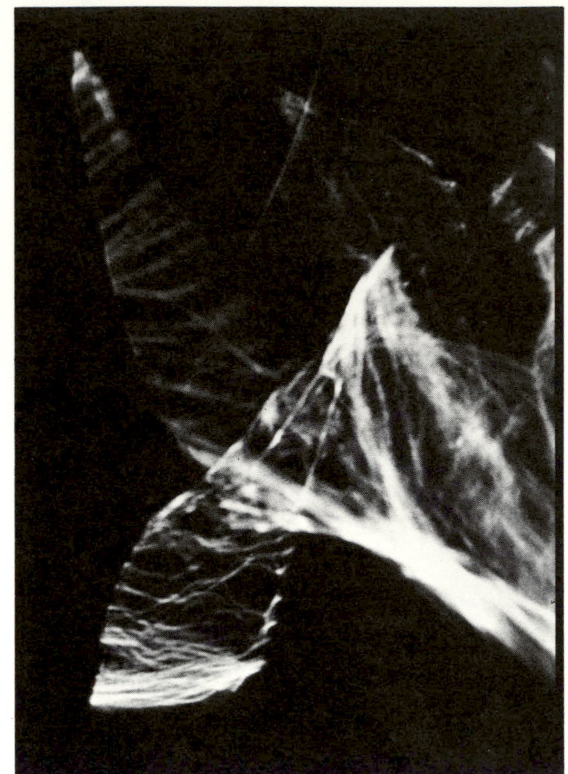

effect can be observed in the viewfinder, and the determination of exposure time offers no difficulties. The automatic mechanism of the camera can be relied upon, though it is advisable to overexpose radically (I used ASA 400/27 DIN film as if it had been ASA 100/21 DIN).

Glass with illumination shining through always produces monochrome images, or images with the same colour as the glass. Very fine colourful compositions result if the camera is set up vertically outside the cone of light and metallic objects used to reflect the light into the body of the camera. Using this method, for example, I have created a series of successful multicoloured pictures, using as a reflecting metal object an old watch-strap.

Since all sorts of transparent and metallic objects can be used for experimentation with these two methods, and since this potential of photography is scarcely known, anyone can here enter into untrodden creative territory—and indeed with very little expense. It is not even necessary to have an enlarger: any lamp can be used, as long as its shade can be covered except for a small opening.

12: TIME EXPOSURE

As already described in the previous chapter, the shutter serves the purpose of deciding the duration of exposure time. Under specific circumstances, however, it is possible to use other means to carry out this task. For example, the illustrations in this chapter were produced in a completely darkened room, in which the shutter could readily have been left open for an even longer time, since the duration of the exposure in a dark room can be regulated by switching the light on and off.

Which method is chosen generally depends on convenience. For subjects such as those shown in *Figs 56–59* the automatic exposure system is not used, and long exposures are called for (up to 20 sec). Under certain circumstances the following method may be the most expedient. Fully darken the room, switch the light off, and then open the camera shutter. With the help of a darkroom timer (highly convenient—but you can count in seconds too!) the light can now be switched on for the required time. After the exposure time has elapsed, close the camera shutter again, of course, before the room lighting is switched on. (How to ascertain the correct exposure time for such subjects is explained in the section on exposure measurement.)

All four photographs feature a simple piece of bent wire (*Figs 56*, *57* and *58* show the same piece, bent at right angles; *Fig 59* shows another, quite irregularly formed). This wire was placed on a record player turntable, illuminated from the side with a slide projector, and then photographed at an exposure time of between 10 and 20 sec, while the turntable was in motion (16 rpm). In *Figs 56* and *59* the wire stood roughly vertically at the turning axis, while in *Figs 57* and *58* it was askew and outside the axis.

The bright strips (particularly clear in *Figs 56* and *57*) are interesting. These were caused by the bright/dark phases of the alternating current. Many people make use

56

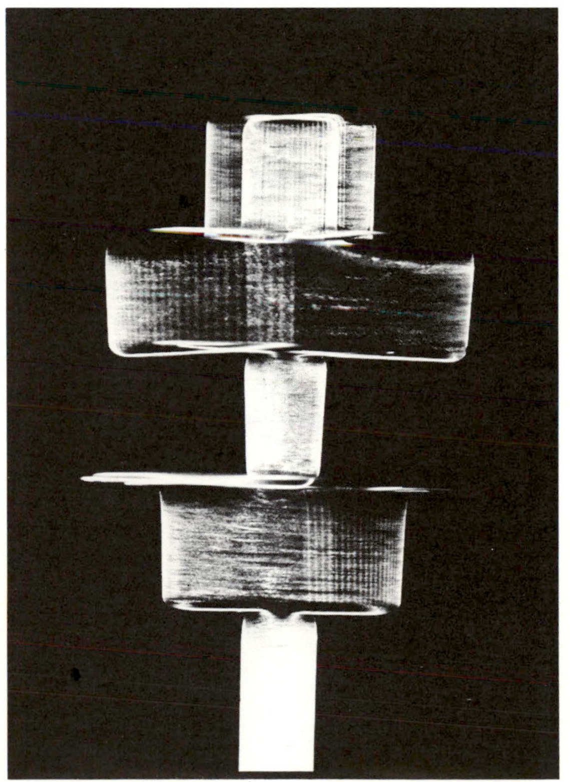

57

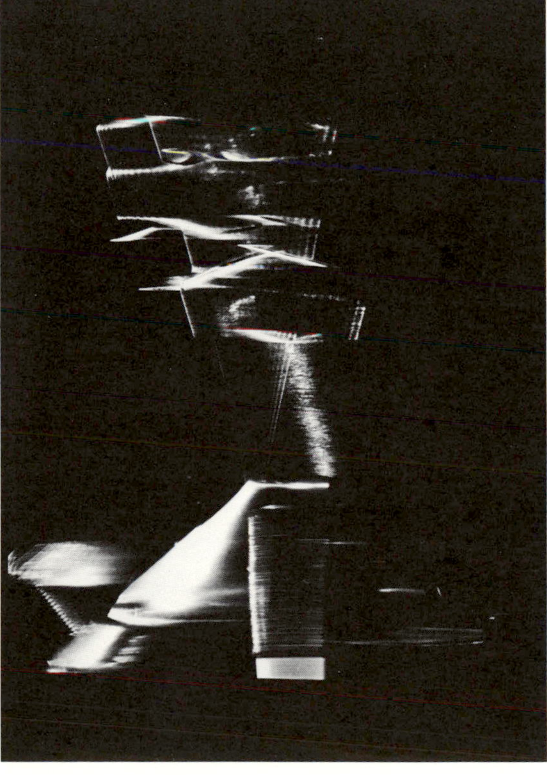

58

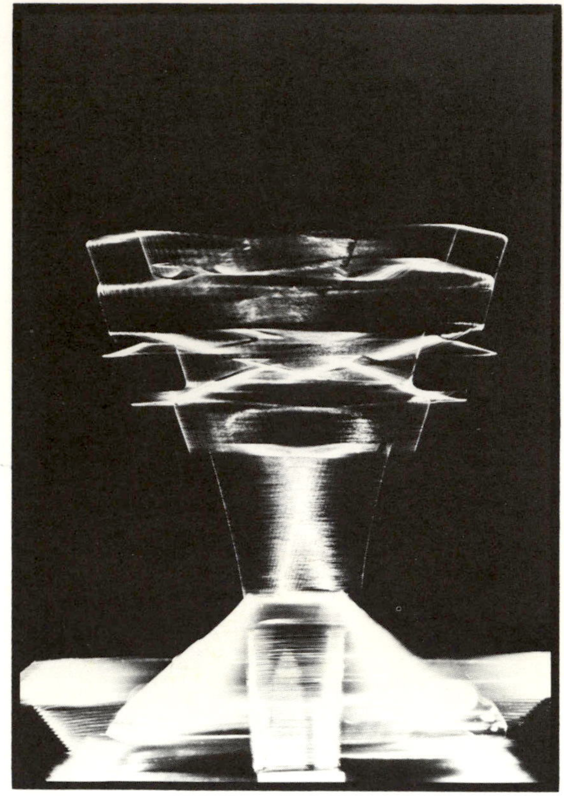

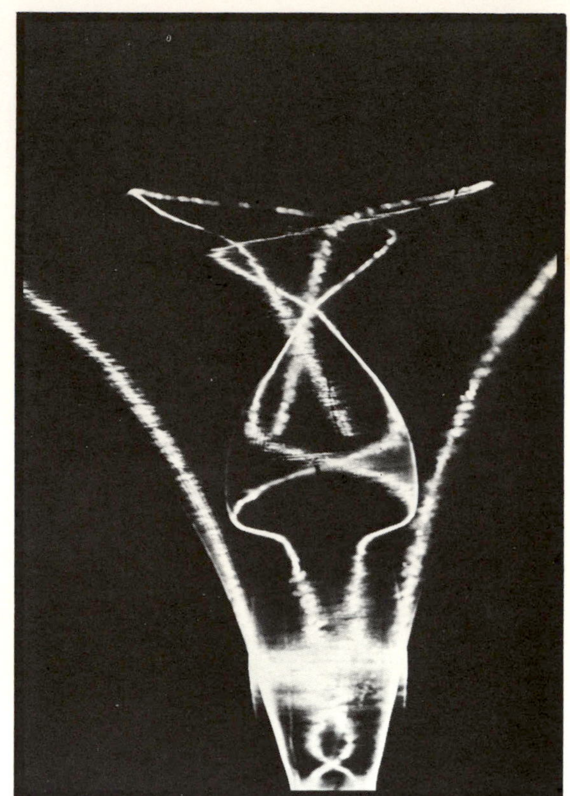

59

of this phenomenon, in order to test their camera shutters. If you set an electric bulb swinging, extended on a long lead, and photograph it at various shutter speeds, on the negative it is possible to count the bright points and dark pauses. Since the frequency of the alternating current is known, the duration of the respective shutter speed may be ascertained.

The details of such an experiment can be worked out by the reader quite easily, and will not be expanded upon here, as the concern of this book is rather with creative possibilities. The potential uses of this method are by no means confined to the relatively 'exotic' representations of rotating objects and the like, as described above, but in practice are often more conventional, as will be explained in succeeding chapters.

13: REPRESENTATIONS OF MOVEMENT

Most objects move in some sort of way. Anyone who has tried to photograph, for example, cut flowers in a vase, is aware that parts of such static objects, under the heat of floodlights, often move visibly. It is not necessary to discuss here subjects such as children, animals and cars. In a perfectly peaceful landscape too, there is a certain amount of movement; a slight breath of wind is sufficient to set leaves and clouds in motion and to make water stir.

Remember also the camera operator—all of us, even the most placid, shake to a greater extent than is desirable for a truly sharp photograph. Since almost everything has some natural movement during exposure it is theoretically represented in a photograph as unsharp. This is only 'theoretically' true, because most of these movements are so slow or so insignificant that the unsharpness caused is insufficient to be recorded by any photographic apparatus (that is to say, the track of a movement cannot be recorded on film if it is less than the diameter of the known circle of confusion). On the other hand, other movements are so appreciable that they appear as 'streaks' on the negative or transparency.

There are two distinct ways of choosing to represent movement:

1 To attempt to 'freeze' all movements as far as possible, and thus record all parts of the subject sharply.
2 To select the conditions for photography in such a way that all or many of the parts of the moving subject are portrayed as unsharp.

Which of these two procedures is chosen depends in the final analysis on what kind of impression of the scene is to be presented to the observer, as technically both methods are possible.

In order to 'freeze' all movement as brief a shutter opening as possible is required. As far as movement of the camera operator is concerned, there is an old rule of thumb which states that, in order to avoid camera shake, the exposure time should be at any rate as small as the reciprocal of the focal length; for instance, 1/50 sec for a focal length of 50 mm, and 1/250 sec for a focal length of 200 mm. To achieve maximum sharpness, however, these values will not suffice; the figures should at least be halved, or—much better—a firm tripod should be used, if the natural camera shake is to be overcome. Unfortunately, in practice, it is frequently the case that with the requisite brief exposure times, such large apertures have to be used that depth of field is severely limited.

However, in doubtful cases there is a good rule to follow: better a really sharp image with limited depth of field than an image with great depth of field and camera shake. (The person who wants to be confident of invariably making sharp pictures uses a tripod!)

Setting aside the matter of camera shake, the question remains: what exposure time should be used if all moving objects are to be represented sharply?

The answer to this question depends upon three factors:

1 Speed of movement.
2 Direction of movement.
3 Scale of image.

It is immediately evident that the necessary shutter speed depends upon the speed of the moving object. *Fig 60* represents the direction of motion and its effects. On the right there are two moving objects (b), whose speed is symbolised by the arrows. The length of the arrows (a) indicates the path travelled by the objects during exposure time. The diagram shows that the object moving across the camera viewing field traces a discernible smear, while the position of the object which moves towards the camera does not alter at all. Its image during exposure merely becomes slightly larger, as it comes nearer and hence is represented on a larger scale. From this observation a rule can be formulated stating that exposure time for a movement of constant speed must become shorter as the path runs more parallel to the film plane. For

60

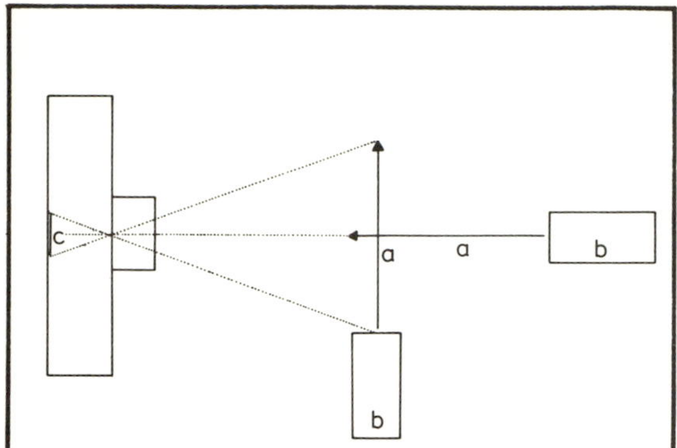

61

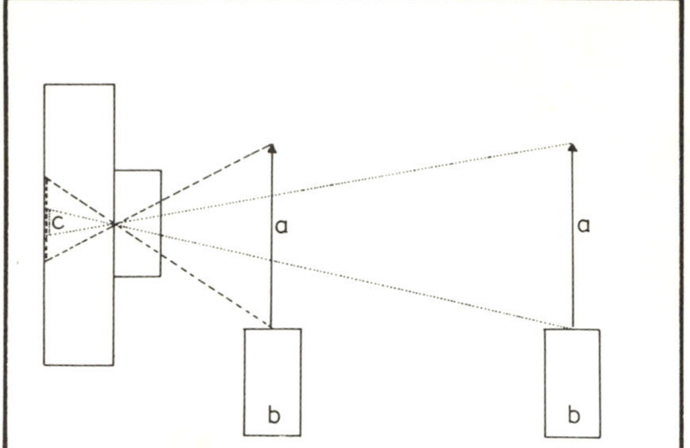

example, take a car in the street travelling at about 30 mph, with a 50 mm lens at a distance of 30 ft (10 m). The necessary shutter speed will be 1/1000 sec if it is travelling parallel to the camera, but only 1/60 sec if it moves directly towards the camera.

Scale of image operates in a different way, however, with regard to movement unsharpness. *Fig 61* shows two representations of the same object moving at identical speed. The distance of the object from the camera is different and the object is therefore represented on the film in two different scales. It can be seen at once that movement blur decreases the further the object is from the camera. The car travelling along the street will serve again as an example. At a distance of 15 ft (5 m) an exposure time of 1/2000 sec is necessary if the object is to appear sharp, while at 75 ft (25 m) an exposure time of 1/500 sec is sufficient.

There are tables which give the necessary exposure times for a whole series of subjects. These tables are very useful if you only photograph fast-moving objects occasionally. However, for intensive work on a theme involving motion (eg sport or motor racing), then there is no substitute for personal experience collected over a period of time.

Uniform movements, such as that of a car in motion, represent a special case. Generally, subjects move at irregular speeds. Consider for example a pole-vaulter. As he leaps upwards he is moving at his fastest: the swift upward movement continues until at the highest point of the leap he comes to a complete standstill, whereupon the downward movement begins. It is obvious that at the 'high point' of the action much longer exposure time can be used than at any other portion of the 'flight'. It is very fortunate that such apparently static moments in the action generally provide inherently dramatic shots. Thus, with an effort, the precise instant can be captured on film.

If the movement is to be rendered as a 'smear' or blur, there is a choice of two different procedures, which can also be combined with each other. Firstly, the camera can be held still—preferably on a tripod—and a shutter speed selected which is slow enough to ensure that the moving object appears unsharp. Here this rule applies: the faster the motion of the object and/or the longer the exposure time, the more blurred the object appears—and the stronger the 'smear effect', the faster the motion depicted will appear to the observer.

For this kind of representation of movement, there are upper and lower limits. If the blur is too modest, the subject merely appears unsharp, and there is no real impression of movement. On the other hand, if the exposure time has been too lengthy, the opposite effect occurs: the moving object becomes scarcely recognisable. This can indeed reach the extreme where a moving object is not recorded on the picture at all. It could occur, for example, where the exposure time has been so lengthy that a car passing through the scene was there for only a small fraction of that time. *Fig 62* shows an example of a photograph which falls roughly midway between these two extremes. The camera was set up on a tripod about 40 ft (12 m) from the passing car. The shutter speed was 1/60 sec.

Fig 63 demonstrates the other possible way to represent motion. During the

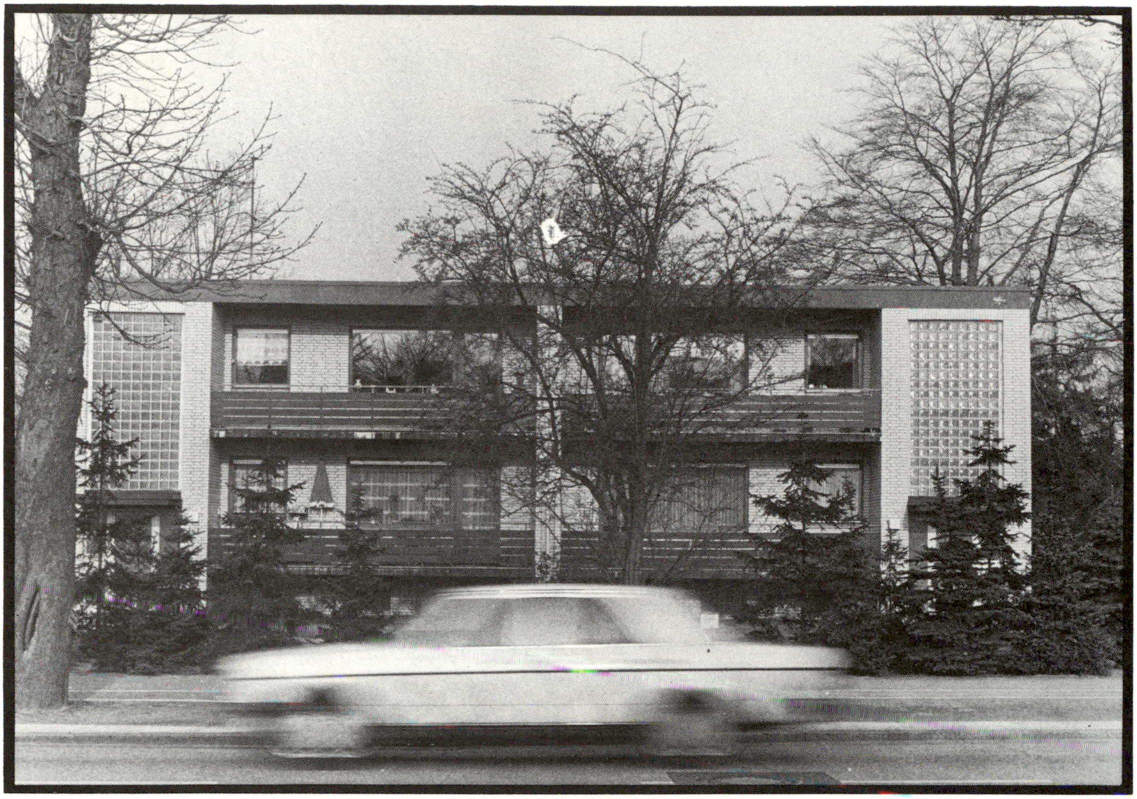

62

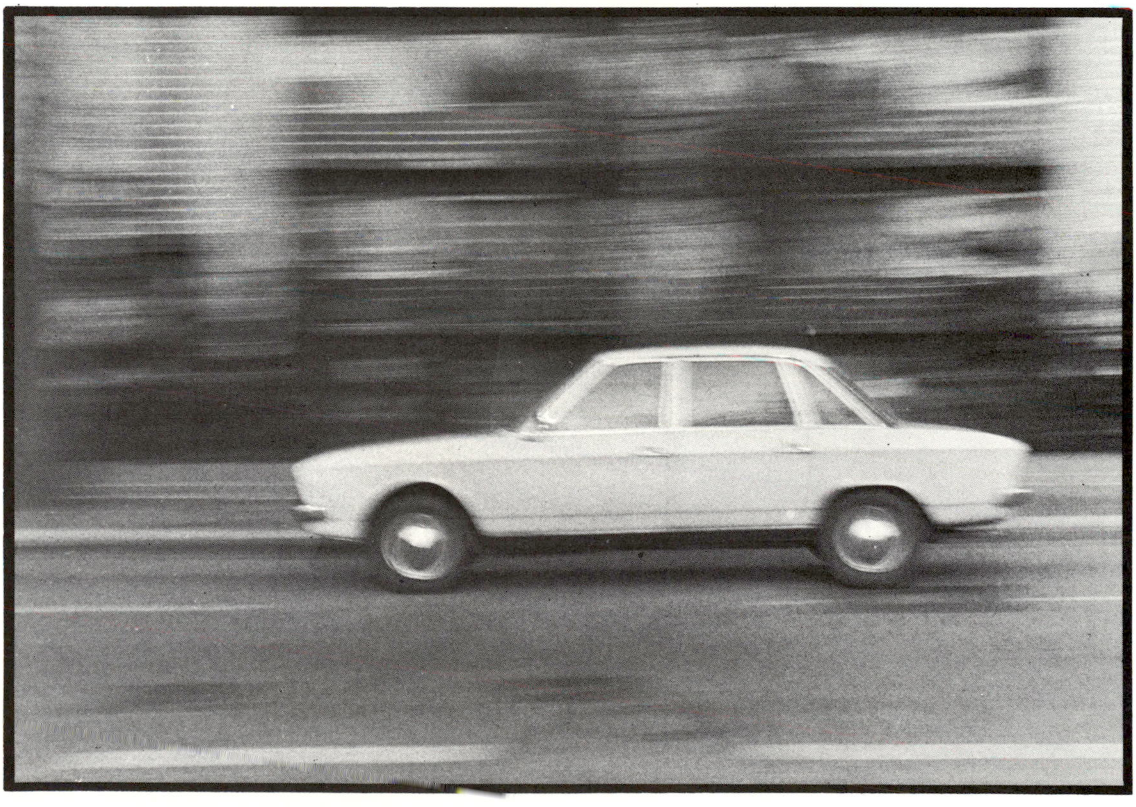

63

65

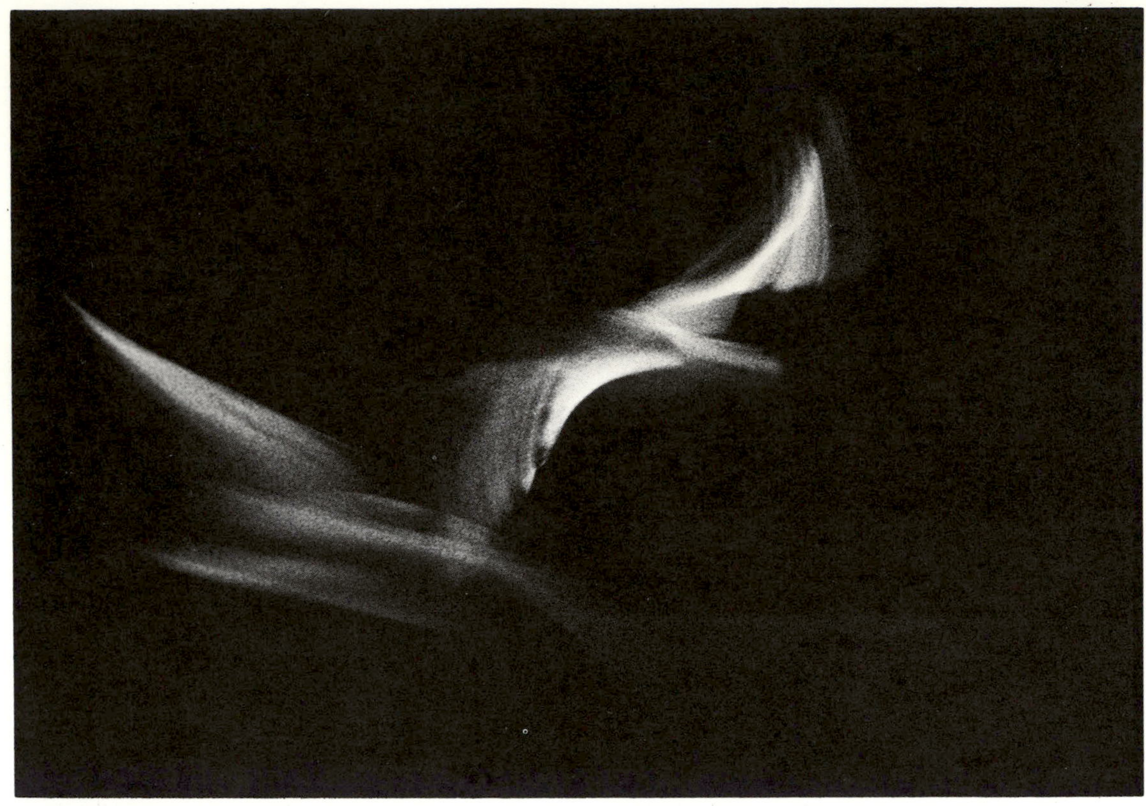

exposure time the camera was 'following' the moving car, with the result that the background was lost in a blur of movement, while the car was (to some extent) sharply delineated. (All other photographic data are as in *Fig 62.*) As it is normally impossible, especially with long exposure times, to move the camera round in absolute synchronisation with the object, such photographs usually include both kinds of movement unsharpness. Only when really brief exposures are selected is it possible to portray the main object (eg a racing car) really sharply.

Moving the camera with the moving object is technically quite simple. First, set the distance the car (for instance) will be from the camera as it passes; select, according to the effect desired, the appropriate shutter speed and centre the car in the viewfinder before exposure. Then move the camera in such a way that the car is held as precisely as possible at the same point in the viewfinder, and press the release as soon as the best position has been reached. It really could not be simpler. It is important though to bear in mind that to be confident of a satisfactory outcome, it is necessary to practise this procedure a good deal. Where possible, it is advisable to take several photographs of the same subject.

Such movement pictures are particularly impressive in colour, since in the blurred areas the colours of the individual parts of the subject blend with one another and can produce the new colour tones. However, very interesting and impressive compositions are also possible in monochrome. Some examples are shown in *Figs 64* and *65*. Although (or perhaps because) they are so simple, they symbolise the lightness, elegance and swiftness of the flying seagulls most strikingly. Whether the second picture (*Fig 65*) goes too far into abstraction or not is a matter of taste and depends on the individual viewer. In any case, it is to be hoped that these and all the other photographic examples will inspire the reader to individual experiments in this area.

14: FLASH AND EXPOSURE

There is a shutter speed on most cameras 'X', corresponding generally to 1/100 sec, at which the release of the camera may be synchronised with an electronic flash unit. In other words, the flash is set off in such a way that its period of illumination falls exactly into the time-span during which the shutter is fully open. However, this does not imply that the flash duration and the total illumination time are of equal length. On the contrary, while the 'X' shutter time of a camera may last 1/100 sec, a flash unit can offer illumination periods extending from 1/600 sec to 1/40 000 sec (according to setting and brightness). The fact that synchronisation does not operate the shorter shutter speeds has nothing to do with the duration of shutter or illumination times. It is simply because at the moment of the flash the image field is not completely revealed.

Fig 66 shows a subject lit with flash according to instructions; whereas for *Fig 67* the automatic system was overridden. Instead of using the synchronised time a shutter speed of 1/250 sec was used. On the lefthand side of the picture about ⅓ of the negative area is not illuminated, as it was concealed by the partly open shutter blind. If this series is continued with still shorter exposure times, the unlit area becomes wider and wider, until at 1/1000 sec only a very narrow strip of picture remains at the righthand side. There is no point in showing appropriate illustrations, because a predominantly black image field is really not very informative. Instead, it can be shown what happens in the opposite direction, that is with a combination of flash and long exposure times.

Fig 68 was taken using 1 sec and flash, and *Fig 69* using ½ sec and flash. In these instances the camera was moved during the entire duration of exposure; for *Fig 68* with irregular vibrating motion, and for *Fig 69* with quite a smooth swing from right to left. In these pictures, it should be possible to detect the movement unsharpness, or blur, which was discussed in the two previous chapters. But quite certainly it is easy to see that, alongside the unsharp movement tracks, a sharp 'main image' or 'basic image' has emerged. The explanation of this phenomenon will become clear by reference to Chapter 12.

If the experiment had been carried out in a completely darkened room, the operation of the flash unit during the lengthy exposure time would have worked in the same way as switching the light on and off. A completely normal and correctly lit picture would have been obtained. No movement blur would have appeared, as the movement of the camera during the short actual exposure time could not have been recorded. This is changed only if the subject is provided with additional illumination. In that case, during the entire period while the shutter remains open, the image can be recorded on film and any movements occurring during this period appear on the picture as blurs. This offers numerous possibilities for visual creativity, because the effect appears not only with movement of camera but also with movement of subject. For example, in this manner representations of movement can be enhanced, by means of a sharp 'main image'. There are, however, considerably more possibilities in this case, since the flash unit can be operated quite separately from the camera. With some equipment, there is even a choice between manual and automatic operations. (Details concerning the manual use of the flash unit would be found in the camera instruction manual.)

If the flash unit is used separately from the camera, it is possible to incorporate several phases of a movement in one picture. A simple example of this is shown in *Fig 70*, which depicts two stages in the procedure of pouring liquid from a jug. The photograph was taken in a completely darkened room. A black cloth served as a background. The camera was set on a tripod and pointed at the selected picture area. The flash unit was hand held and directed at the subject. Precisely at the start of the movement, the shutter was opened, with the aid of a cable release (at position 'B'), while the flash unit was at the same time fired twice in rapid succession. Immediately after that the shutter was closed. The result was the representation of a continuous movement in

66 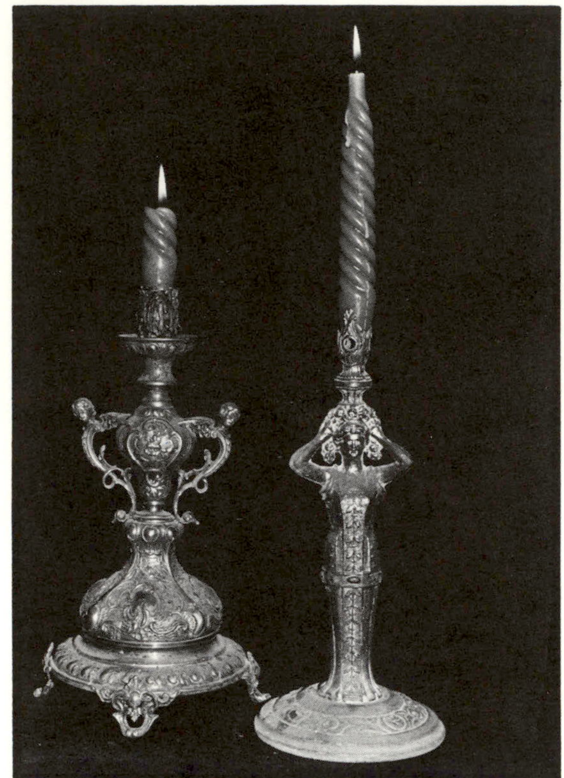

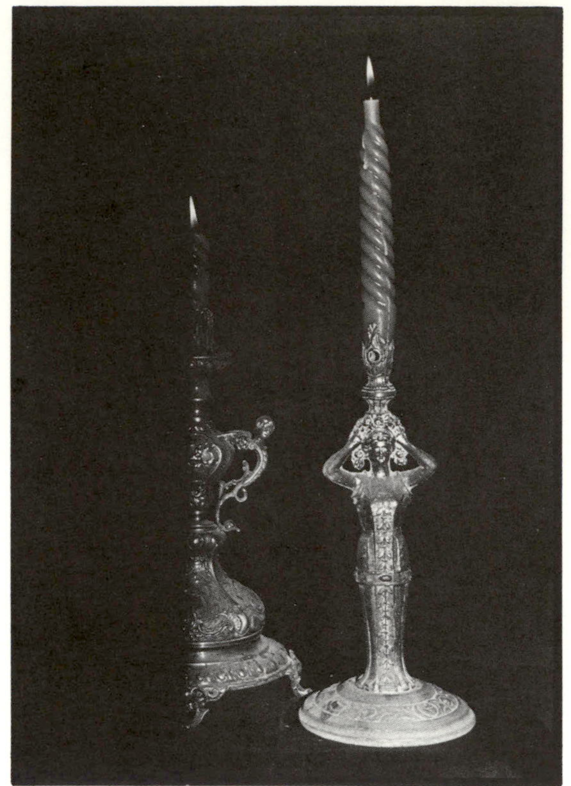 67

68 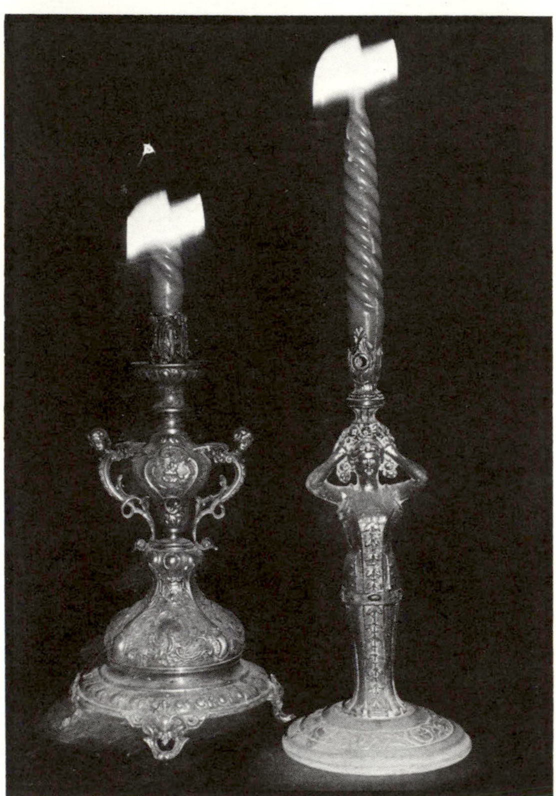

two phases—as shown in the illustration.

To help avoid errors, there are two pieces of technical advice which are useful to know. If the two individual parts of the picture overlap, as occurs in *Fig 70*, expose as few partial images as possible in superimposition, so that the picture does not become too confused. In addition, remember that the amount of light exposed to the film doubles in those areas where part of the subject is lit twice, so that the aperture must be slightly less than indicated. (Details concerning the correct procedure are given in the next chapter on multiple exposure.) If the movement extends over the entire subject area, and the moving subject is portrayed as being very small, a large number of partial light exposures can be made without the picture becoming indistinct.

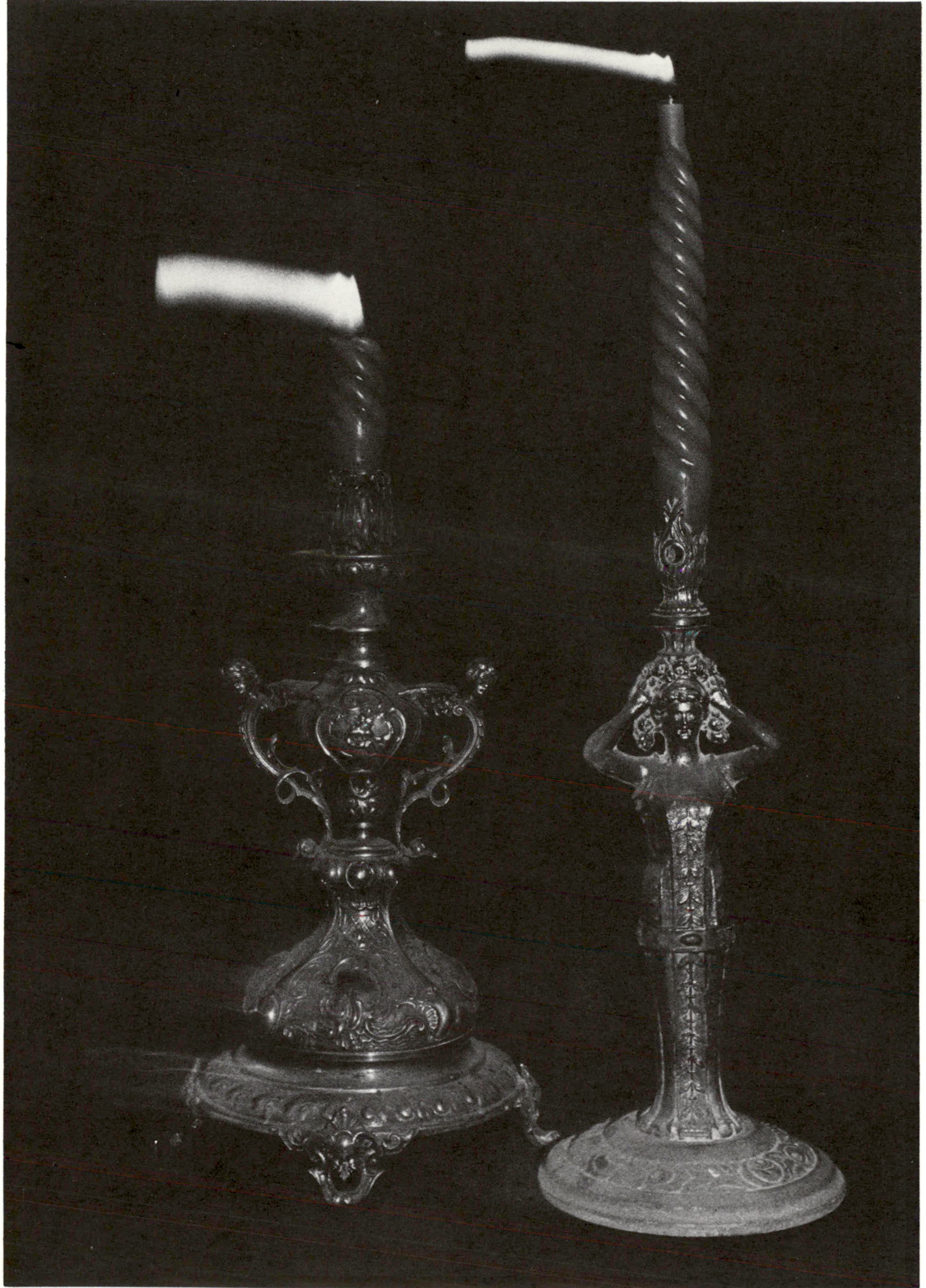
69

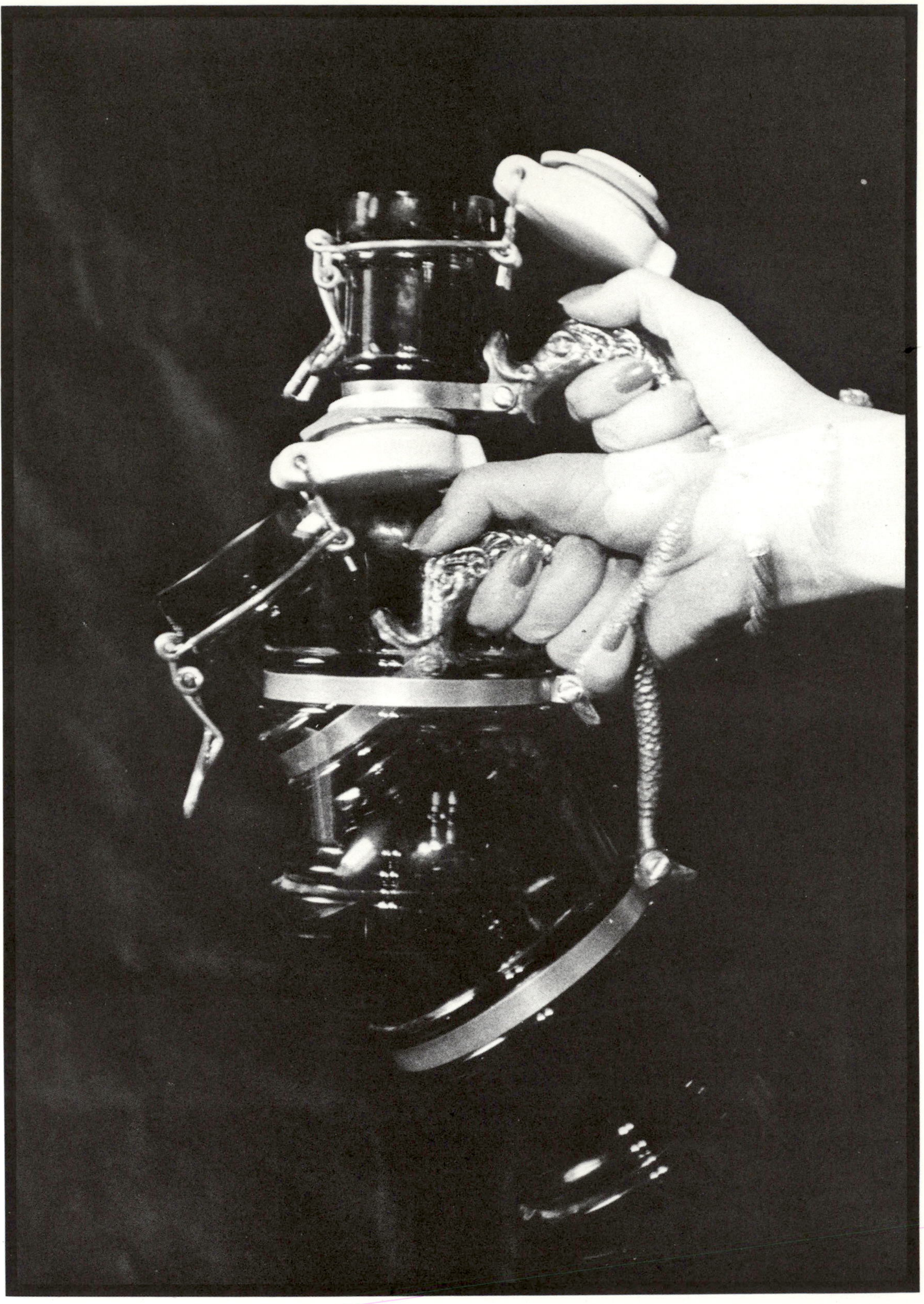

15: MULTIPLE EXPOSURE

Multiple exposures can in theory be produced equally well either by releasing the shutter repeatedly or by switching the light on and off. This is only in theory, however, for with each sort of multiple exposure, one procedure or another is preferable. Most of the multiple exposures dealt with in this chapter are in practice feasible only with a camera whose double-exposure prevention lock can be switched off at will.

In the past, double exposures were categorised as infrequent faults, occurring because shutter and film transport had to be operated separately. Then someone jumped to the crafty idea of coupling the two together in such a way that release of the shutter was possible only after the shutter was cocked and the film transported. Nowadays, with all miniature cameras both procedures are accomplished in one action, so that this kind of mistake is quite impossible.

The trouble was that it had become established among photographers, during the development of this technical innovation, that double and multiple exposures represented an interesting photographic creative medium. Suddenly this had to be given up owing to the security system built into the camera. The logical consequence was that the better (and more expensive) cameras were provided with the facility of overriding—switching off the double-exposure prevention lock. The upshot is that it is now possible to take up this area of photographic creativity once again. This is very fortunate, as multiple exposure can be one of the most interesting photographic techniques. It has, however, been somewhat discredited for a time, and there are three main reasons for this:

1 For some years multiple exposures were impossible with most cameras.
2 Multiple exposures were (and still are) misused for kitsch productions such as 'Naked Girl in a Bottle' and similar rubbish. But why throw out the baby with the bath water and forgo this creative facility because of this type of horror?
3 It is often said that multiple exposure is 'old hat', and so a lot of people will not wear it. In this regard it should be pointed out that this criticism is generally levelled at stereotypes such as those referred to in Point 2, which indeed have existed for too long. Besides, why should multiple exposures be considered 'old hat'? Photography itself has existed much longer than multiple exposure, and yet photography is still with us. This applies also to other creative possibilities described in this book. The decisive factor is not whether it is new or not: it is what you are going to make of it!

Fig 71 shows a threefold exposure. At first sight the effect is of a completely conventional photograph. It becomes recognisable as a multiple exposure only when the colourfully iridescent stretch of water is noticed—and then only if the viewer is aware of how this effect came to be.

It is well known that in colour photography light is separated into three primary colours blue, red and yellow and combined in the film itself. The various tones are composed of mixtures of these three basic colours. Consequently, it is also possible to filter the light used for the photograph in such a way that with one exposure, only the light of one primary colour falls on the film. Now if you record three exposures in succession in the three primary colours on the same section of film, a picture in natural colours must result, just as it does in a single exposure with the whole spectrum of colours falling on the film at once. This is the case in theory, but with one modification. If during the individual partial exposures something changes in the picture, through movement, all the portions of the picture do not retain the necessary amount of each colour. This should become clearer if you refer to *Fig 72*. In this case during the separate partial exposures various persons were in different parts of the scene, so that they appear as coloured figures in the picture.

In *Fig 71* the water of the lake appeared in each of the partial exposures, so that the correct total amount of light fell on the film; but owing to the differing reflections in the water whose surface was moved by the wind, the light was split up into multicoloured areas. No further explanation is needed to show that this can provide highly interesting creative potential for the representation of movement. The technical prerequisites needed to produce such a picture are as follows. In addition to a camera with provision for multiple exposure, and as firm a tripod as possible, a 'repro-filter' (red, blue and green) is necessary. Simply place the camera on the tripod and expose the picture once through each of the three filters. Measure the exposure through the filter each time, and take half the assessed value. It should be noted that each of the three filters calls for a different value, so for each exposure there must be a separate assessment. The different values are not put into practice by altering the aperture, but by appropriate choice of shutter speed.

This method of determining exposure time is not quite exact, with the result that changes in the colour balance may appear in the final picture; but the precise determination of appropriate times would be beyond the means available to the average amateur, and so you must either put up with the slight traces of colouration, or else—if you do your own enlarging—filter these traces out in the darkroom.

There are three proven procedures for the production of this form of multiple exposure but still further possibilities may be found:

1 Photography of moving subjects with a static camera.
2 Photography of static subjects with a moving camera.
3 Minor changes in focusing distance, or strong contrasts in depth of field between partial exposures.

Another group of multiple exposures, not illustrated here, are so-called 'double image' photographs which are surely familiar to everyone. These double image pictures can be exemplified by a room of normal appearance with the same person appearing twice in it—perhaps once on one side of the scene as waiter, about to serve himself as diner seated at the other side of the picture.

Technically this kind of picture is fairly easy to produce. Cover half of the picture area during the first exposure, perhaps by fixing a black card to the end of a long lens hood or something of that kind. For the second exposure the other side is similarly masked off. If you work with precision, the trick is not evident in the final picture.

I do not intend to dwell on this matter further, because so far I have been unable to think up a layout which effectively demonstrates this effect—and also because particular pictorial examples would be seen as mere illustrations of the procedure, and not as photographic compositions in themselves. This does not imply, however, that you yourself cannot have a good idea for a picture which can be carried out in this way. It is somewhat different with the second kind of double-image photograph, that is, double or multiple representation of one person or object in front of a black background. Seven pictorial examples are given here, to provide some small insight into the manifold creative possibilities of this technically straightforward procedure. It simply consists of incorporating various partial exposures of one subject (theoretically an unlimited number) on one portion of film. The photographer is thus at liberty to alter the placing and arrangement of the subject, as well as the image scale, the lighting and other features. For this technique, the requirements are only a camera with double exposure facility, a matt black background and lighting equipment.

In practice three difficulties arise, but they are all easily overcome. First of all, even the darkest background reflects a certain amount of light, if it is directed straight at the subject. The result is that this impression of light, absent from a normal photograph, can with repeated partial exposures amount to an uncongenial grey, and moreover can spoil the subject contrast. This can be prevented by setting up the subject some distance in front of the backcloth, and at the same time making sure that none of the light falls on the background.

The classic method consists of painting a cardboard box black, and placing the objects to be photographed on a sheet of glass on the open side of this receptacle. However, reflections on the glass can often lead to thorough confusion. Accordingly, the pictorial examples in *Figs 73—79* were

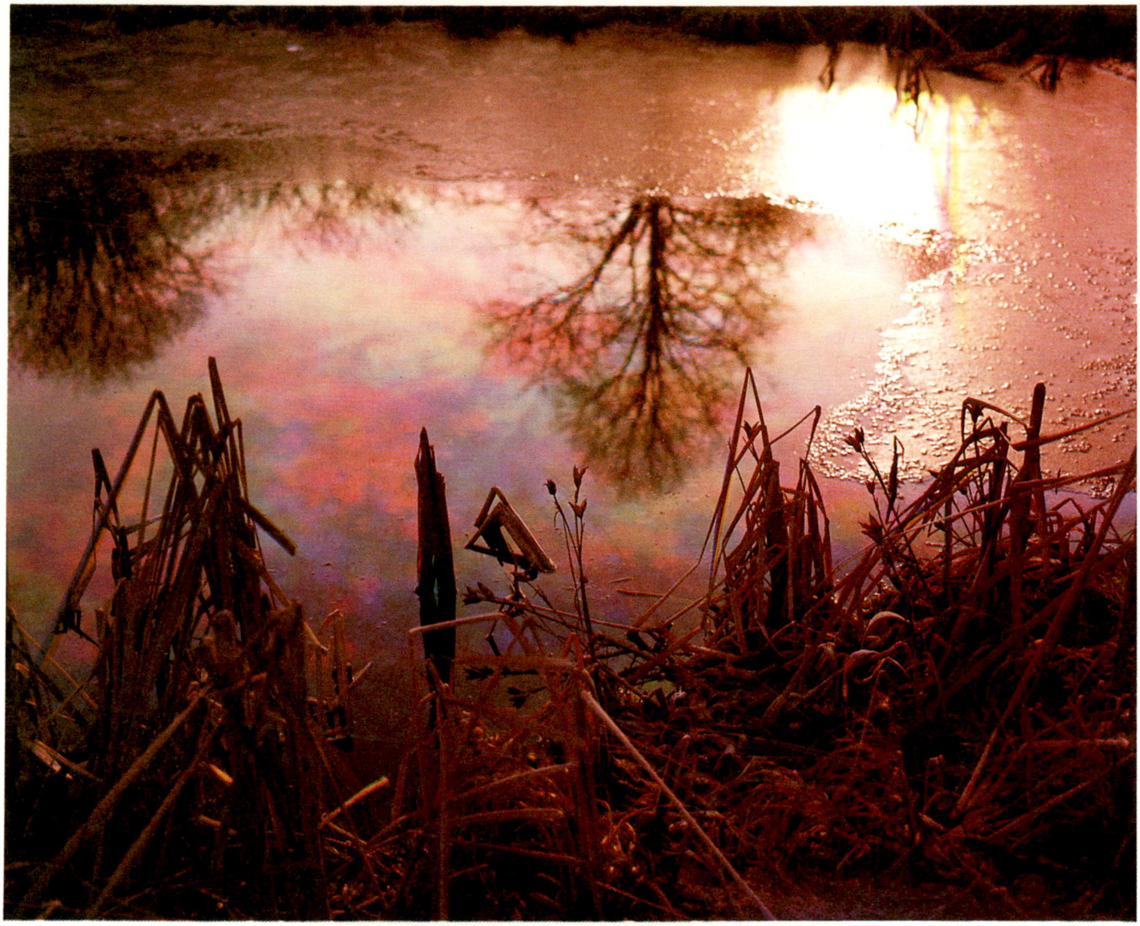

71

72

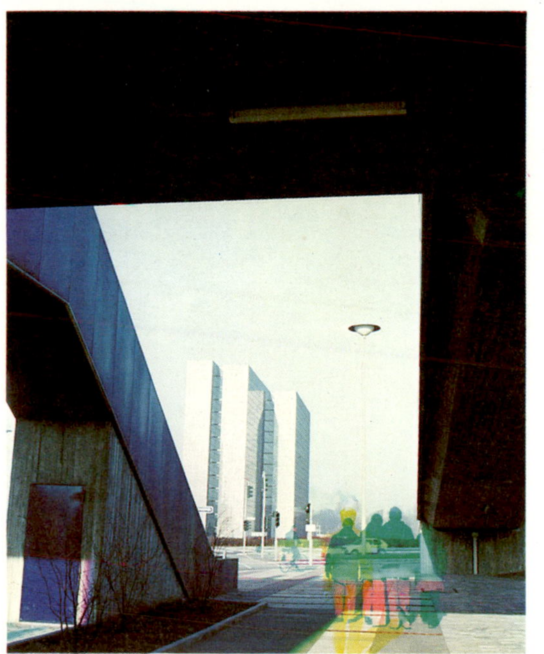

73

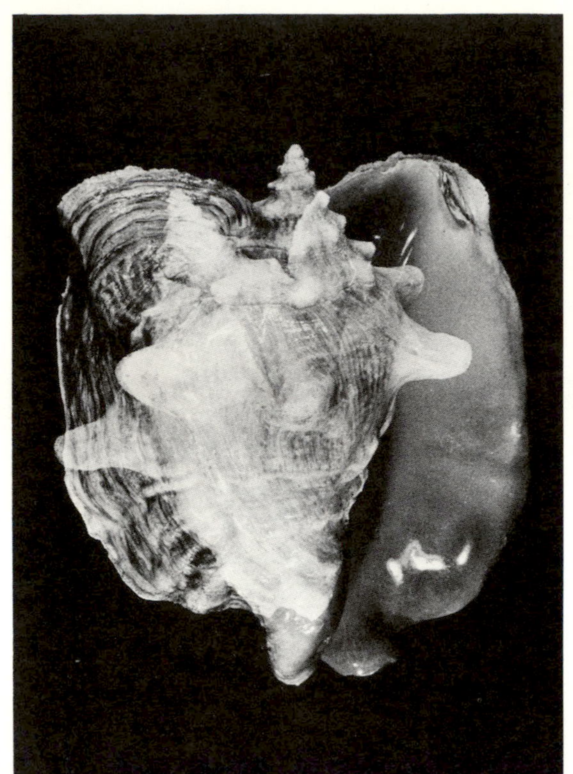

74

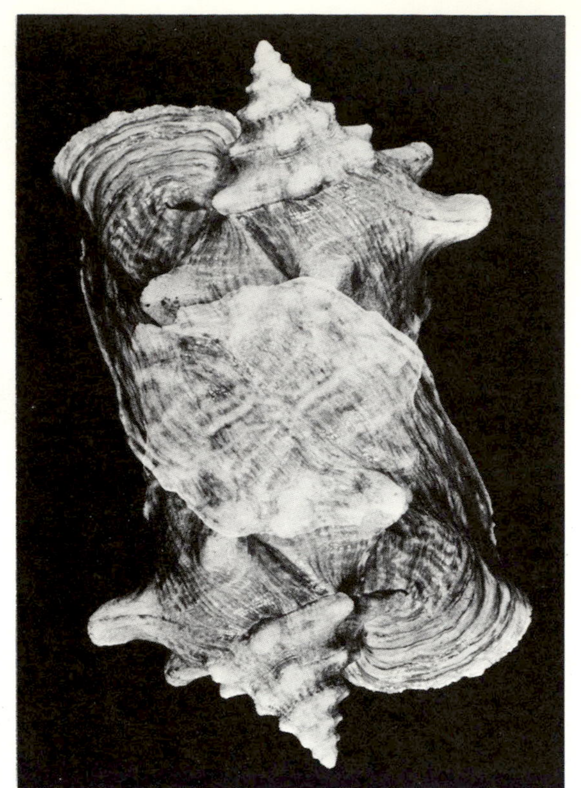

75

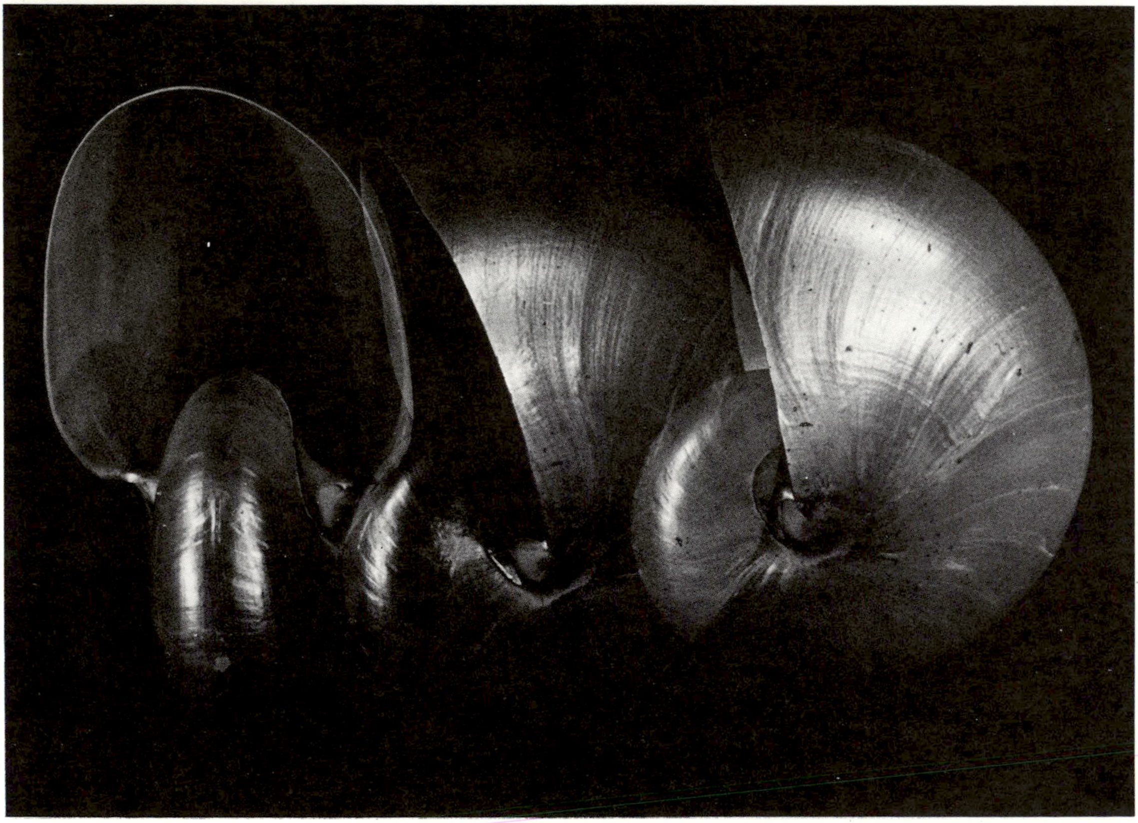

76

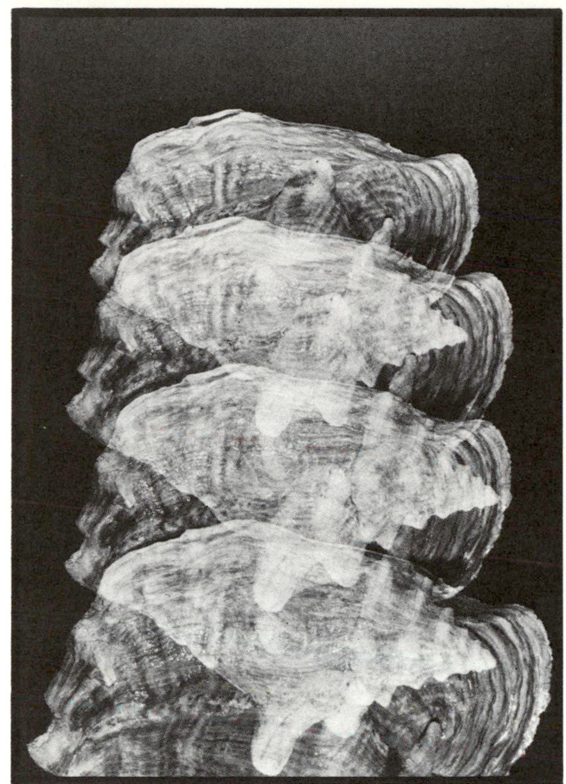

77

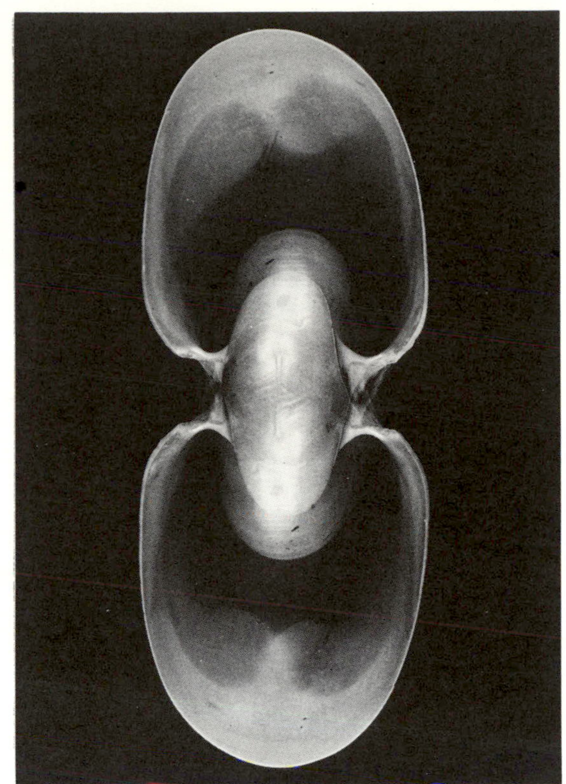

created in another fashion. The base (black velvet) was shaded with black strips of cardboard, which are placed just outside the image field, and the subjects were fixed with modelling clay to bottle corks, in order to keep them the required distance from the base.

The second problem concerns lighting and exposure. By close scrutiny of *Figs 73* and *74*, it is possible to detect that each picture is appreciably brighter in those areas where the two partial exposures overlap. This is a natural consequence of the fact that in these areas, during both exposures, light has fallen on the film, so the negative becomes darker there. This can go so far that in the enlargement, at places where there are several superimpositions, white shapes appear and these strongly impair the effect of the picture.

In order to avoid this, take care that the illumination of the subject is as even as possible. In addition, the exposure time must also be carefully worked out. There is a rule of thumb which states that with double exposures each partial exposure should be for half the normal time, with triple exposures a third, and so on. However, this does not always apply. If the partial images overlap as little as in *Fig 75*, each of the three exposures can be taken normally. On the other hand, if the partial images overlap as much as in *Fig 76* or *Fig 78*, you should in fact use only the appropriate fraction of the measured time for the individual exposures. With *Fig 76*, for instance, four partial exposures of 1/15 sec at aperture *f*8 were used; the measured value was 1/4 sec at *f*8.

Depending on colour, brightness and form of the subject, and on type and number of partial exposures, variations may be made on this procedure, though these can only be done after thorough experimentation and trial.

As far as pictorial composition is concerned, the illustrations demonstrate some ways in which, for example, separate views of one subject may be incorporated into one picture (*Figs 73* and *79*). They also show that, through different arrangements of the partial exposures, the information and aesthetic effect can be varied. The remaining illustrations demonstrate possibilities for the creation of radically

78

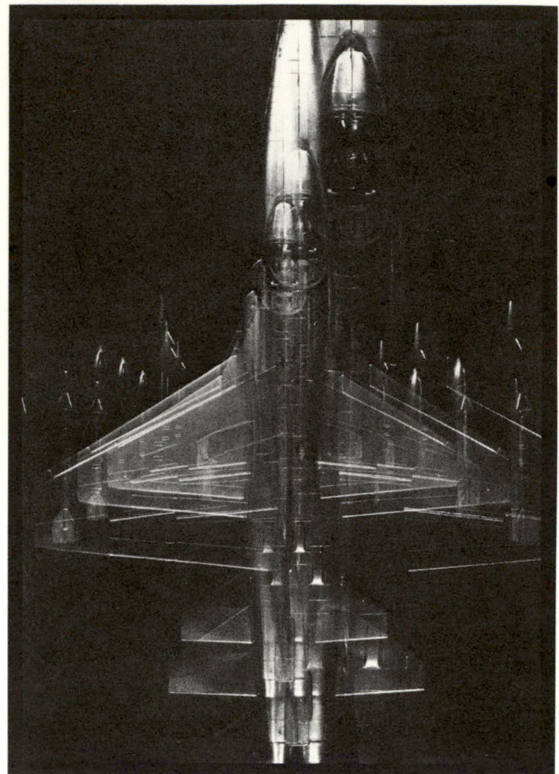

79

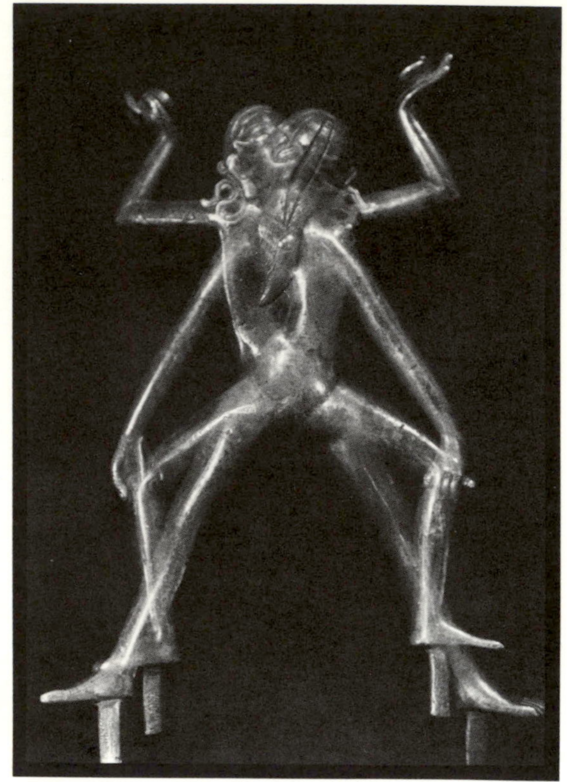

differing visual structures through alteration in position (*Figs 74* and *77*), or in both position and scale (*Figs 76* and *78*).

Exact positioning is the final problem in this area which must be discussed. Arrangements as in *Fig 77* call for a precise positioning of each partial subject. Since most miniature cameras are not provided with focusing screens, with which appropriate placings could be made, an alternative method has to be found. For *Fig 77*, the following procedure was used. After the first partial exposure, the outline of the subject was marked with drawing pins; it was then turned around, aligned precisely, and the drawing pins removed before the second exposure.

Finally, there is one other interesting phenomenon to note. Some reflections are also double exposures. Two subjects can be combined and photographed with one exposure. *Fig 80* was produced in this way. It is a picture of a room indoors, which has been photographed through a window, on which the surroundings of the house were reflected (*f*2.8/21 mm lens). No further explanation of this picture is necessary in order to suggest that natural reflections too represent an interesting area of photography.

There are naturally many other creative possibilities in addition to those indicated in these few examples, but this area is not technically difficult, and there are many possibilities in composition. Anyone can experiment further at will.

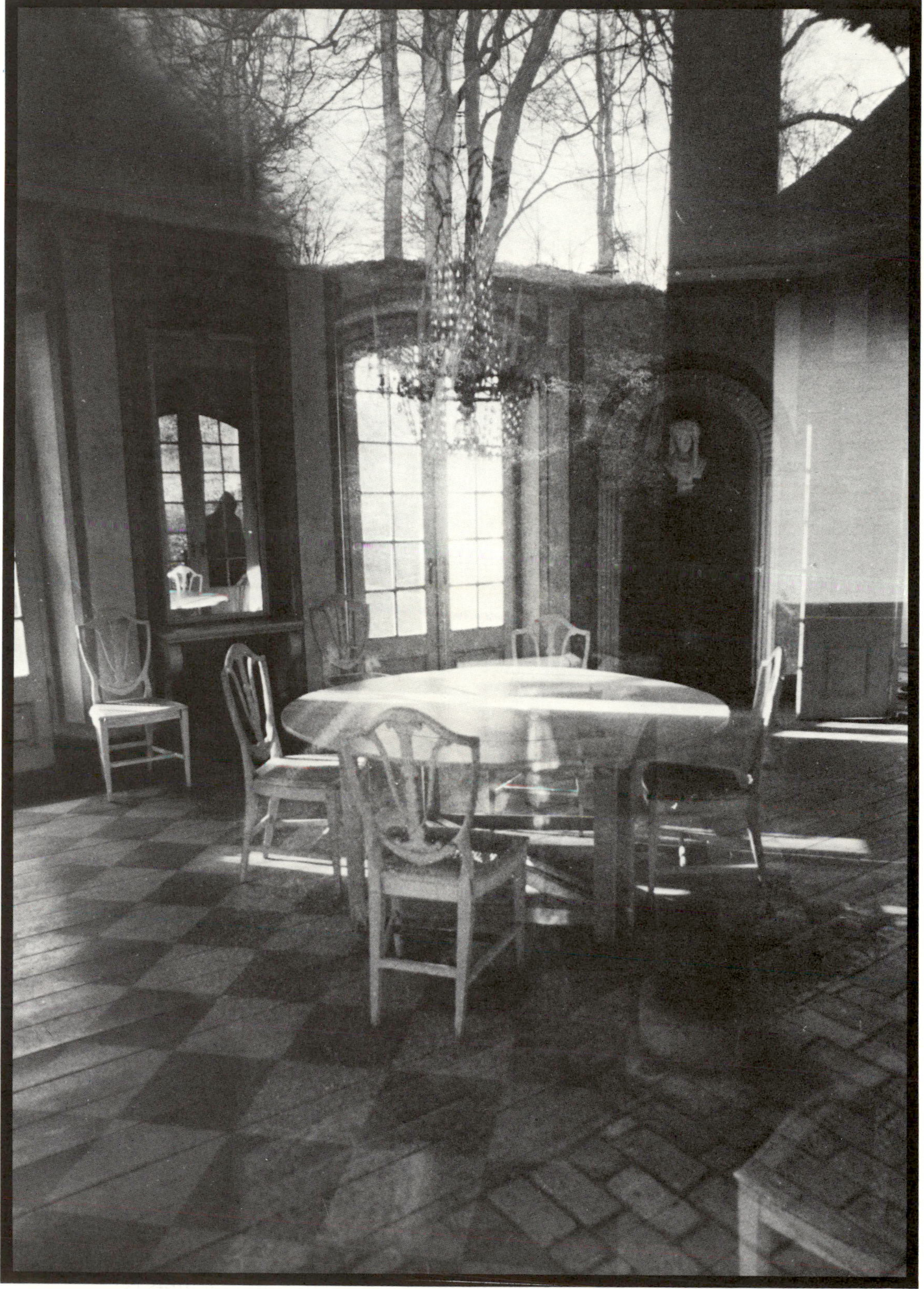

80

16: THE SHUTTER: POWER DRIVE WITH MOTOR AND WINDER

This chapter on power drive comes under the subject of the shutter simply because the power unit not only drives the film transport but also cocks the shutter. The photographer only needs to operate the release. Thus a camera with automatic exposure control and motor or winder may, without qualification, be called 'fully automatic'.

What are the advantages and disadvantages of this sort of automated camera, and how do motor and winder differ in the creative potential that they offer?

There are three main disadvantages:

1 Cameras with motor and winder are naturally more expensive than those without.
2 The cameras are larger and heavier. (At this point let me make a quite personal comment. The trend nowadays is towards designing cameras as small and light as possible. But if you have hands as large as mine, you can hardly use some of these cameras without a winder, since you cannot grasp them properly. Besides, you should also bear in mind that the lighter a camera is, the stronger the tendency towards camera shake. In my experience the maximum acceptable camera weight is well over a kilogram. This critical remark applies to practically all modern cameras from all manufacturers; and everyone who selects a camera because of its small size and light weight should remember that he is not only going to carry it; he is going to take photographs with it!)
3 The cameras are more noisy than 'hand-driven' ones.

There are several basic differences between the two types of camera. In outward appearance a motorised camera is normally larger and heavier than one with winder, and it is also much more expensive. The motor camera has its motor built in, while on other models the winder may be detached. Without entering into details of construction, the only other difference is that with the motor camera it is possible to expose upwards of four pictures a second, while with the winder camera the maximum is generally two.

Now the obvious question to ask is: What can be undertaken in general with winder and motor cameras, and when is one or the other superior?

The principal advantage of the winder camera over one that is hand driven is that you are free to concentrate on the subject and you do not need to remove the camera from your eye between exposures. This is very important, particularly with extempore shots, and with all other kinds of picture which depend on seizing the right instant. Into this category come portraits too and also such specialities as winder-controlled multiple exposures, such as were dealt with in the preceding chapter.

So far, winder and motor have been regarded as simply a question of convenience and not as a 'must'. The matter becomes more interesting when considered in relation to the representation of movement. Apart from an infinite variety of possibilities in science and technology, the motor-driven camera comes into its own with sport (including dance) and wildlife photography. One thing, however, must be realised at the outset; to use a power winder or motor drive to record visual sequences of movement and of processes merely in order to select the best picture later, leads to laziness which will be duly punished by enormous expenditure in film stock.

Just take a look at some of the sporting photographs of past decades! It is immediately obvious that it is not essential to have a winder or motor drive to capture dramatic moments in a fraction of a second. For this a more important requisite is a sharp eye, together with as far as possible a good knowledge of the subject with which you are dealing. You should not, then, use winder and motor simply to save yourself the trouble of winding on. It is preferable to use them to produce a series of shots, conceived as a series and saying more in their entirety than individually.

The comparative advantages of motor and winder lie in the subject matter. The faster the process, the more pictures can and

81

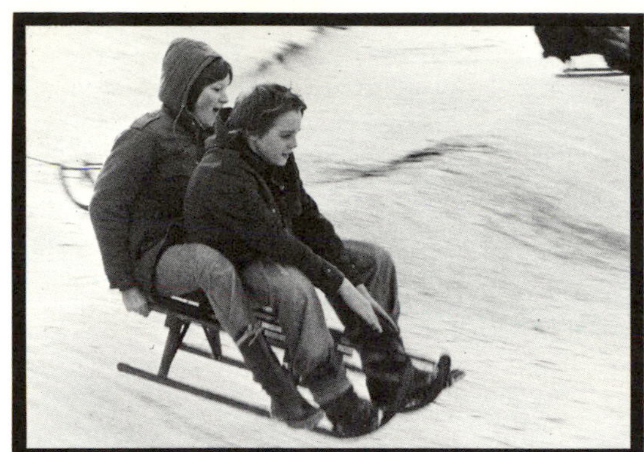

82

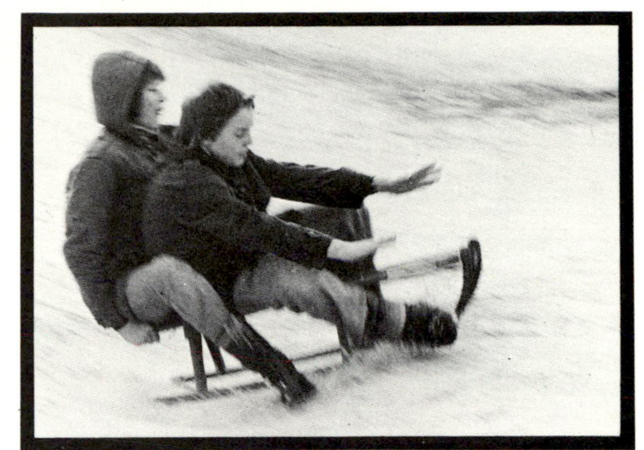

83

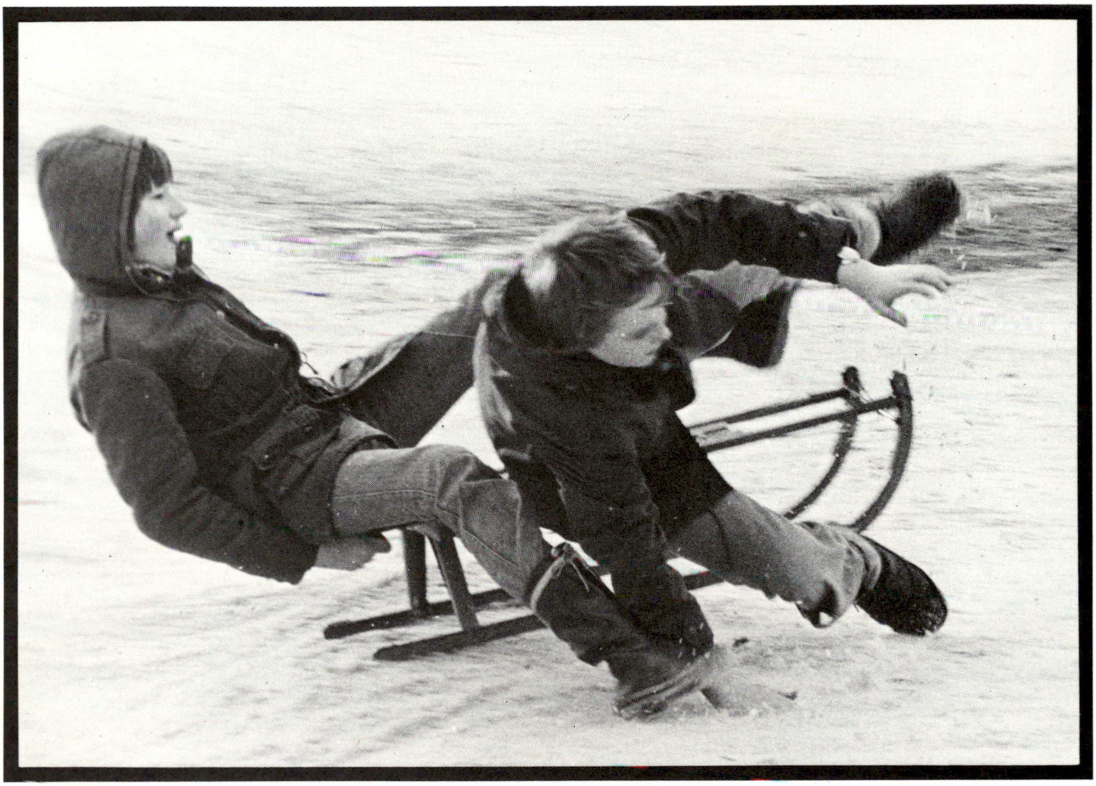

84

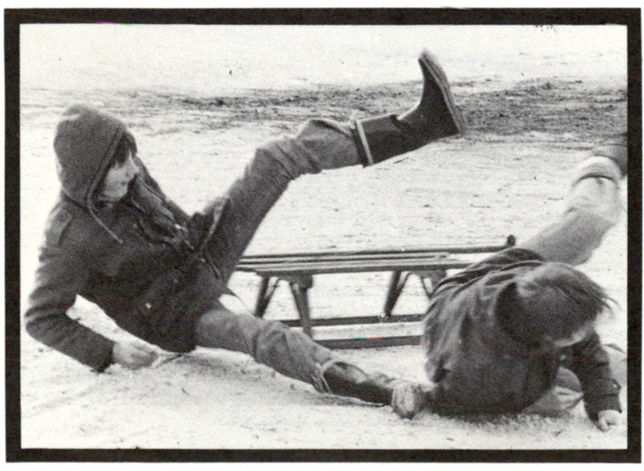

85

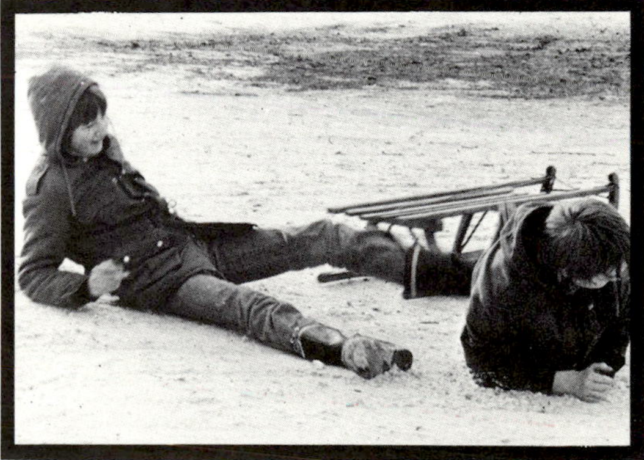

86

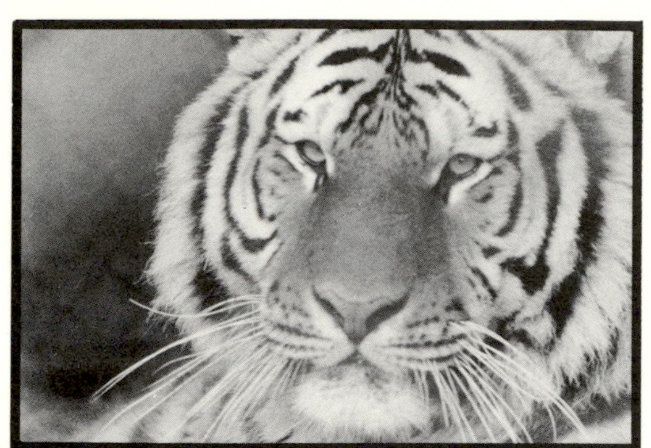

87

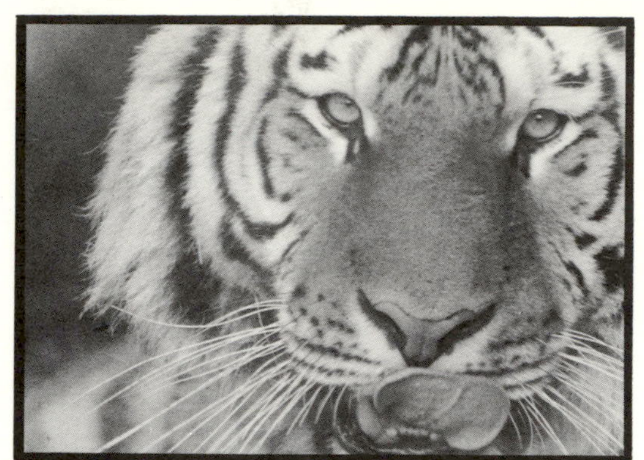

88

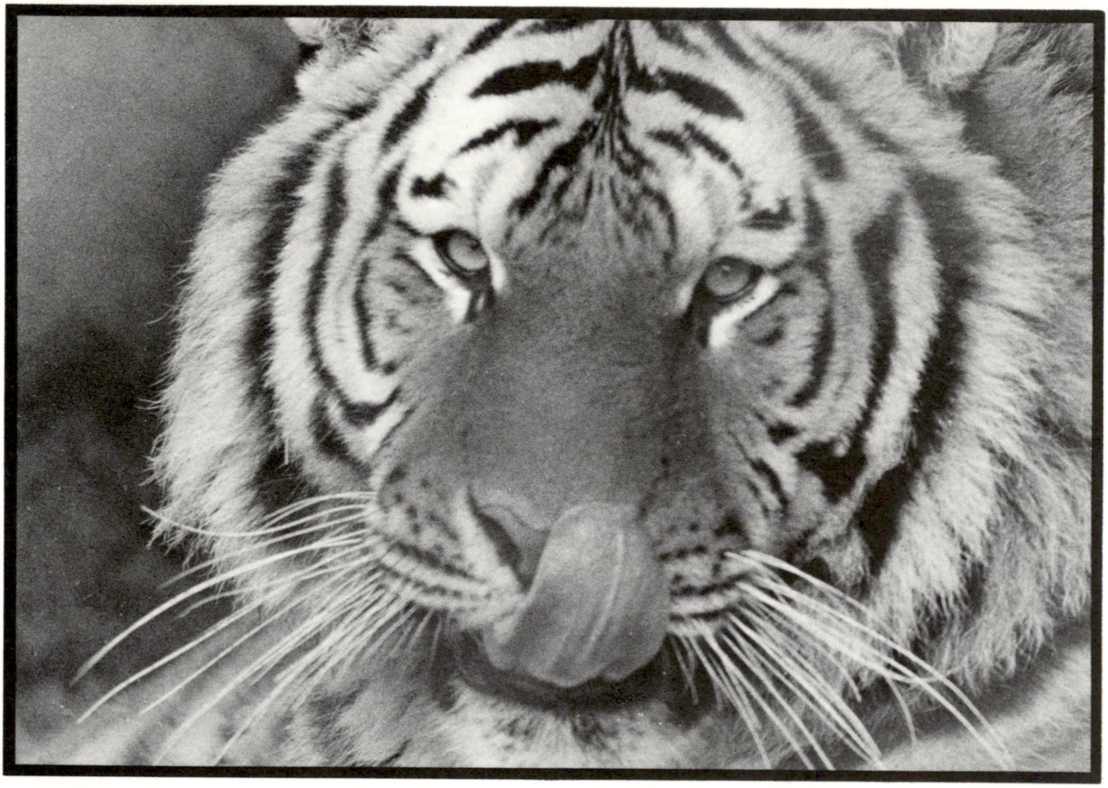

89

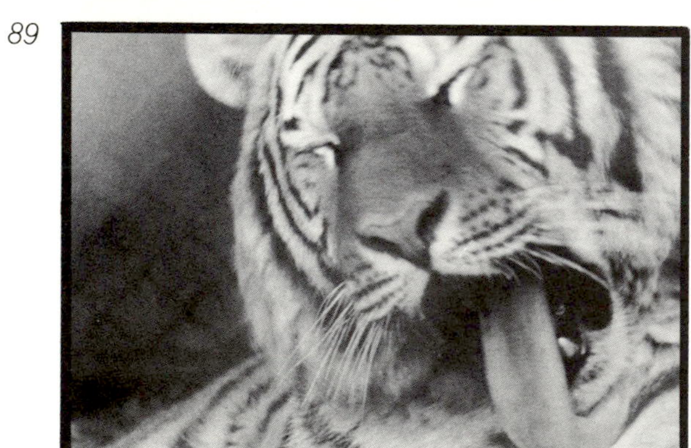

90

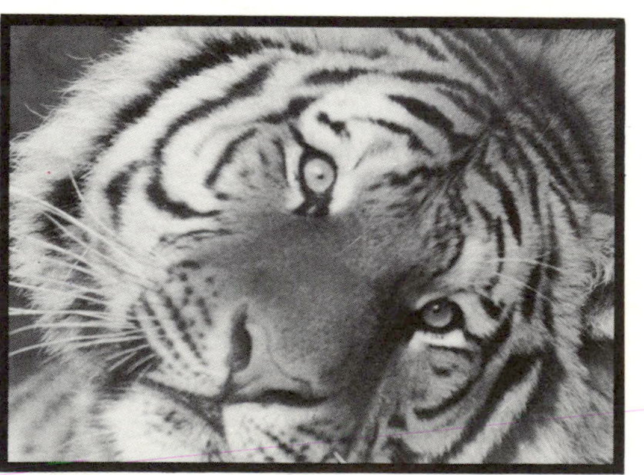

should be taken of it—and for this a motorised camera is needed with the facility to produce the greatest possible number of exposures in a given time. For slower activities, generally pictures spaced more widely are sufficient—and here the winder camera comes into its own.

The two sets of pictures exemplify these different uses. *Figs 81—85* consist of five consecutive photographs taken from an action sequence. The series was photographed with a motorised camera taking about four pictures a second. (Other data: automatic exposure control, *f*5.6 at 1/100 sec.) These five photographs in fact illustrate characteristic stages in the event, and it may clearly be seen how each individual phase in the action develops from the previous one. It is easy to imagine how much would have been lost in such a situation using a winder, by looking at *Figs 81*, *83* and *85*. The sequence no longer 'works' as a record of an event, but only as a set of separate pictures.

The ideal province of a winder, then, is not a fast-moving event. A series such as *Figs 86* to *90* is much more suitable. The photographs were produced by separate exposures at irregular intervals of between 1 and 3 seconds. They do not combine to form a continuous representation of movement; they depict rather a series of situations during a lengthy event.

By this differentiation of the general possibilities for the motorised camera on the one hand and the winder camera on the other, the conclusion emerges that the special facilities of the motorised camera are called into use so infrequently that a winder camera is generally more useful.

17: EXPOSURE MEASUREMENT

Basic considerations

The measurement of exposure is certainly one of the most vital factors influencing a photograph.

Unfortunately the advent of the built-in meter, and especially the spread of automatic exposure systems, has had, among its many benefits, a very negative aspect. Too many amateur photographers allow an automatic system to take over not only the work of exposure assessment but also their (photographic) thinking. They are often unaware that occasional corrections of measured values are necessary in order to produce technically first-rate pictures. Not only that, they are also unware that the expression 'technically first-rate' in creative photography should be taken as a starting-off point. Most subjects may be exposed in radically differing ways—and the way which is selected depends exclusively on the effect desired.

The beginner in photography is extremely happy to find anything at all in his pictures—and to this end the automatic exposure system is a great help. Only later on does it begin to dawn on him that, occasionally or perhaps frequently, things should and could have gone better. Eventually the time comes when he turns his attention to the fundamentals of exposure assessment. Let us now make a start at this. (Persons who classify themselves as beginners should omit the following paragraphs and turn to the section headed *Practical examples.*) This book is not concerned with technical and optical principles, but exclusively with a practical description. The technical knowledge is not directly necessary here for practical purposes.

First of all it is necessary to clarify a basic point. There are two kinds of exposure measurement—that of 'light intensity' and that of 'brightness'. The difference is quite simple. When measuring intensity the amount of light is measured which emanates from, or is reflected by, the subject. Camera light meters work on this principle, as do most hand exposure meters. When measuring brightness, on the other hand, it is the amount of light which falls on the subject which is assessed. Since this procedure is employed mainly in copying work and in scientific photography, it is unnecessary to consider it any further here.

In the measurement of light intensity, in turn, there are two distinct methods—integral measurement and spot measurement. As most camera light meters work according to the first of these principles, this method is considered first.

The light which passes from the subject to the camera is what is measured. It is integral; that is to say, the measurement is not taken from just one part or another of the subject, but is an average value, built up from the various light or dark parts of the subject. From this it can be deduced that the light and dark parts of an average subject always mix and add up to the same 'average grey'. This means that if a piece of card is photographed which has been painted an average grey, then the light meter of the camera (or a manual exposure meter) always gives the same value, produced by the average grey colour of the card. It is thus irrelevant whether the card is photographed at night with a very long exposure time or at midday with a very short one; if the value supplied by the light meter is kept to, the card is always depicted as equally grey. (In practice, there are deviations owing to reciprocity law failure and so on. These are not discussed here, to avoid complicating matters unduly.)

Here, then, are the parameters of this kind of exposure measurement. The light meter naturally cannot distinguish between a white, grey or black card. It provides in each of these cases a value which gives a rendering of the card on film as middle grey—irrespective of its actual colour. (Here too there are limitations which are not discussed here.)

Fig 91 gives a practical example of this. The subject combines the very bright (snow) with the very dark (the shady wall). The picture was planned in such a way that the individual brightness zones of the whole scene mix to form a quite acceptable middle grey (*f*3.5/100 mm lens). The automatic exposure system of the camera gave, for the

91

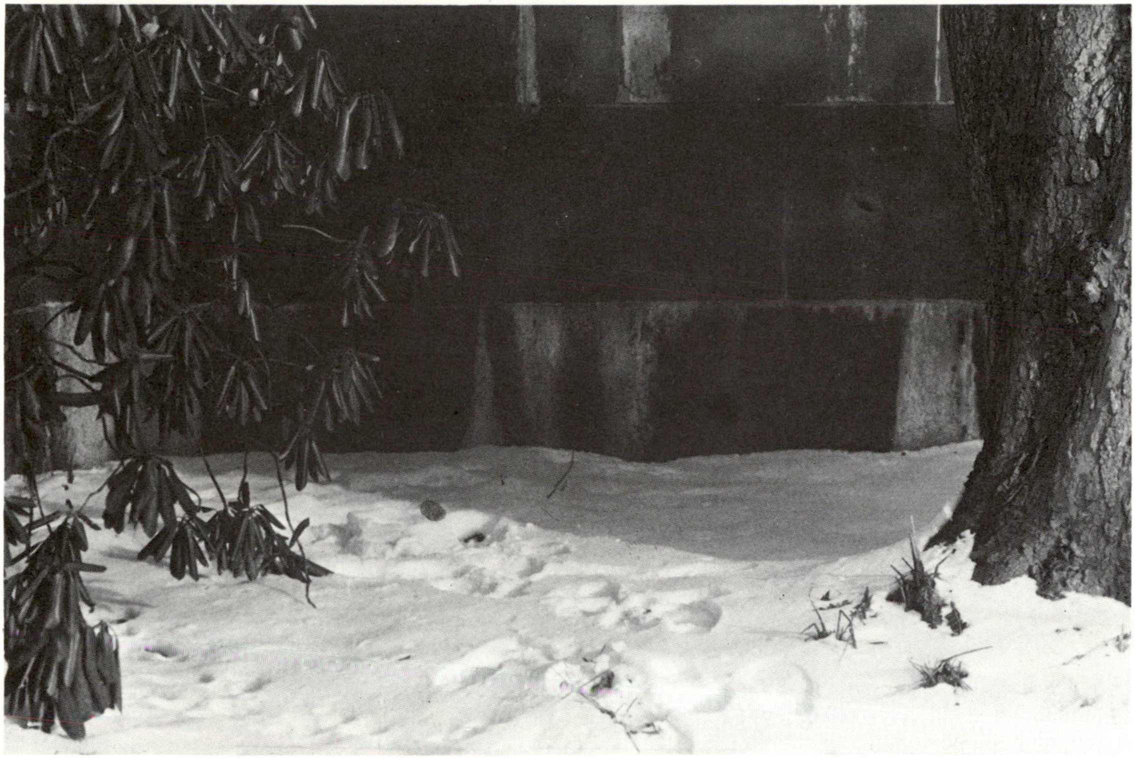

91a

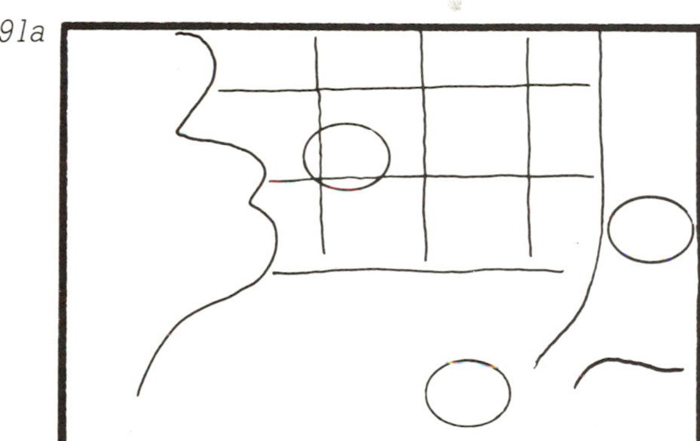

chosen aperture of *f*8, 1/125 sec as the correct shutter speed. (Since this 'basic picture' is to be the starting point for other comparisons, all the rest of the photographs—up to and including *Fig 99*—have been enlarged to the same extent, in order to give an idea of how much the individual negatives differ from each other.)

In *Fig 91a* three areas of varying brightness have been marked, which are examined more closely later. *Fig 92* shows how these areas of varying brightness in the subject and in the negative relate to one

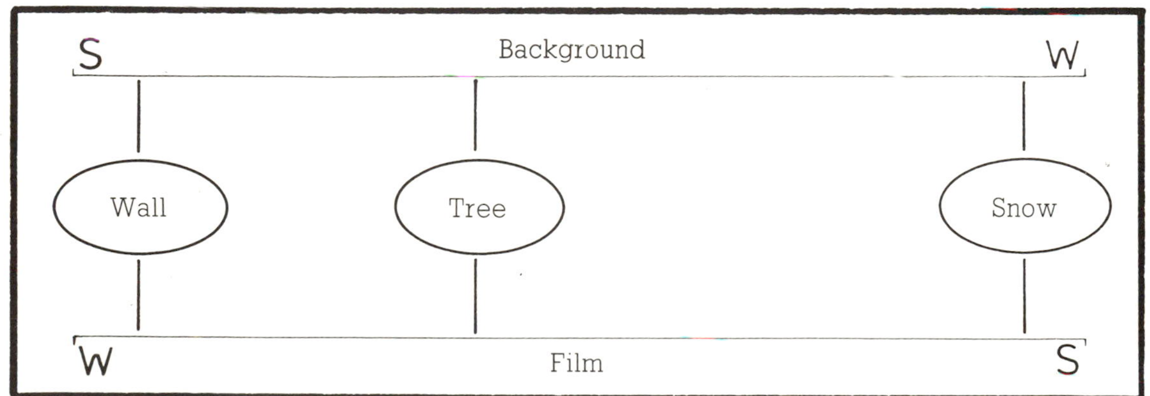

92

93a

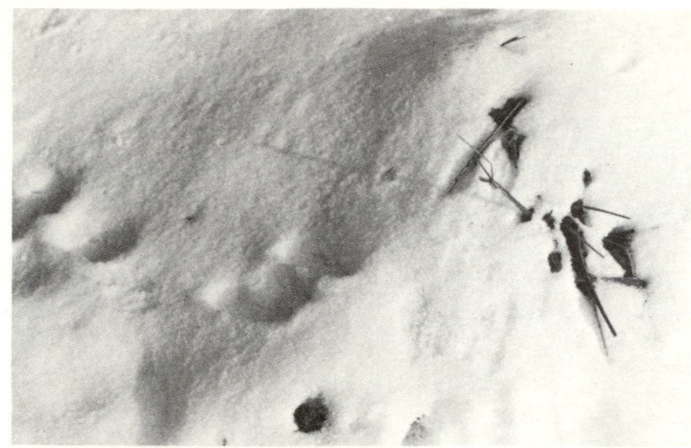

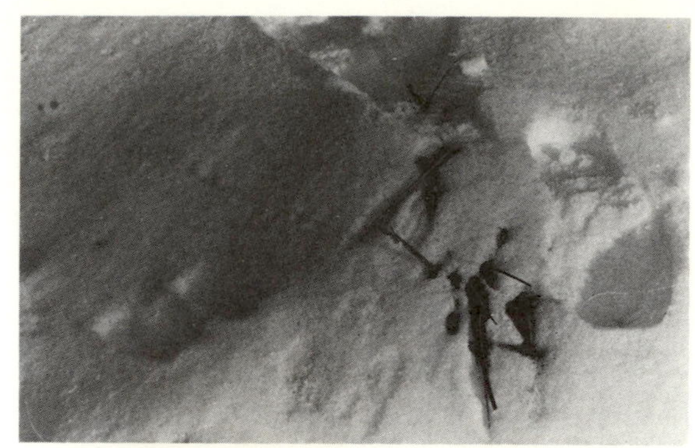

93

94a

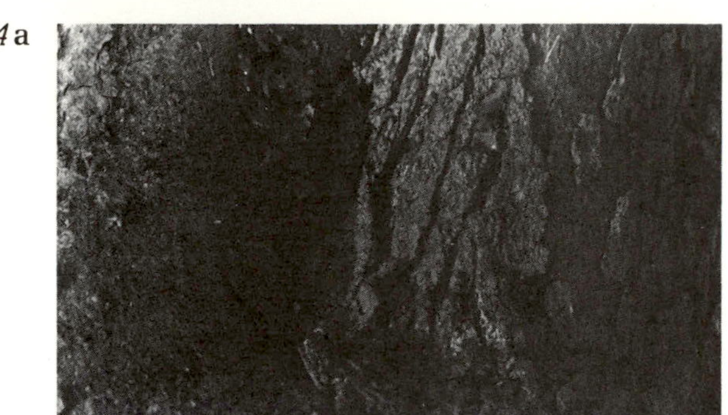

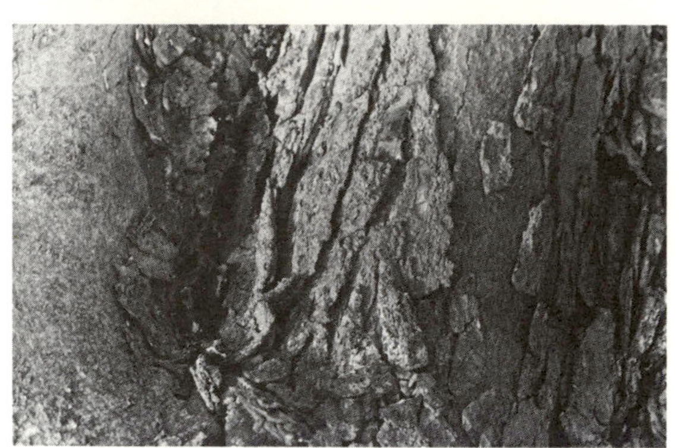

94

another. The upper line represents the scale of grey tones in the subject from black (left) to white (right), while the lower line represents the relevant ratios on the monochrome negative film. The shapes in the middle of the diagram are intended to symbolise with their borderlines the three grey values of snow, tree and wall on the film. *Figs 93a—95a* show these three details. For these photographs the automatic exposure system was switched off, and they were all taken at the average value given for the original photograph (aperture *f*8 at 1/125 sec). Consequently snow, tree and wall all appear in the same brightness relationship to each other as in *Fig 91*: the snow very bright, the tree somewhat dark and the wall almost black.

For *Figs 93b—95b*, the automatic exposure system was switched on again and the value provided each time by the automatic system. For the snow the shutter speed was 1/750 sec instead of 1/125 sec; for the tree about 1/80 sec; and for the wall 1/50 sec! (In each case, of course, at an aperture of *f*8.) The negatives are correspondingly different: the snow is very much darker, and the wall and the tree are much brighter than in the previous pictures. These results occur because the light meter reading is based always on a middle grey—irrespective of the actual grey value in the subject. *Fig 96* shows the differences in measurement between the two picture series again represented schematically.

What then is the correct exposure? To answer that question look again at the photographs. The snow in *Fig 93a* looks more natural. However, although the tree and wall look more natural in *Figs 94b* and *95b*, because the exposure method used takes into consideration the actual brightness inherent in the subject, the overall brightness of the conditions is not taken into account.

What is the cause of that? It is owing to the fact that the concept of 'snow' is associated with the idea of 'whiteness', and consequently people, unwittingly, expect snow in a photograph always to appear very bright. Trees and walls, on the other hand, do not involve this kind of expectation. Accordingly any representation of them appears natural to us as long as it does not go to extremes; if it is a little brighter or darker, this does not matter, as long as in the picture

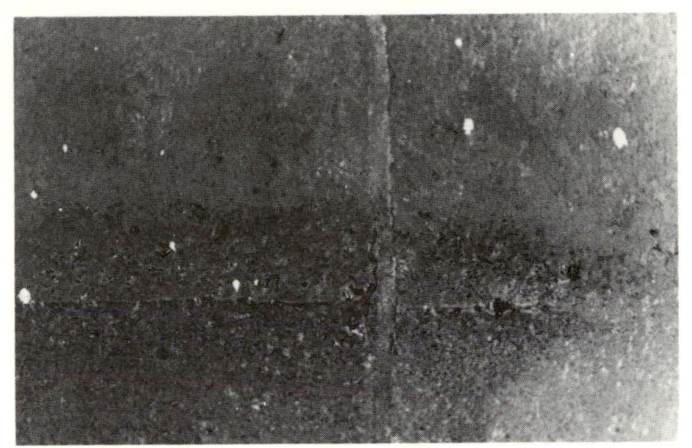

95b

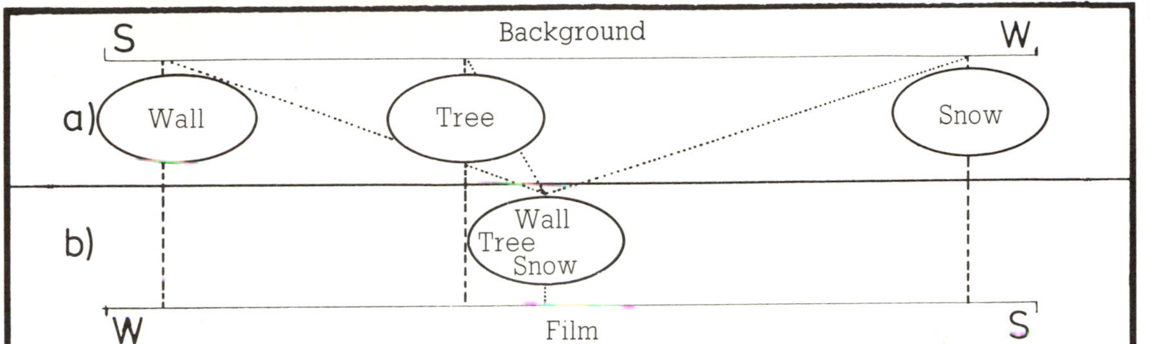

96

clear points of interest appear—for example, white snow, or in a portrait the whites of the eyes.

To recapitulate; the integral measurement based on average values always provides a 'correct' exposure for the average subject. Subjects which are very much brighter or darker than average are always rendered as middle grey, irrespective of actual conditions. If this effect is not desired, longer exposures must be given to bright subjects and shorter exposures to dark subjects, in order to compensate.

In this connection, the film's capacity for representing contrast is important. Every film is capable of encompassing a particular contrast range. That is to say, if the brightest and darkest parts of the subject are represented with equal clarity (namely, as neither pure white nor jet black), then the contrast range of the film suits the subject. 'Contrast range' means the difference between the brightest and the darkest grey values which the film is capable of rendering simultaneously. *Fig 97* illustrates the point that this measurement has to be taken into account in exposure. In *Fig 97* the film was exposed for such a long time that the brightest parts do not register any more; here the contrast range of the film was exceeded. In *Fig 99* the situation was exactly reversed; the film was so briefly exposed that the darkest parts of the subject permitted no light to reach the film. Only the middle negative (*Fig 98*) was exposed in such a way that the brightest and also the darkest parts of the subject lay within the contrast range, with the result that both registered. From this evidence it can be deduced that there is no such thing as exposure latitude in itself. Only in the case of subjects with limited contrast can the exposure be varied without exceeding the rendition capacity of the film.

With 'normal' subjects, 'normally' photographed, such considerations are of course irrelevant—just switch on the camera, and leave the rest to the automatic system. But as soon as you come to consider less conventional subjects with unusual lighting, it is important to have a clear idea of the contrast range of the subject, and also of how well the film can cope with it.

Practical examples

The following three photographs have been

97

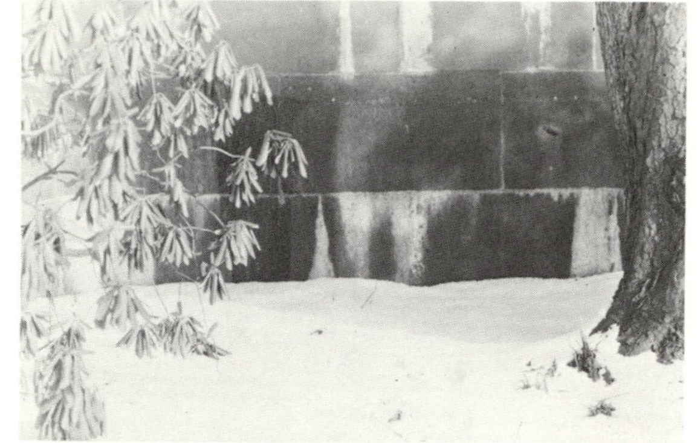

97

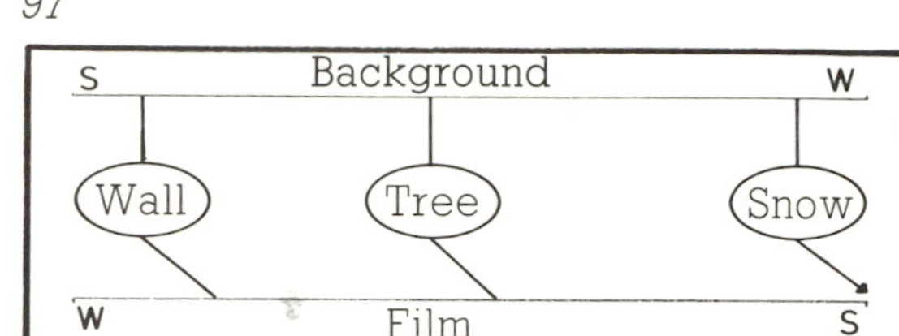

98

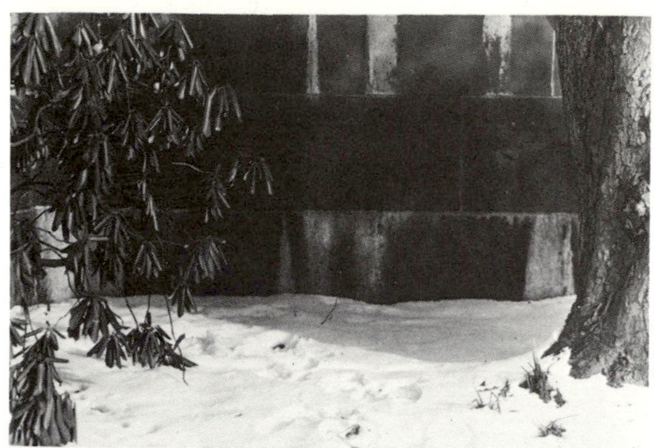

98

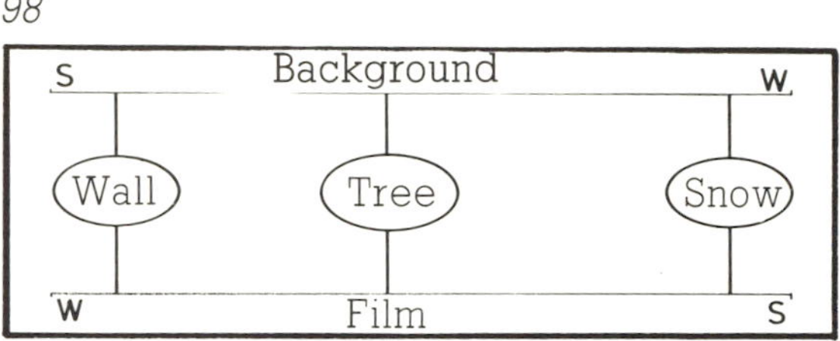

99

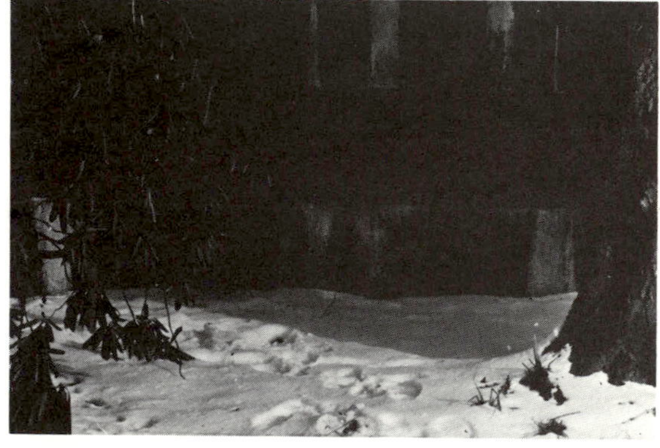

99

S Background W

Wall Tree Snow

W Film S

selected because, despite their similarity of subject in the establishment of exposure time, each was handled differently so that a characteristic visual effect would be achieved for each picture.

Fig 100 shows a large room, illuminated by only one very small window. It is easy to appreciate that the difference in brightness between the window and the greater part of the room was so great that it easily exceeded the contrast range of the film. In such cases it is customary to expose for either the brightest or the darkest part, so that at least one of the two will be well defined. In this case neither of these things was done, but instead exactly the middle value was chosen, with the result that the negative shows mainly black and white areas, together with a limited use of grey. The aim of this course of action was to emphasise the contrast between the cool darkness of the room and the dazzling brightness of the 'outer world' forcibly penetrating into the room.

To make this calculation, first of all, estimate the exposure time for the brightest

100

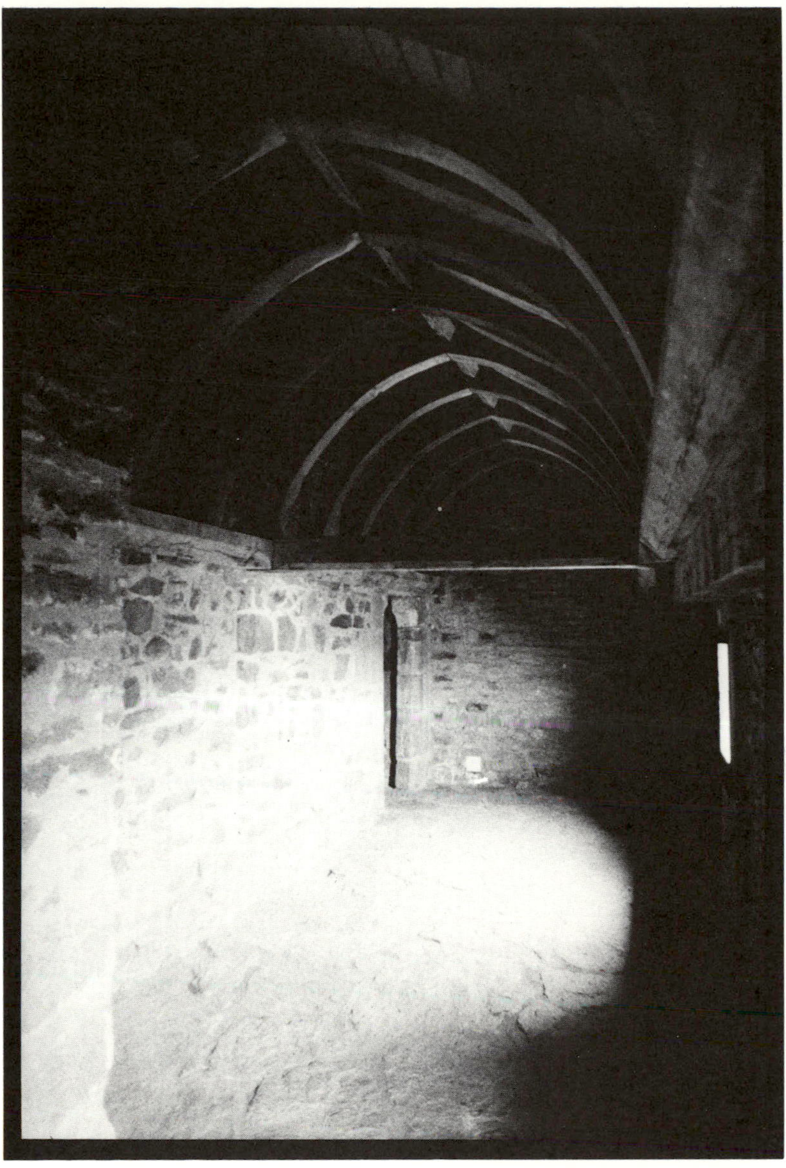

and darkest parts of the subject. The best way is naturally using a manual exposure meter with viewfinder and indicated measuring field. Alternatively, it is possible to go up to the specific areas with the camera and use its integrated light meter. For *Fig 100* the following values were indicated: darkest part of the subject, 2 sec at *f*16; brightest part of the subject, 1/500 sec at *f*16. Since each doubling of exposure time indicates a doubling of the amount of light falling on the film (this applies also to the space between one aperture stop and the next), these readings mean that in the brightest part of the subject the film receives 1024 times more light than in the darkest! Working from the principle that a monochrome film, at best, can achieve a subject contrast range of from 1:500 to 1:1000 (the latter only with high-sensitivity film after forced development) it must be concluded that the subject contrast in this case exceeds the efficiency of the film. There are, then, three possibilities for establishment of the correct exposure, and these are set out in the following table:

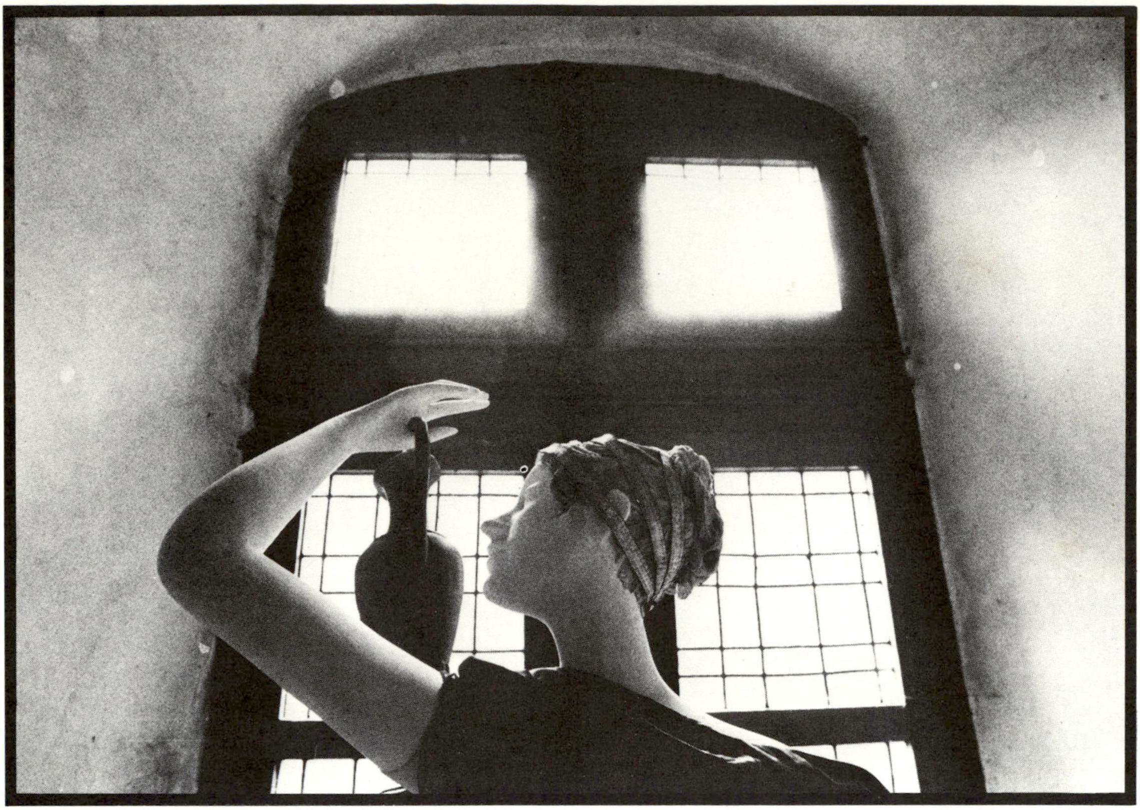

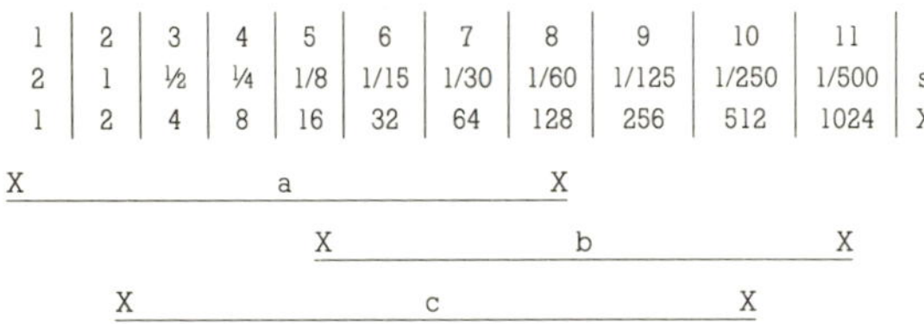

1	2	3	4	5	6	7	8	9	10	11	
2	1	½	¼	1/8	1/15	1/30	1/60	1/125	1/250	1/500	s
1	2	4	8	16	32	64	128	256	512	1024	X
X				a			X				
				X			b			X	
	X				c				X		

The first line in this table is a sequence of consecutive numbers. The second line indicates the exposure times appropriate to the chosen apertures for the subject. The third shows the respective multiples of the amounts of incidental light. The fourth line finally indicates by the example of a 100ASA/21 DIN monochrome film—which has a total contrast range of 8 aperture stops—which range of subject contrast, with the three exposure possibilities, will acctually be recorded on film.

1 Exposure 1/4 to 1/8 sec (aperture *f*16): the entire dark area of the subject will be rendered, while the bright area will be lacking.
2 Exposure 1/50 to 1/125 sec (aperture *f*16): the entire bright area of the subject will be rendered, while the dark area will be lacking.
3 Exposure 1/15 to 1/30 sec (aperture *f*16): the extremes of bright and dark areas will be lacking, and the emphasis will be on middle values. In the final picture pure white will be retained.

In *Fig 101* the lighting conditions were similar to those of the foregoing picture. Here, however, the intended visual effect was different. The shop-window figurine standing in the dimly lit room, as main subject, was to be recognisable in detail, so the dark parts of the subject were to be more strongly emphasised. If a similar table had been compiled for this subject as for *Fig 100*, the choice would necessarily have fallen on (1). Such a disregard for the brightest parts of the subject naturally produces a strong 'irradiation' of these areas (as can be seen in the picture). In this case, however, this effect was specifically intended, since the profusion of light entering from outside gives a solid symbolic effect.

Fig 102 shows a completely different

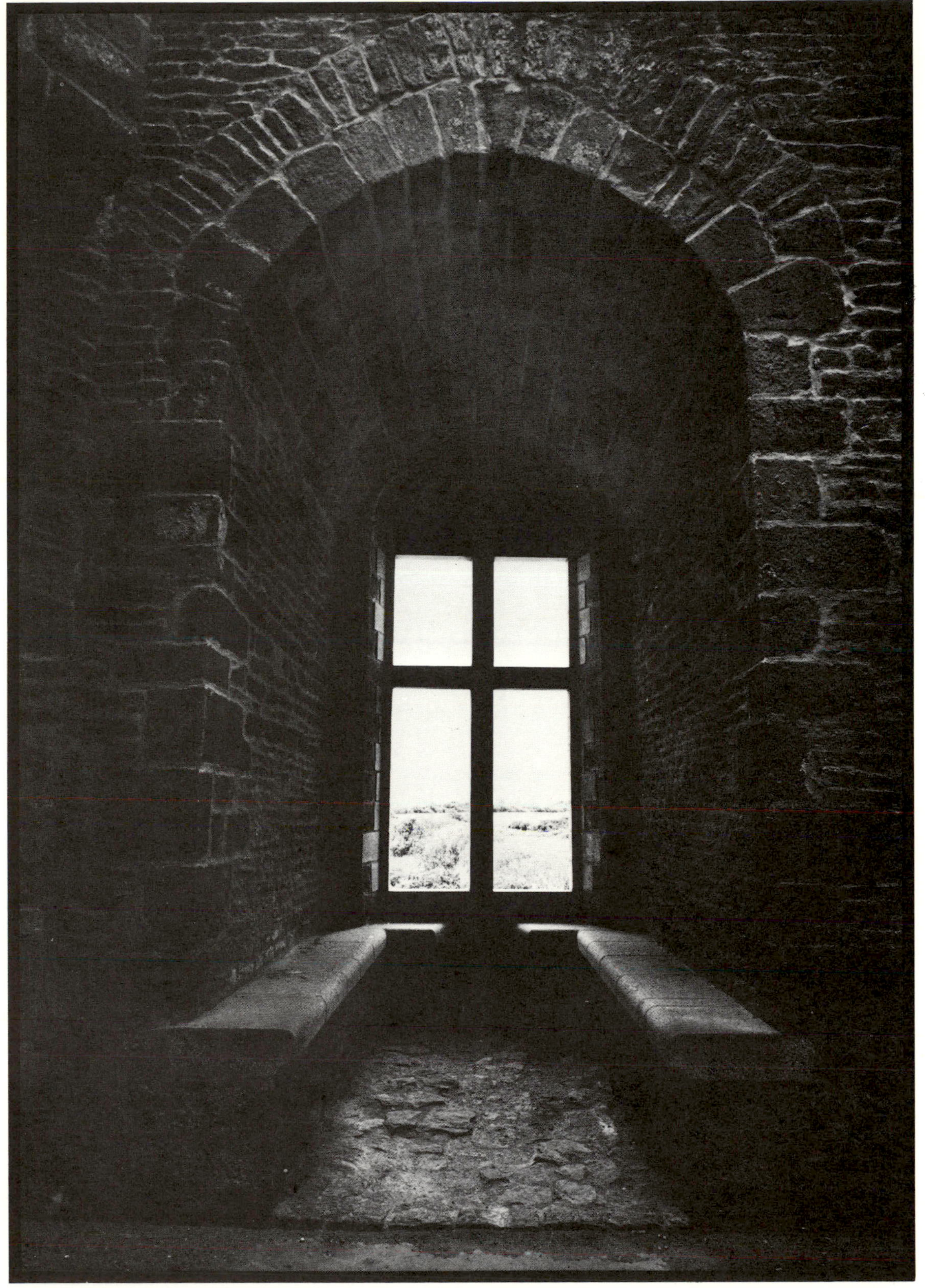

approach. Here the equally high subject contrast was to be faithfully rendered. For this purpose a film of high sensitivity (400 ASA/27 DIN) and wide contrast range was used, so that the brightest and darkest parts of the subject would be registered.

Incidentally, photographs against the light, such as *Fig 3* in the first chapter, do not differ from the illustrations provided here as far as assessment of exposure time is concerned. In each case, whether the intention is to emphasise the bright or dark parts, or to work uniformly as far as possible, the exposure must be adjusted accordingly. In this instance it is not necessary to use tables and calculations. Here there is nothing to equal personal experience—even in comparison with the most scrupulous of computations.

For readers who do not yet have the benefit of wide photographic experience and might feel uncertain about these exposure assessment methods the following list summarises the main points again:

1 Integral exposure measurement (the automatic system in a camera) always provides correctly exposed negatives of 'normal' subjects.
2 Normal subjects are those in which bright and dark details are fairly evenly distributed.
3 Normal subjects have a relatively limited contrast range of about 1:30, so that minor deviations will fall within the exposure latitude of the film.
4 The more the subject strays from the customary bright/dark distribution and from normal contrast, the more precise and careful the exposure measurement must be.

Since most photographic beginners start their careers with conventional and straightforward subjects, it fortunately turns out that at the outset the labour-saving automatic system of the camera can be completely relied upon. Only after considerable experience and a desire for original photographic creativity do the problems dealt with in this chapter arise and accordingly require to be solved.

Thus there are in general three possible courses of action:

1 Exposure measurement for brief and sudden events (such as extempore shots, reportage, sport and wildlife photography) should always rely on the built-in system of the camera.
2 Subjects such as portraits, conventional landscapes and so on may also be photographed with the camera's automatic system. (To take advantage of the creative possibilities of depth of field, the automatic timing system should be employed.)
3 Static subjects of all kinds, particularly those which radically differ from normal themes in distribution of brightness and in contrast, can be photographed with the aid of the automatic system, as long as you use your experience to make corrections beforehand. However, the person who desires precise control should in such cases utilise a manual exposure meter and ascertain the correct exposure.

The best procedure to use depends basically on personal temperament. People who are always in a hurry will certainly not bother to wander through the neighbourhood with an exposure meter, carrying out at least three assessments for one photograph.

There are also those amateur photographers who take all possible kinds of subject, simply because this gives them pleasure, or because they wish to have a visual record for the future. They are generally quite content with the kind of picture quality available with the aid of automatic integral exposure systems.

In conclusion, it can be summed up that integral exposure systems nearly always produce pleasing pictures—and sometimes outstanding ones. Only when you are aiming high and wish to have precise control of visual effect should you renounce automation, as then it is not a matter of merely producing usable negatives, but of producing negatives good enough to use for making significant photographic statements. This applies particularly to transparencies, since it is impossible to correct them after they have been taken.

18: THE PHOTOGRAPHIC OUTFIT

I read recently in an American photographic journal the following dialogue:

Question: 'What is the difference between a painter and a photographer?'

Answer: 'When two painters meet, they can talk for hours about their profession without mentioning a single time the type and quality of their paint-brushes.'

This quotation, which, if I remember rightly, stems from Charles Harbutt, makes it beautifully clear that indeed in photography far too much is spoken about technology and apparatus and far too little about pictures.

And yet . . . a lens or a camera body generally costs more than a brush or a canvas, and it is perfectly understandable that the enthusiastic amateur photographer wishes to learn more about it before investing in a photographic outfit. For this reason in the following pages a few pieces of advice are offered about the assembling of a photographic outfit. To be sure, there is a proviso. What equipment you require depends exclusively on what you wish to photograph—and how you intend to go about it. This proviso applies particularly to special subject areas such as sport, wildlife photography, copying work and travel photography. Here the choice of apparatus arises necessarily from the technical requirements of the photographic situation.

It is more interesting to deal first with the very wide field of general creative photography, which is not confined to specific themes or photographic situations. At this point, the same familiar questions always arise, such as: 'What do you recommend as standard equipment?' or: 'What else do you require if you already have a basic outfit?'

To start at the beginning, most amateur photographers enter their single-lens reflex careers in a conventional way, by purchasing a lens and camera body—and here already it is possible to make a mistake.

A single-lens reflex camera is a camera designed for alternative lenses—and even if at the start you buy only a camera body and lens, both should be selected so that later on further equipment can be added. The outfit should fulfil all basic requirements without being too expensive and elaborate.

If you could have a look into my photographic bag for 35 mm equipment, you would generally see (among other items) the following: two camera bodies (one with motor and one with winder); three lenses (*f*4/17 mm, *f*1.2/50 mm and *f*3.5/100 mm macro); an angled viewfinder; a manual exposure meter; a cable release; a firm clip camera stand and various filters. For financial reasons that is not to be recommended as basic starting equipment for the beginner, but it serves as a general guide. The best universal standard equipment should at least include a camera body and three lenses: a wide-angle, a telephoto and a normal lens.

If you possess only a single wide-angle lens, it should be somewhere in the middle of the wide-angle range, preferably however towards the short rather than longer focal length end. While a 28 mm lens is usually recommended for wide-angle, I generally advise something like an *f*2.8/24 mm lens, because I believe that the wide angle demands more experience in pictorial composition if it is more pronounced. Besides, from the point of view of angular field, the 24 mm lens is such that it retains its usefulness if, eventually, you obtain an additional wide-angle lens.

As a 'normal lens', as far as resources permit, it is worth the expenditure on something really good: either a very fast lens, such as *f*1.2/50 mm, or perhaps a macro lens, such as *f*3.5/50 mm. But at this very point opinions differ radically. For example, it is in many cases highly questionable whether such a high-speed lens as an *f*1.2/50 mm can be used efficiently, while on the other hand there are thoroughly convincing arguments in favour of the 100 mm as a macro lens (as against the 50 mm).

To try and clarify this problem the various possibilities are set down in the following table:

Wide-angle	Normal	Telephoto
*f*2.8/24 mm	*f*1.2/50 mm	macro *f*3.5/100 mm
*f*2.8/24 mm	macro *f*3.5/50 mm	*f*2.5/100 mm
*f*2.8/24 mm	macro *f*3.5/50 mm	*f*2.8/135 mm

If a universal standard photographic outfit is to consist of one or other of these combinations, the first decision is to select a suitable camera body to go with one of these lenses. It is not exactly a straightforward matter, and it could be difficult to choose from among these lenses.

In recent years, another possible solution has arisen. It is not an ideal remedy; nevertheless, if financial considerations permit, it is a particularly good solution to the problem of choice. Your initial choice could be a zoom lens, for example, *f*2.8/40—80 mm, with close-up facility. With this lens alone it is possible to carry out a very large proportion of photographic techniques, and further acquisitions later can be contemplated calmly and without panic.

To sum up:

1 Recommended basic equipment: a camera body with a zoom lens, perhaps *f*3.5/50—135 mm.
2 Recommended additional standard equipment: basic accessories, such as an *f*2.8/24 mm lens and an *f*2.8/135 mm lens (or if you have a special interest in close-up and macro photography, an *f*3.5/100 mm lens instead).

Now that the question of lenses has been at least briefly discussed, the camera body can be considered—and it will be evident why this is in second place.

As, by force of circumstances, most people have a very positive idea of the limit to the cost of their proposed camera outfit, the following three alternative possibilities arise:

1 To acquire a highly versatile (and expensive) camera body, which would fulfil all possible ambitions, and supply it with a high-grade lens, such as an *f*1.4/50 mm.
2 To purchase a camera body of mid-range, and fit it with the same lens or one slightly more expensive.
3 To look for the lens which pleases you, and then purchase the body which you can still afford.

In my opinion the third alternative is the best. A versatile lens (say *f*2.8/40—80 mm) provides appreciably more creative possibilities than does an expensively designed camera body as, apart from the viewpoint of double exposure facilities, the more expensive bodies are designed chiefly with ease of operation in mind, and not to provide extra creative potential. In addition, if in the course of years your photography becomes more ambitious, the moment may arrive when you want a second camera body (for example, to enable the use of different types of film alternately). By that time you should know what facilities the new body should have.

It is best, therefore, if you have sufficient financial resources, to select at the start a camera body incorporating every conceivable facility, with automatic time and aperture control, manual override, double exposure facility, attachable winder and so on. If resources are limited, however, buy a basic camera body and an *f*2.8/40—80 mm zoom lens rather than an advanced type of camera body and an *f*1.4/50 mm lens.

Having provided some reasonably sensible and stimulating information about basic standard equipment, I should like to mention an accessory which I find continually useful, though often it is left in the background. This is the angled viewfinder which enables you, without acrobatic dislocation, to take photographs from ground level or at any rate below normal eye level. It is quite possible that the height of the viewpoint is of decisive importance for the effect of a picture, and the angled viewfinder is generally used for wide-angle photographs. The reason why so many amateurs are not aware of this is simply that, because they do not possess an angled viewfinder, they nearly always photograph from eye level. In this regard it is fair to say that the acquisition of an angled viewfinder extends creative potential just as far as the purchase of an alternative lens and is very much cheaper.

All these accessories naturally cost money—even a lot more money! But there is one inescapable fact—never in the history of photography was so much first-class equipment available for so little cost as there is today. It should also be remembered that you can start modestly and spread your expenditure over several years. (Just try buying a ski for the right foot for the coming winter season, in anticipation of purchasing

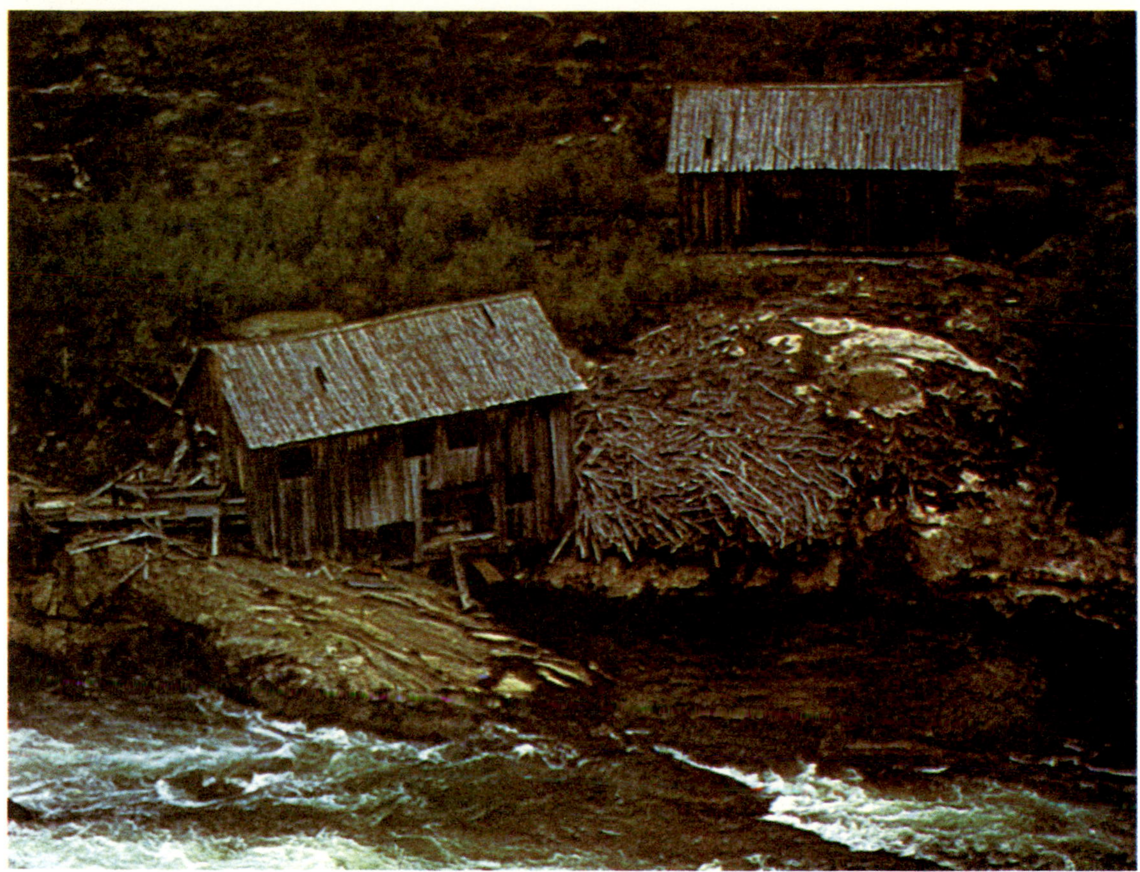

the left ski next year . . .)

Joking aside . . . as described in Chapter 2, you can even take 'real' photographs using an old cigar box. The art is merely in getting to know the available equipment and exploiting it to the full. The information given in this book is intended to be helpful in this respect.

Finally, there is a piece of equipment which is just ideal for those people who have no liking at all for technicalities; for those who want to be able to take photographs with the maximum of ease and the minimum of equipment. I refer to the single-lens reflex camera which takes 110 type miniature film. Some of these very small cameras in fact incorporate a remarkable number of facilities.

It is possible to find a camera of this type which incorporates a zoom lens corresponding to 50—100 mm in a camera of conventional format, with which, at macro setting, you can take a close-up photograph of an object field of about 12 × 9 cm; you can select an aperture from between *f*4.5 and *f*16 and the built-in automatic shutter mechanism may be corrected to provide deliberate over- or underexposure. Despite these really impressive statistics, many people have reservations about this format. This is generally because they attribute an inadequate picture quality to the 'pocket format'. There are two reasons for this:

1 It is an unfortunate fact that commercially processed, big enlargements of pocket-format negatives (in colour or in monochrome) are nearly always appalling.
2 Most amateurs working with pocket cameras forget the lessons learned in the 'photographic childhood'. All is unsteady and jerky, the distance is not properly set, no lens hood is used when its use is essential, lighting is not checked, and in fact everything is done wrongly which *can* be done wrongly.

This does not of course have to happen. On the contrary, quite the reverse can take place—but only if two conditions are fulfilled. Firstly, that when using the pocket format you should work just as meticulously as with a larger format. Secondly, use reversal film or develop your negatives yourself and make your own enlargements. This must be done with the greatest of care, for with such a tiny format faults and imperfections in processing become very strongly evident (and usually disastrous) as compared with the conventional miniature format (which is already vulnerable in any case).

As the intricacy of this work is not to everyone's taste, the best solution is to use reversal film. At best, you can smuggle into a slide show a few good examples of this tiny format, without revealing the fact to the audience, and probably be surprised at their acceptability. Naturally, there are some limitations, which should be borne in mind to avoid mistakes.

1 Such a small format will not accommodate as much physical information as a larger one. With slide projection this does not apply to the same extent, as the screen texture and viewing distance set limitations to the viewer's appreciation of detail and powers of discernment.
2 For highly detailed subjects with subtle colour gradations (for instance, wide landscapes with vegetation), the film material is stretched to its limits. However, provided the matter is given a little prior thought, there is no need to expect real difficulties.
3 For enlargements on paper, you can count on good results only with self-processing. (Unfortunately I cannot say anything about colour negative film, as I do not use it).

Fig 104 is a whole-page reproduction of a monochrome enlargement made from pocket-format film. The technical quality of the print speaks for itself—but if you have any doubts as to how much quality is lost in book reproduction, try it for yourself.

Fig 103 originated in a colour transparency with very subtle colour gradations, which is not generally recommended for pocket-format photography—but in this instance it has turned out well nevertheless. *Figs 105* and *106* are particularly interesting. Both show practically the same subject, one photographed on normal miniature film and one with pocket format. I leave it to the reader to decide which picture was taken with which size of film.

It is notable that there are cameras of pocket format with a high-quality mirror reflex optical system, which has much creative potential. Although this advanced type of pocket camera is somewhat larger than other simpler cameras of the same kind, there is nevertheless no problem about carrying it with you anywhere. So the motto of the pocket camera ought to be: 'Better a pocket camera in the hand than a miniature camera in the house'!

There are no general universal rules governing the assembly of a photographic outfit, because the choice of apparatus depends on the type of photography that interests you and on how you intend to go about it. The information advanced in this chapter has been merely offered as a starting-point, to prevent unfortunate initial choices. In the course of long practice you will discover what else you require.

104

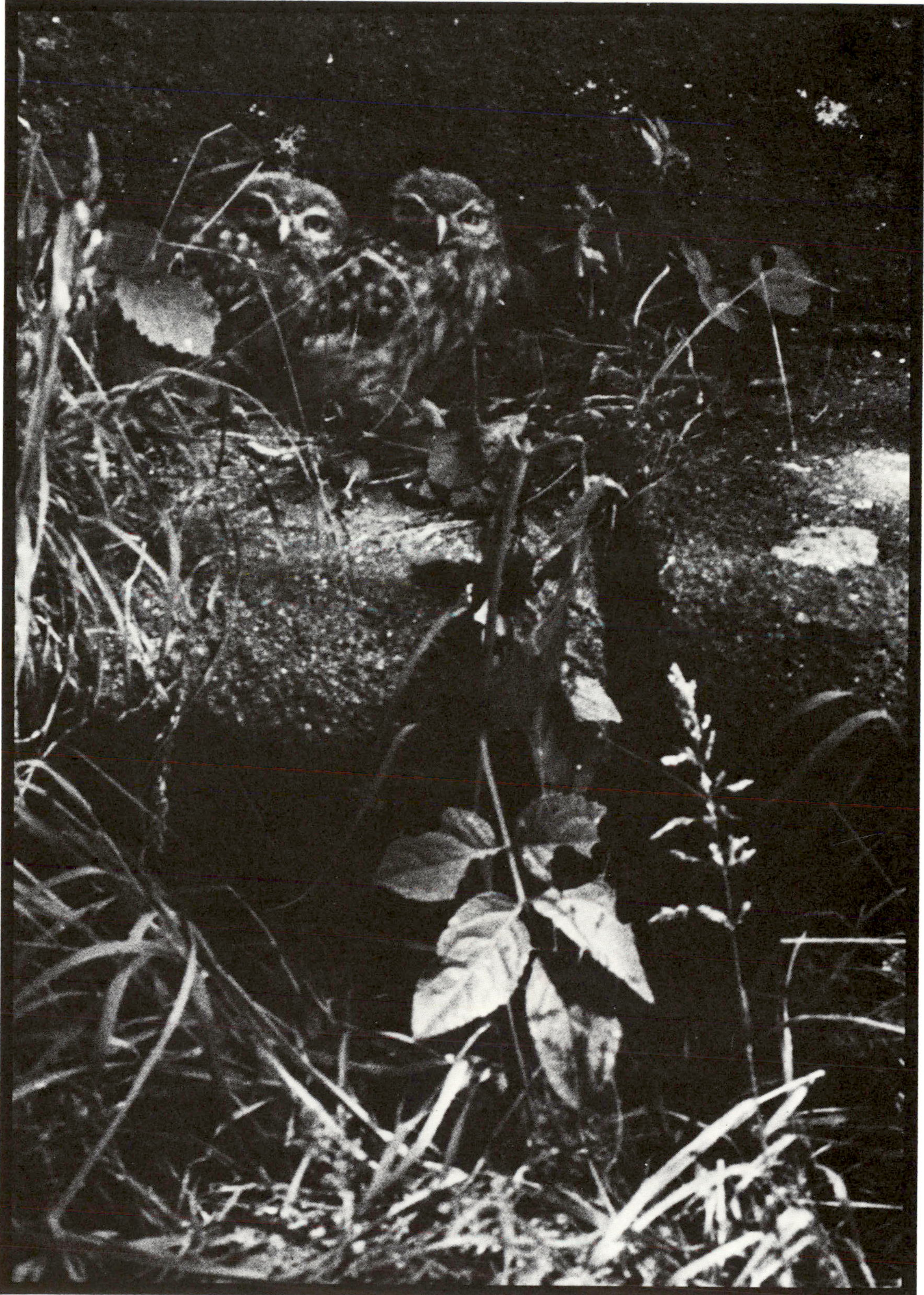

105

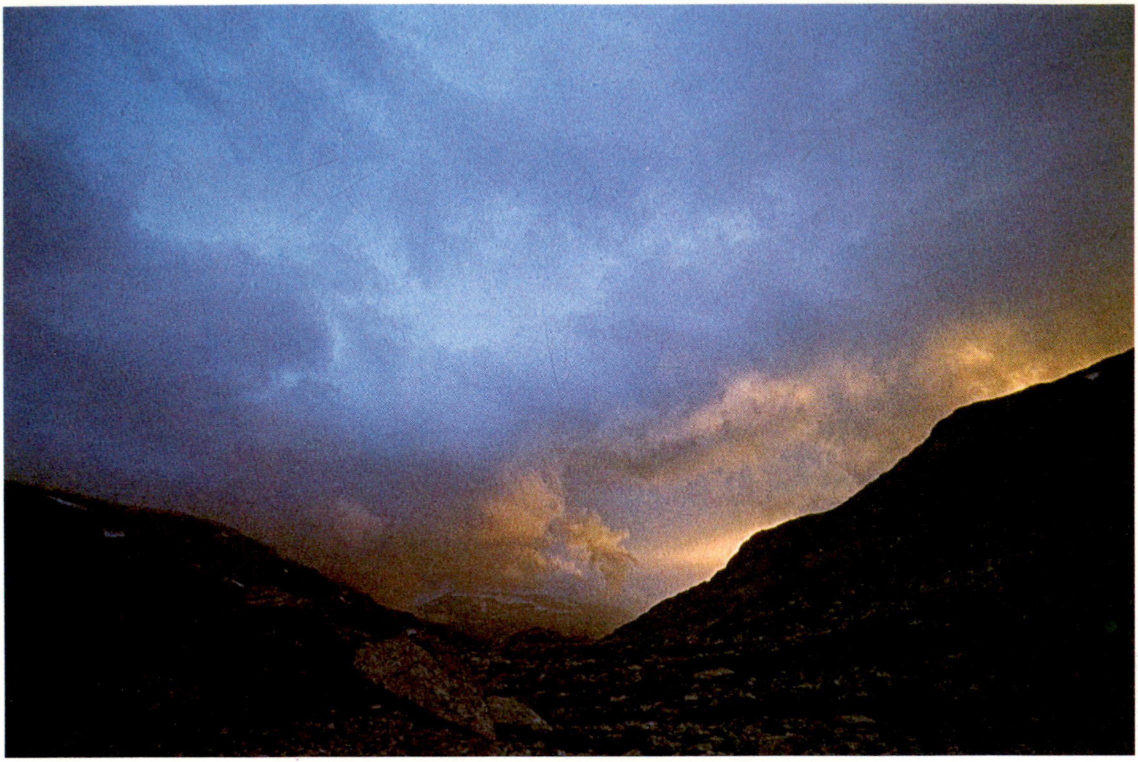

106

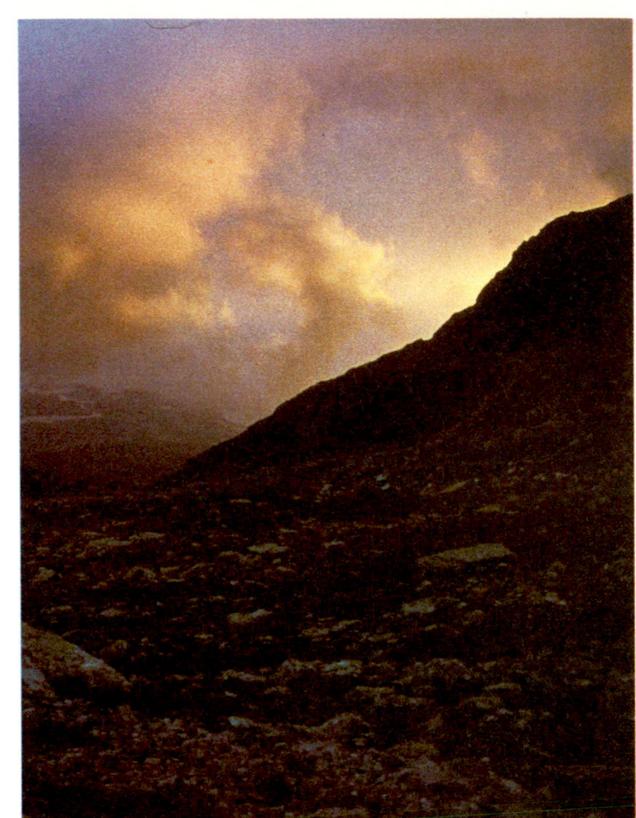

19: COLOUR AND/OR MONOCHROME?

In the previous chapter it was remarked that at some point in your photographic career you would feel you required two camera bodies. This applies, for example, if you frequently wish to take colour and monochrome pictures in alternate sessions or during the same session.

Many amateur photographers spurn monochrome photography—or indeed colour photography. It is, therefore, useful to discuss at this point the differences between these two processes and to suggest some advantages and disadvantages. Such considerations are always a cause of disagreement, since every photographer advocates his own personal views with a vehemence which is not necessarily founded on logic—and I do not exclude myself from this criticism.

There are two possible basic attitudes. The arguments for both are given here.

Firstly, it is often said that beginners ought to start with monochrome photography, since it is easier than colour. That is quite wrong. It would be more accurate to say that monochrome photography is so much more difficult than colour, that many people do not even become aware of the higher subtleties in an entire lifetime. As proof of the greater difficulty of colour photography, technical arguments are advanced which stem from the early days of photography. It can surely no longer be asserted today that colour photography is technically more exacting. The materials for taking and reproducing are so much improved, and the processing so much simplified, that anyone with determination can cope with it.

In what way, then, is there greater difficulty in monochrome photography? Monochrome photography, through the transformation of colour into grey values, forms abstractions to a very much greater extent than colour photography. The photographer can, therefore, have a much more telling influence on visual effect. This demands not only considerable knowledge and experience, but also an extremely apt use of imagination with regard to the effects of the photographic process on the picture. Thus monochrome photography is more difficult than colour photography.

The second argument, from the opposite point of view, would be as follows. It is said that monochrome photography is so much more exacting than colour. That is quite wrong. It would be more accurate to say that colour photography is so much more difficult than monochrome that many people never even begin to come to terms with it.

The reason for this is not purely technical. It is rather that the abstraction processes essential for the kind of visual composition appropriate to colour photography, through additional involvement with colour, have become so intricate that the transition from making pretty pictures to devising colour photographs which make genuine statements, calls for much greater creative effort than that required for monochrome photography.

You can see that both arguments begin at the wrong end! I do not wish to stretch the discussion any further, as I hope that, having considered the matter, you will agree with me that there is not a single logical argument to support the notion that either form of photography is 'better' or 'worse' than the other. It is far more important to realise that each form has an equal standing in its own right. The choice of which to use in any particular case is certainly worth some deliberation, since according to the proposed effect and subject, sometimes colour and sometimes monochrome is to be preferred. Anyone who stubbornly confines himself to one or the other is throwing away an appreciable amount of photographic material.

From this the question naturally arises of when this or that kind of photography is to be chosen. Unfortunately there are no rules which govern this, because the decision depends purely on what the picture is to say. The best rule of thumb is that when such a problem crops up, weigh up in your mind whether the colour in the picture is destined to provide information which is important for the statement you wish to make, or whether a monochrome treatment makes an abstraction possible that heightens the general impression.

107

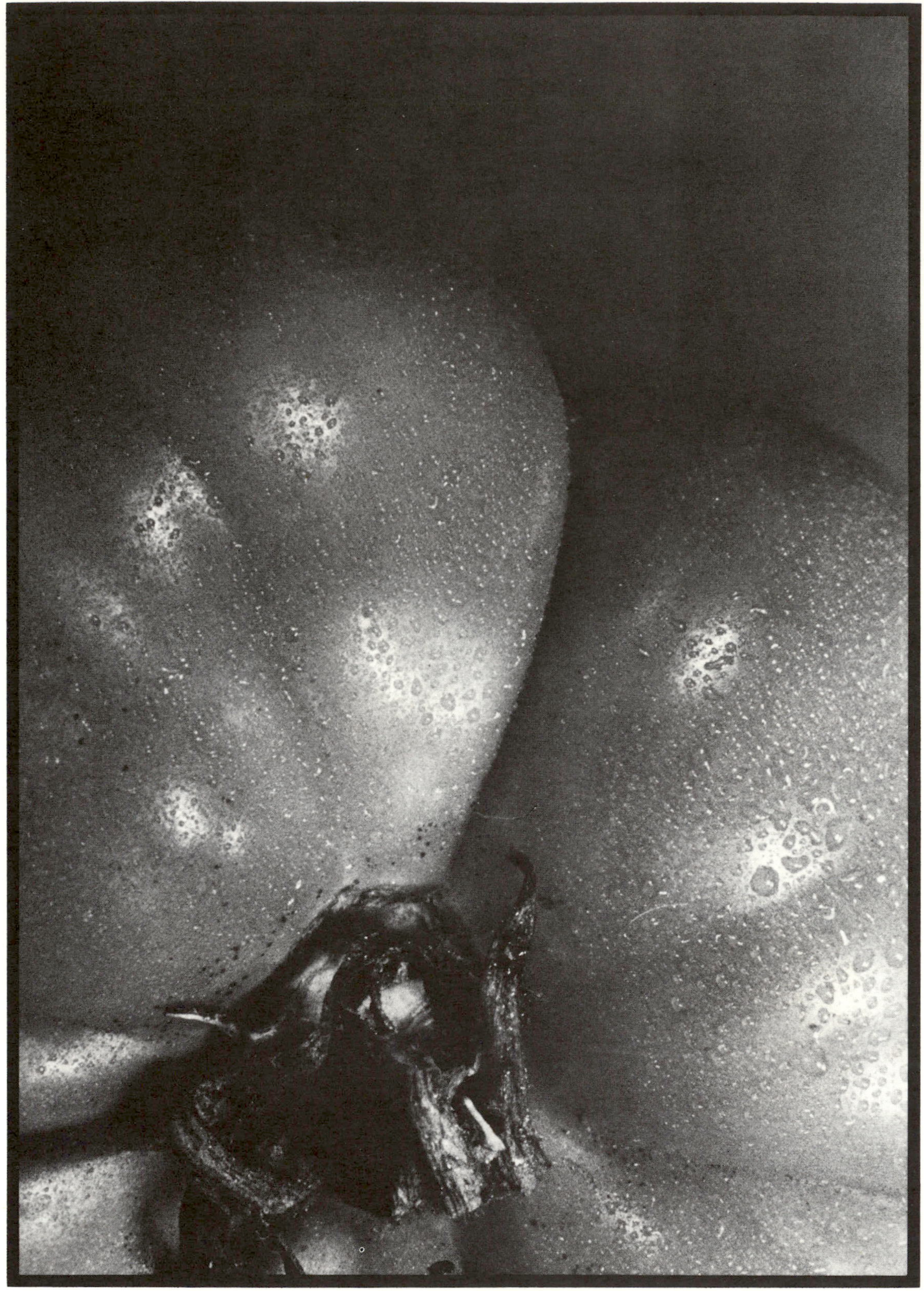

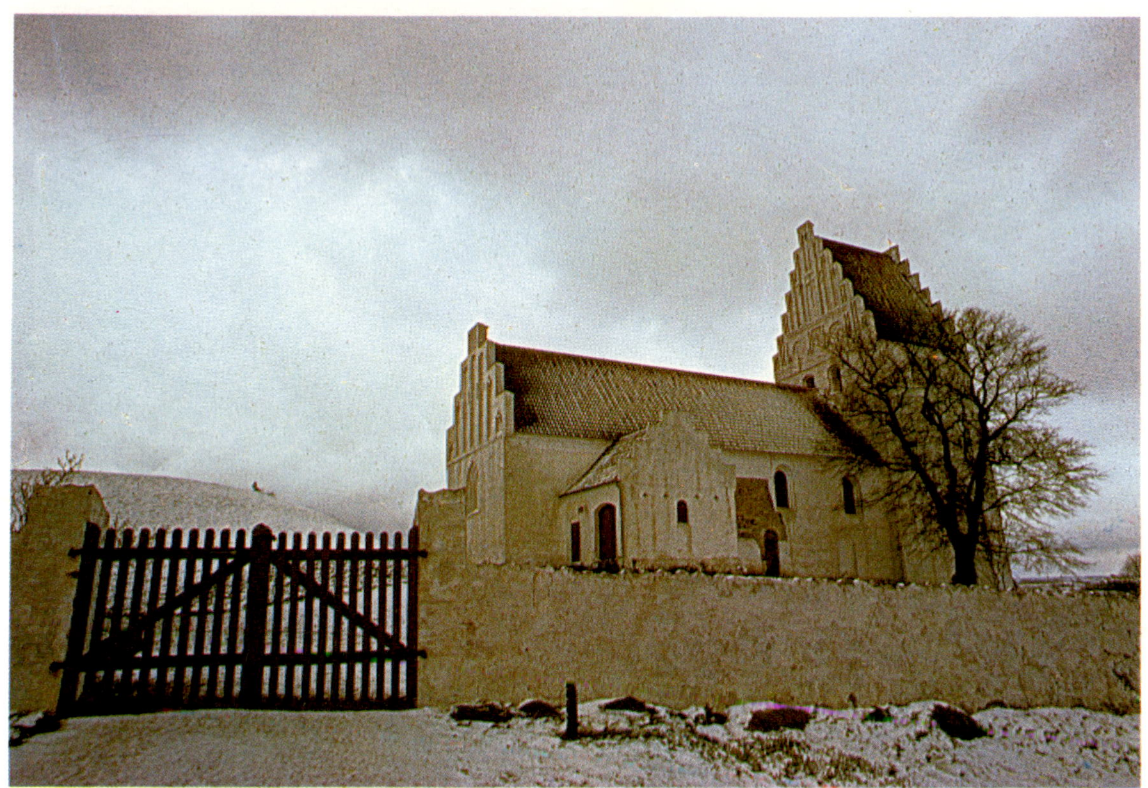

108

The two pictures selected to illustrate this point achieve their unique attraction not least because they contradict the usual expectation.

First of all, consider *Fig 107*. This portrays part of a ripe tomato. The obvious question is to ask why this photograph was not taken in colour, to show the fine deep red hue that is characteristic of this fruit? As a representation of a tomato, this picture would doubtless have gained in strength through the addition of colour. However, something else is intended here. In fact, the shape bears a striking resemblance to a certain portion of female anatomy (this has been confirmed by the immediate response of observers to whom I have shown the picture)—and this relationship in shape, which is the purpose of the picture, is evident only in a monochrome version. Colour would have concealed it by an overemphasis on reality.

In *Fig 108* the situation is exactly reversed. The subject presents almost exclusively grey tones, and hence it would be normal to choose a monochrome representation. But that would be wrong, because only in a colour photograph is it clear that the subject has only grey tones—and thus the strangely disturbing and cold atmosphere of the picture is achieved.

These two illustrations help in making clear how vital the decision between using colour and monochrome sometimes is, and also that it is well worthwhile to devote some thought to it.

20: LANDSCAPE

According to amateur photographic statistics, the landscape in its widest sense—involving buildings, population, towns and so on—is far and away the most popular of all photographic subjects. In my opinion there is also no region of photography in which so much rubbish is concocted than that of the landscape.

In most cases the reason for this is not a technical one. It would be much nearer to the truth to say that for successful landscape photography, in addition to the correct equipment, a certain attitude of mind or mental alignment is principally required which is appropriate to landscape. This requires some training, since the genre is inherently 'unnatural'.

This may perhaps sound distinctly strange, and you will certainly be asking what it all means. To help understand this, think back for a moment to your last holiday journey, or your last extended walk, and try to call to mind *how* you perceived and experienced the landscape. You will in all probability discover that this is by no means a simple matter, for generally a person recollects a unified experience rather than its component parts. This is contrary to a widely held view.

Even if you stand at a particular spot within a landscape, you receive an impression from it, involuntarily and unconsciously, which is composed of the totality of your experience. In other words, you might experience for example heat and cold; hear the wind, and perhaps also animals or the crackling sound of wood burning. You are aware of what is to your left and your right and beneath you (because you have seen it). You have also had the experience of reaching that specific place—and so on. All these sensations and experiences coalesce and add up to your impression of a landscape. And then you press the camera release.

In that instant you have recorded a picture of a memory, that is, a picture which, when you view it later, will bring back the shadow of that experience from your memory. The great disillusionment generally comes, however, when you exhibit this photograph to another observer. As a rule, you must begin with the assumption that the viewer of a picture has no prior knowledge or preconceived attitude to provide a direct relationship to the picture. This was possible for you, as creator of the picture, since you were personally involved with its origin and its milieu. In other words, the only way an outside viewer can relate to a photograph is with the use of what he can extract from the picture itself; whereas you as creator of the photograph have at your disposal an additional resource in the shape of an experience and an impression not available to the other viewer. The aim, then, must be to make all this evident from the picture.

I trust that you will not now ask: 'What in heaven's name has all that got to do with photography?' In my opinion, this consideration is indeed the cardinal point of every kind of photography (except scientific), because at some time you have to make a decision between two possibilities.

To make a photographic record, you have only to photograph something which is involved as closely as possible with the event, location or experience. If you look at this photograph later, it will bring back the total memory for you. This signifies nothing more than that a record photograph is merely a 'trigger'. The essential factor, namely the memory, is held by you and is completely separate from the photograph.

It is quite the contrary with pictures which are to be shown to others. Your sensations, or your idea, or whatever you wish to convey to outsiders by means of your picture must be contained in the picture itself. To arrive at that should be the object of your photographic endeavour.

If, therefore, the provisional definition of a 'good' photograph is a photograph that embodies for the viewer a deliberate statement which 'registers' with him and stimulates thought in him, then it follows that the photographer must have something to say before proceeding to make such a picture. This 'statement' might quite simply involve a personal reaction to a particular feature in the landscape. But something constructive must be done about it—lying around on the beach sunning yourself is

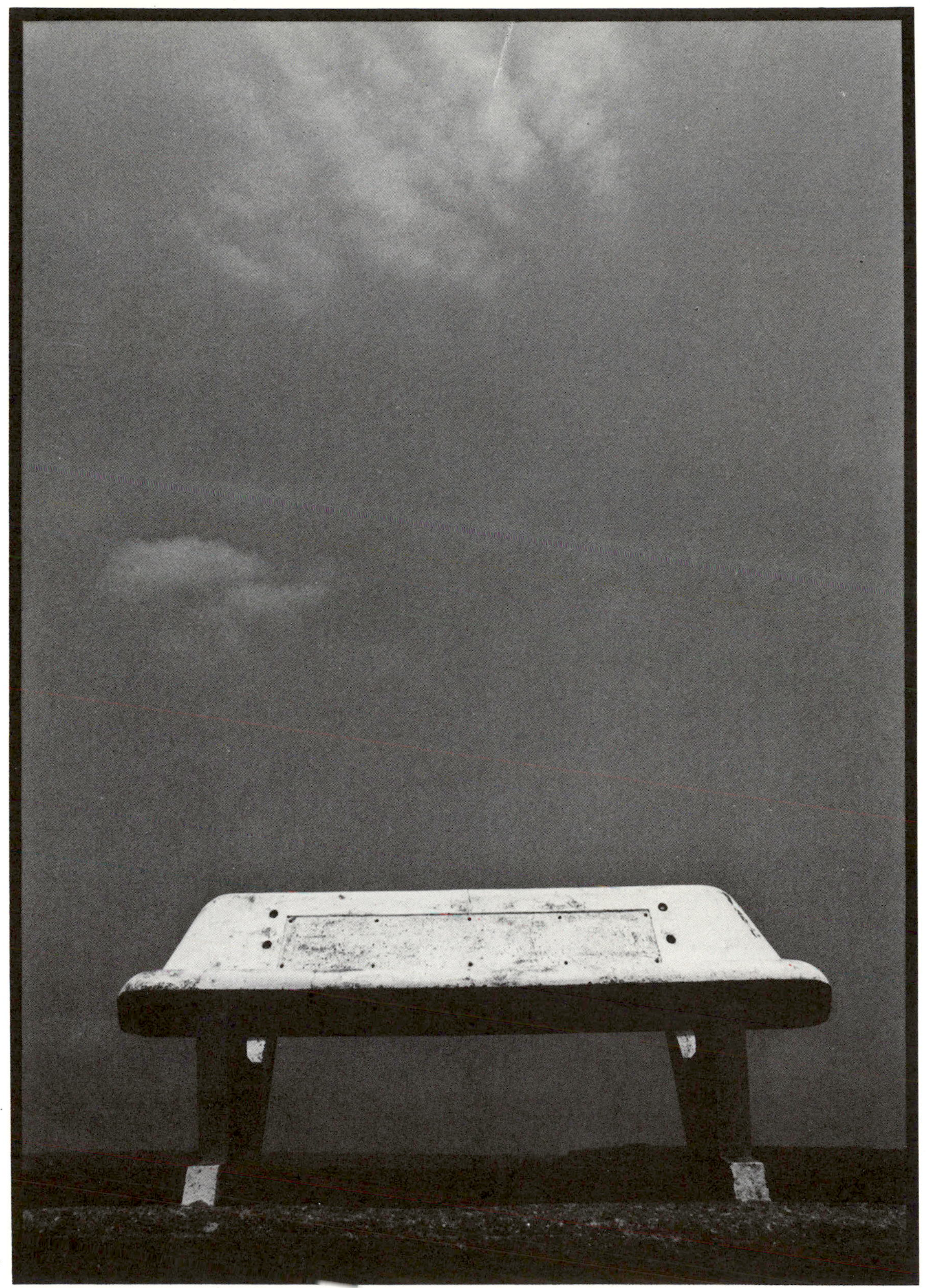

admittedly a congenial occupation, but not necessarily a photographically productive one. These considerations form vital mental equipment for the photographer.

Some years ago I was tormented by the thought that it must be feasible to demonstrate these arguments visually in photographs. Accordingly, I entered upon the task with a series of pictures on the theme of 'benches'. This series, which grew to quite a number but was never completed, was intended to show that even a quite familiar object, such as a bench, can form the basis for an expressive photograph—provided, by photographic creativity, it is successfully involved in a picture which fascinates the viewer.

The subject of *Fig 109*—a bench in a French harbour—is indeed an everyday object, on which people sit, but to which no-one gives a second thought. The photograph of this object, however, arouses a strong feeling in the viewer and demands from him detailed observation and reflection.

In the case of this illustration, two factors have had the strongest influence on the visual effect: focal length and height of viewpoint. The bench was situated on top of a low wall, so it was possible to hold the camera so low that the photographic viewpoint was for practical purposes below 'ground level' (represented here by the upper surface of the wall). In this way, and by means of very short focal length (using an *f*2.8/21 mm lens with angled viewfinder), a photographic view of the subject is created which is a physical impossibility to an actual observer.

The picture gives an impression of alienation. Some observers have expressed this by stating that they felt they were not looking at a bench but at a UFO—at any rate at an unearthly, disturbing object. The unusual allocation of light and shade caused by the low-level view, giving the effect that the sky is darker than the subject, contributes to the general impression.

It is interesting to compare this picture with the other photographs of benches in Chapter 4. There, using other means but basically similar subjects, a completely different visual statement is made. From this comparison it can be deduced that creative possibilities arise not only from technical sources such as alternative lenses, but also from waiting for the correct lighting or the right weather. (In some circumstances this can take some time: for the correct kind of mist for the two benches shown in Chapter 4 I waited over a year.)

With regard to the next photograph (*Fig 110*), it is useful to discuss in more detail the particular properties of extreme wide angles in landscape photography. The strange effect of this photograph (of an old castle on the Isle of Fuerteventure, Canary Islands) is created by the juxtaposition of the large stone, bearing the number 116, and the small castle in the background. It is obvious to the viewer that in reality the size of the objects depicted is reversed. This contrast between the actual objects and their representation in the photograph is responsible for the ambiguous atmosphere of the picture.

It is easy to see that the very wide angle of the 17 mm lens used, together with the practically unlimited depth of field, made the odd structure of this photograph possible. A corresponding photograph, taken with a telephoto lens, would have resulted in the inclusion in the picture of an unimportant part of the background—and this would have been outside the range of the depth of field. Thus the wide-angle lens opens up two possibilities in landscape photography.

Firstly, individual objects can be endowed with a special significance by exaggeration of their size and can also be brought forward in the composition, in such a way that a particular relationship between the single picture elements can be forced upon the viewer. On the other hand, the phenomenon of exaggeration of size differences between foreground and background can be employed for the purpose of relegating unimportant or less important elements to the background. An example of this is shown in *Fig 111*. As the boat was the principal subject, a lens angle of 35 mm could have been used. I chose a 21 mm lens instead, because I wanted to make the distracting objects on the coastline (for example, the houses) as small and insignificant as possible, and thus also to draw the attention of the viewer away from the background.

At this point I must comment adversely on some 'recommendations' which are continually being made, especially in

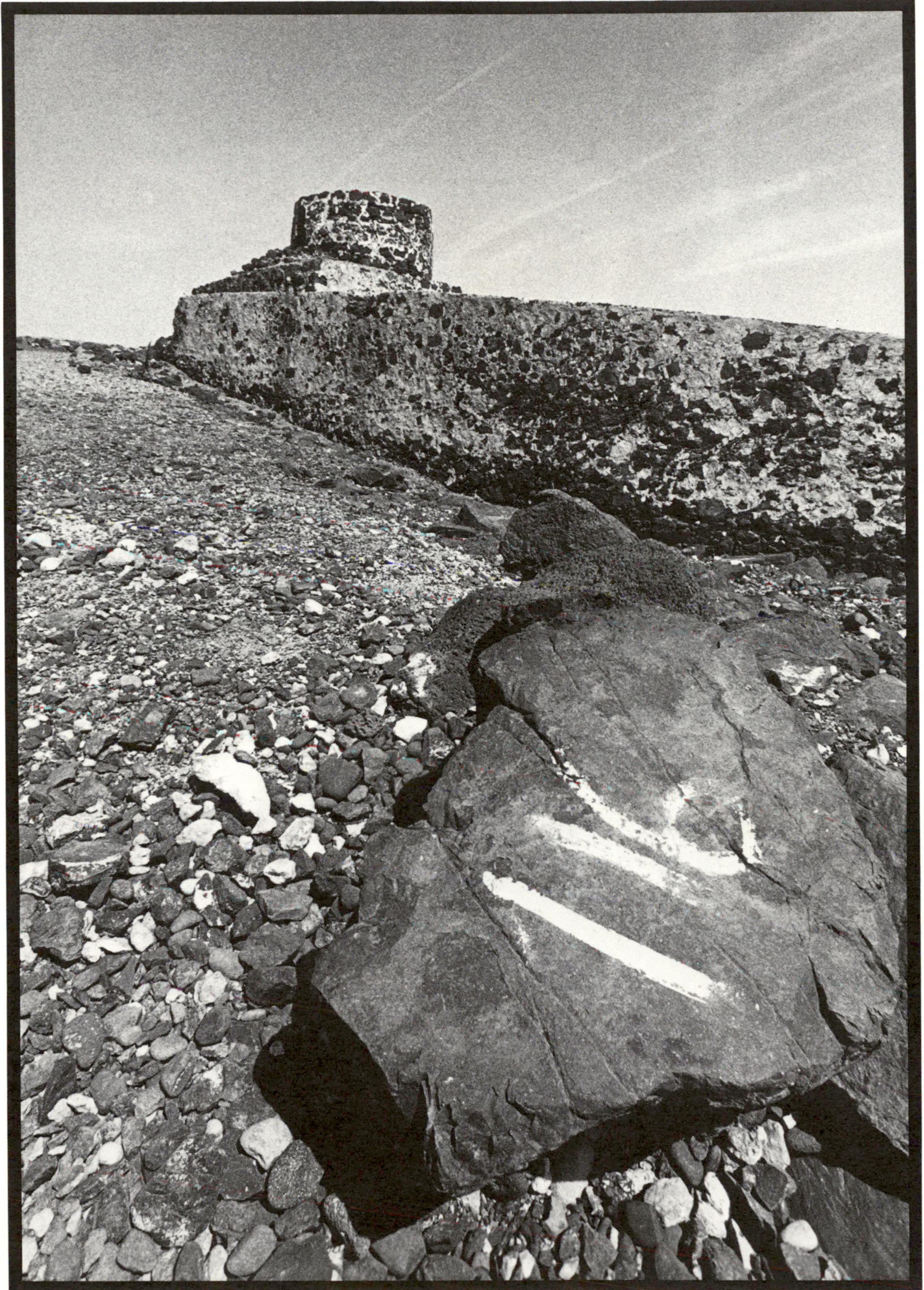

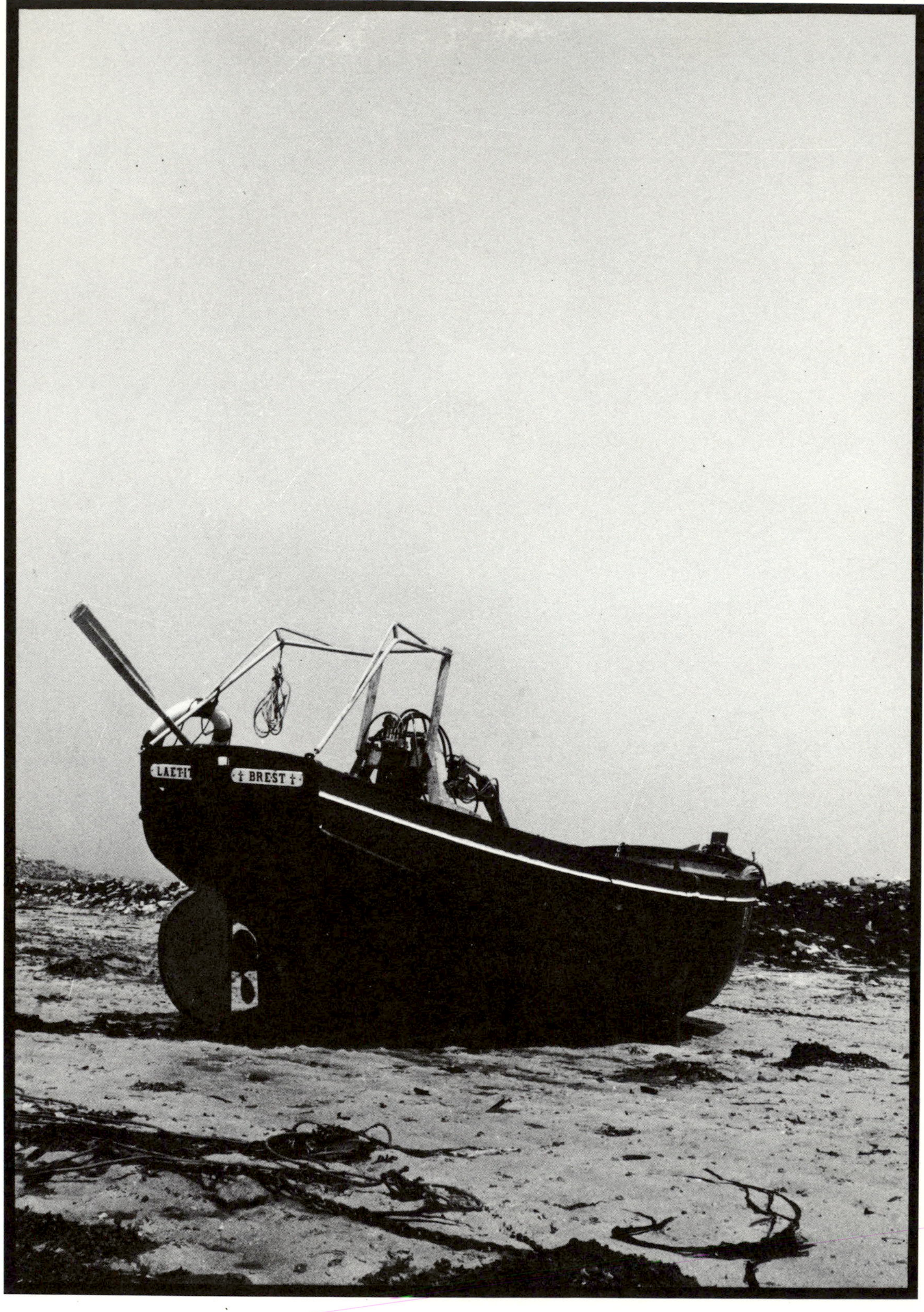
LAET-IT
BREST

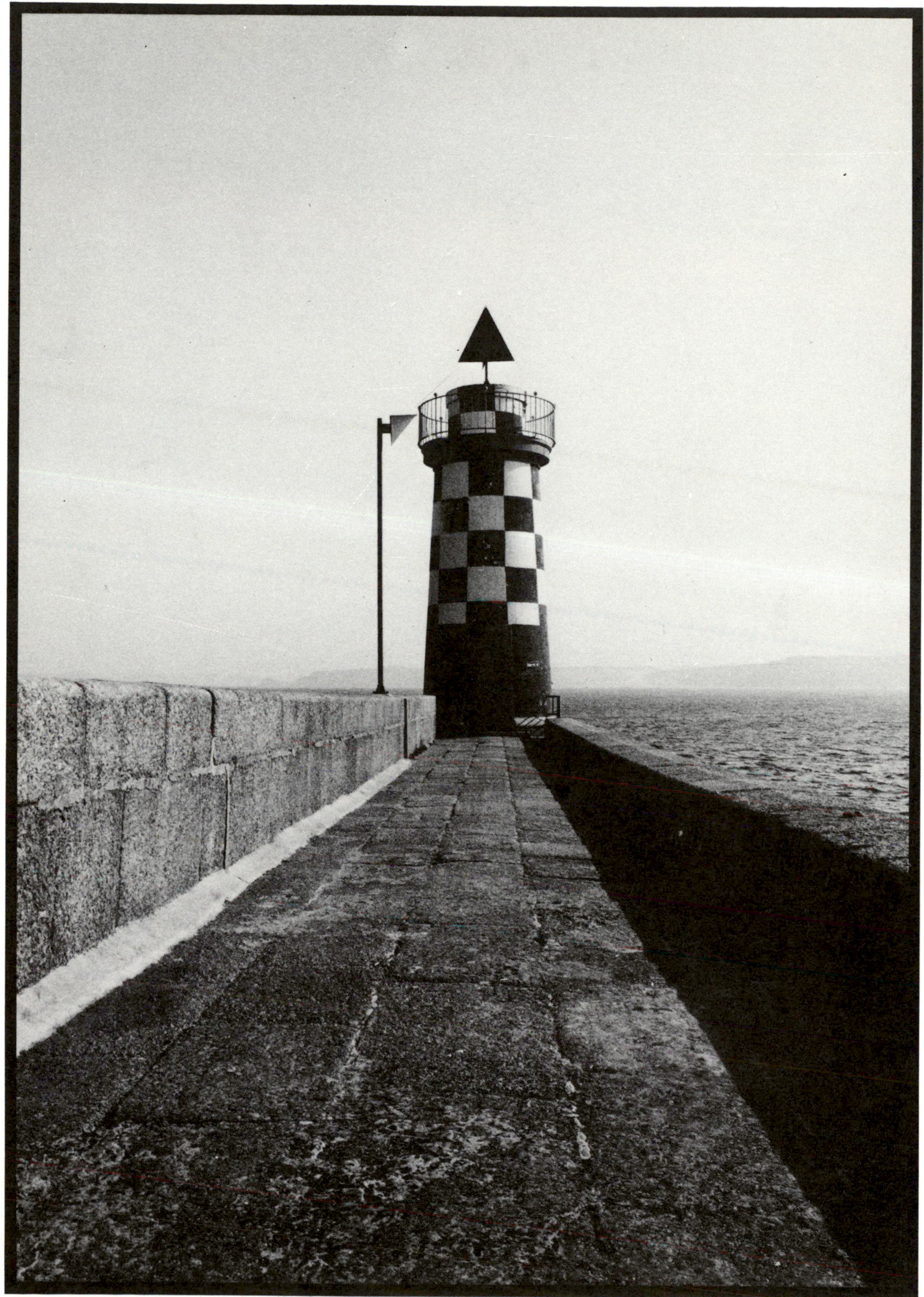

connection with landscape photography. For instance, it is often suggested that a foreground must be found for a picture. The usual examples shown are the branches of a tree hanging from the top or the side of the picture—or else a female companion (do not forget the red pullover if the picture is in colour) draped artistically on a rock. To be honest, such arrangements in my opinion are meaningless. There are sufficient photographic possibilities to allow the inclusion in the foreground of items to suit individual tastes and inclinations to the full. Such accessories as those indicated in the above-mentioned 'recommendations' are in this respect superfluous since they do not arise naturally from the general concept.

Another of these 'recommendations' decrees that the horizon should never go through the middle of the picture, as this has a dull effect. Have another look at *Fig 110*. Do you really find it dull because the horizon exactly bisects the picture?

Fig 112 shows two 'offences' against 'golden rules'. The horizon passes right through the centre of the picture and besides, there is no foreground at all. Strictly speaking, then, in accordance with the 'classic rules of composition', there is absolutely nothing of value in this picture. Yet to most viewers it seems to have had a unique and fascinating attraction, which has been in no small measure due to these (conscious) offences against the rules, and also to the exaggerated spatial effect provided by the *f*4/17 mm lens.

(Perhaps at this juncture I should remark that in this second section of the book the great majority of my illustrations have been exhibited or otherwise shown to the public, with the result that the quoted reactions of viewers of these pictures are genuine and not mere conjecture; I have sought out these reactions primarily in order to be able to incorporate them in this book.)

The vital point which is being emphasised here is that no purpose is served in applying generalised rules to an individual picture. The entire conception of a picture must develop from within itself and have independent existence. Picture postcards are a good illustration of this point. In general, these are composed according to the 'golden rules', with fleecy clouds above, those notorious red blobs in the foreground and the subject 'bang in the middle', surrounded by branches and rocks, or perhaps simply by sausage-stalls, buses and droves of tourists. Feel at liberty to take such photographs; but if these conventional rules are applied to a subject, without any attempt to come to terms with them first, the result is usually the same sort of soulless and characterless picture postcard view, which could have been bought at the nearest souvenir shop and would have been cheaper and often technically more skilful.

I should like to apply these considerations to a further example. During my last visit to the French province of Brittany, I spent several nights at a somewhat unprepossessing camping site in the south of the region, where construction was still in progress. Naturally I could have seized the opportunity of taking a batch of record photographs. But whereas photographs of the camping bus or of the sanitary facilities or similar attractions would be less than fascinating (even if I had taken them), two pictures of another kind which I did take there will perhaps be of interest.

Fig 113 shows the remains of a partly collapsed fence in front of a thicket of conifers. There is absolutely nothing to be found here of the camping atmosphere of the place; but this did not worry me. I was much more interested—bearing in mind the texturally fascinating structure of the wood—in the strange contrast between the ruined man-made fence and the impenetrable natural thicket from which it protected the site. Using an *f*2.5/100 mm telephoto lens, I attempted to portray fence and thicket as being as close as possible to each other, so as to emphasise this aspect of the composition, while the viewpoint height, exactly halfway up the fence, stressed the forbidding aspect. The same picture taken with a wide-angle lens from eye level would have showed the fence in such a way that it could be literally overlooked, thus spoiling the effect of the fence as a barrier.

Precisely the opposite photographic thought-process played its part in *Fig 114*. This portrays a quantity of tubes which building workers had laid down just a few metres away from the fence in *Fig 113*, in front of the thicket. This subject suggested to me an illustration of the theme 'technology versus nature'. I tried to introduce this idea

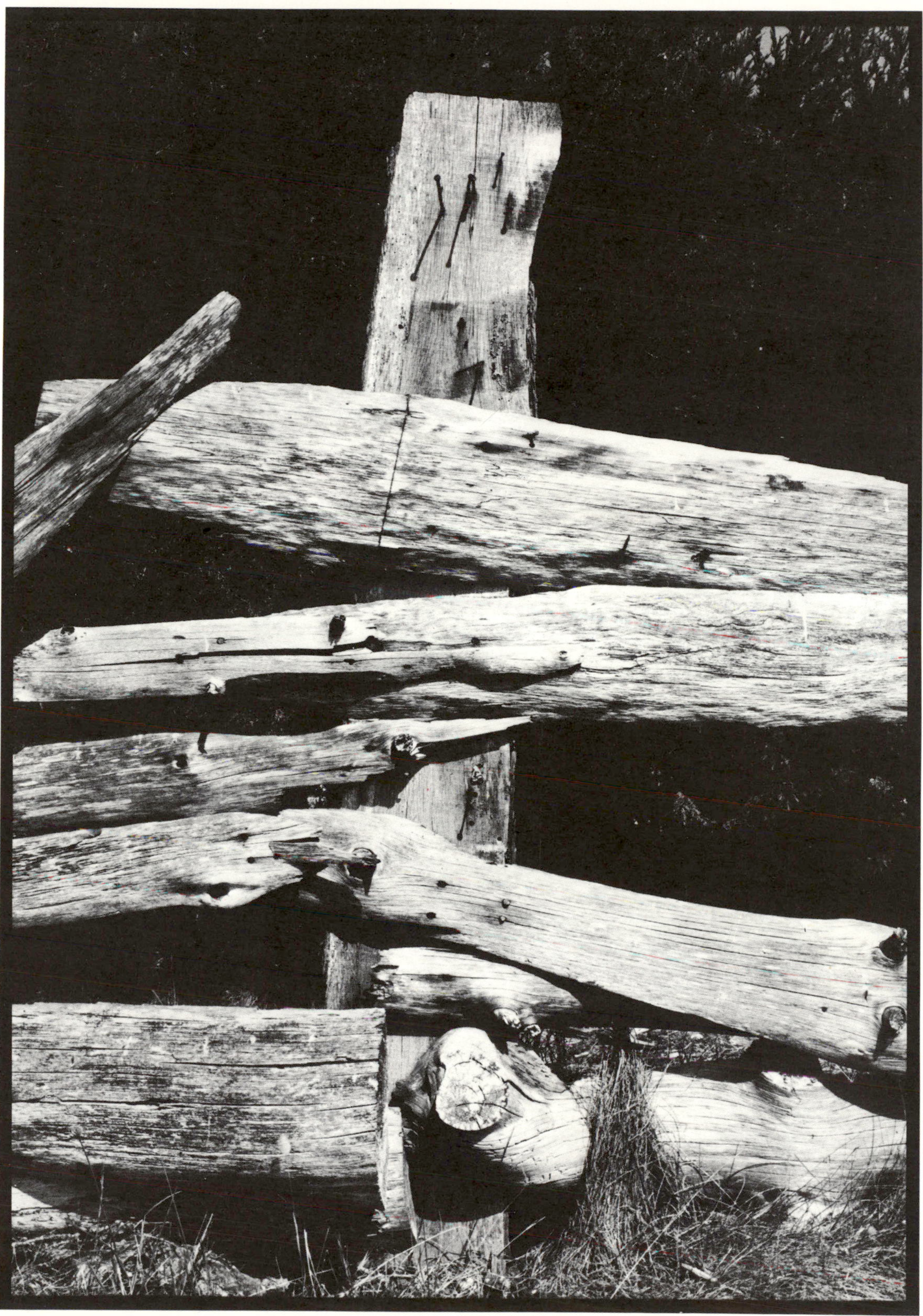

114

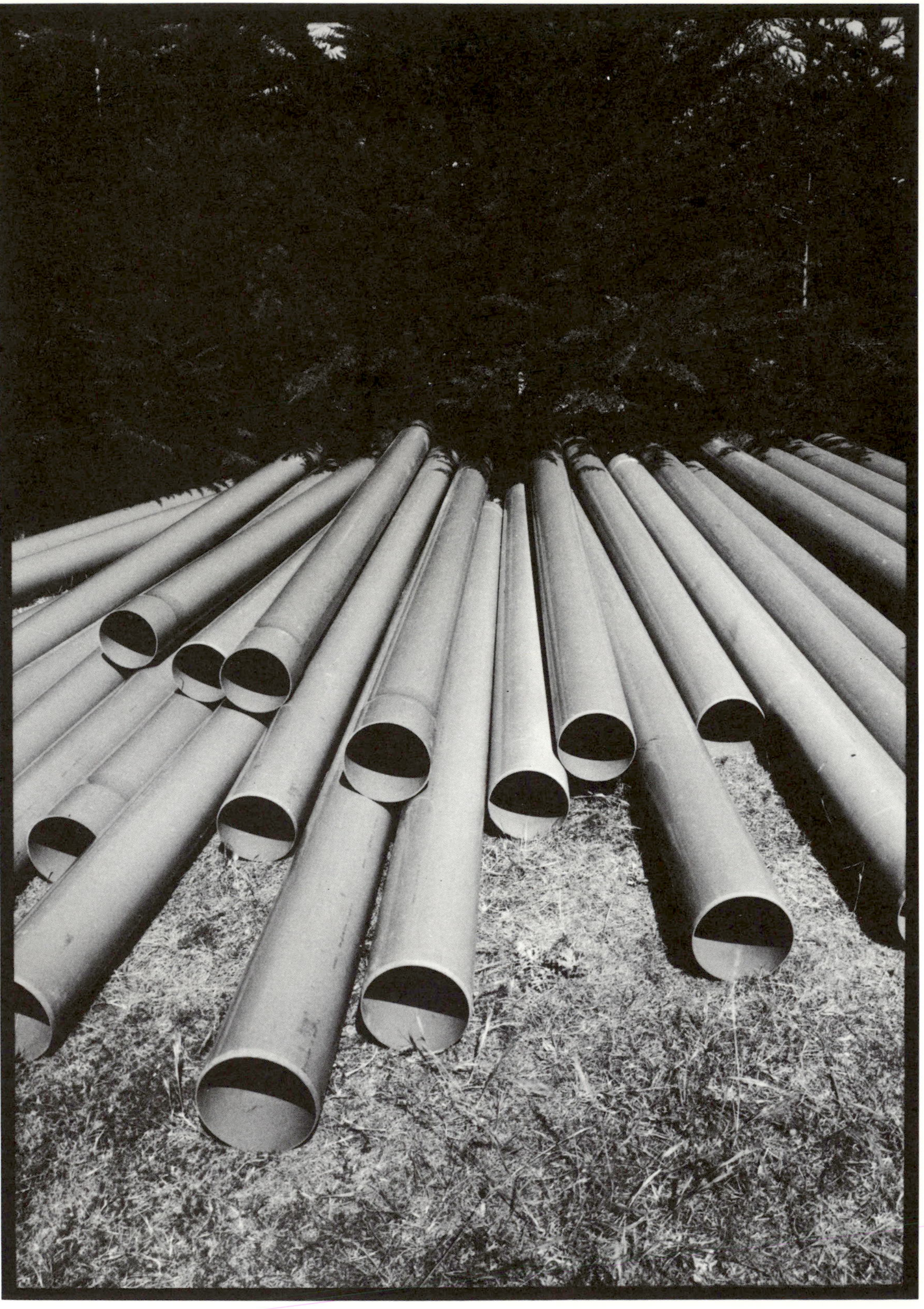

into the picture by choice of focal length, height of viewpoint and angle of the camera.

The use of an *f*2.8/21 mm lens, together with the eye-level viewpoint and the strongly tilted camera, worked in such a way that the long tubes, not in themselves remarkable, tapered very sharply in perspective, thus leading the eye dynamically into the picture—to be brought up abruptly against the almost black mass of the thicket.

These two pictures have been chosen because they demonstrate that almost anything can be extracted from an utterly conventional subject—in this case a camping site. It is often possible to 'see' something in an unpromising scene and if this is translated into photographic terms, a disinterested observer can also extract something from the finished picture.

With this procedure, there is a risk involved which you may have noticed already in examining my illustrations. The more you immerse yourself photographically in a subject, the more personal, and hence expressive, the resulting photographs are. There are of course people who cannot begin to find anything in this kind of picture, as they are, so to speak, on an entirely different wavelength. So you would either have to try to come to terms with this, or else confine yourself to making picture postcards, to which scarcely anyone raises objections, but for which scarcely anyone becomes really enthusiastic. Always remember—*you* are taking the photographs; and if people do not appreciate your efforts, you can also purchase some picture postcards to prove that you were there.

This leads back to the point that everyone should assemble his photographic outfit according to his individual outlook. For instance, it is not necessarily recommended that you follow my example and work with the extreme 17 and 21 mm wide-angle lenses: the focal lengths you use have to suit the particular effects you are aiming at. As copying other people's pictures is certainly not an interesting occupation, in the same way it is as well to select your equipment according to your own outlook and requirements.

Perhaps a few of my readers are disappointed that I have not offered a foolproof formula for landscape photography. But all of you should by this time have learnt for yourselves that there are no foolproof formulae in creative photography. Thus my photographs are not shown here merely so that they can be copied. The comments which I have appended to my illustrations, and the quoted reactions of other viewers, should act instead as a stimulus to original reflections and ideas for individual photographic creativity—and what emerges from that depends on you. This of course does not apply exclusively to landscape photography, but it is appropriate to mention the point here.

As a whole series of varying points of view have come under scrutiny in this chapter, it is useful to summarise some of the most significant before concluding.

The fundamental and uniquely photographic means of expressing your intentions and ideas is the choice of lens. According to the focal length selected, the subject can be transformed and rearranged, so that it presents itself to the observer in a specific manner.

Rules of composition are not to be regarded as significant structural aids if they are simply used arbitrarily in your own picture. The arrangement of the individual elements is vital for the picture's statement, and must therefore comply with your creative intention—and not the converse. It, therefore, follows that before and during the taking of a picture it is important to have an exact conception of the effect of the final photograph, and to be quite clear in your own mind how the technical means at your disposal are to be employed to achieve this end. This is certainly not an easy task. At this point it is apposite to quote a story told of Mozart. It seems that Mozart was asked at one time whether piano playing was very difficult to learn. His answer is alleged to be that it was not difficult at all—it was merely a matter of hitting the right note with the right finger at the right moment . . .

However, do not become disheartened as there are other sayings you could heed instead—such as the one that says: 'practice makes perfect'.

21: BUILDINGS

Up till now in the consideration of landscape photography, the emphasis has been mainly on focal length and the associated problems of viewpoint. It has been shown that the structural facilities provided by the creative use of focal length and viewpoint allow the opportunity of arranging the separate constituents of the theme with regard to their effectiveness in the picture, almost exactly as you wish. There are, however, certain situations or subjects, such as buildings, which for technical or other reasons cannot be placed or rearranged in the picture in the manner we would have wished. What then?

The answer to this question is easy to give, but often very hard to obey. Do not take a photograph at all. Similar advice applies to the later processing and treatment of your photographs. In enlarging, in viewing and selection of transparencies, and even in sticking into the album enlargements fresh from the chemist's shop, there can be no escaping the fact that the most important accessory is a large wastepaper basket! The first vital step on the way to better photography is ruthless selection. Just imagine that you are showing someone a whole box full of photographs: hundreds of fairly good ones and mediocre ones, and amongst them three, four, five or maybe more which are really outstanding items. It goes without saying that the viewer will regard the few masterpieces in this proliferation of pictures as mere accidents.

Be very critical, and leave all those photographs in the cupboard which are even to a small extent unsatisfying to you. You will be doing a favour both to yourself and to others, for there are more than sufficient bad and mediocre pictures in existence, and, as has always been the case, really good examples are extraordinarily rare.

The problem, of course, is once again the decision whether a picture is good or bad. What pleases me is not necessarily satisfying to you—and vice versa. One favourite bone of contention among amateur photographers consists of the so-called 'golden rules' of composition, which allegedly stipulate what makes a picture 'good'. Among other rules, it is laid down that a photograph is good only if it fulfils certain technical requirements. One of these prerequisites is concerned with grey values in monochrome photography.

This rule states that the darkest parts of a picture must embody recognisable details, and that the brightest parts must differ from pure white to the extent of having a very light grey quality, while the intermediate grey scale should be as wide and varied as possible. This kind of assertion certainly renders the assessment of a picture very easy. But it will not do. It is no aid to better photography, because this very possibility of breaking down sections of a subject into pure white or black, and the concentration of the grey scale in other parts of the picture, is an important means to control the impact of a picture.

Fig 115 exemplifies this point. It shows the ruins of a Cornish castle, using a 21 mm lens. The picture looks very powerful and stern. This effect is achieved mainly in two ways. Firstly, the viewer is influenced by the rigid perspective structure with the worm's eye view, made possible by the use of the wide-angle lens. Secondly, and even more significantly, the reduction of the grey scale made this effect possible.

The plain, almost entirely black silhouette of the castle serves as a kind of backdrop, in front of which the bench seems to float. Thus the picture comprises three zones, each of which represents a small section of the grey scale: the black of the castle, the dark grey of the bench and the light grey and almost white sky. Far from diminishing the impact of the photograph, this reduction of the grey scale actually creates the strong effect of the composition. A diffusion of these areas and a reduction in contrast would certainly have destroyed the whole effect of the picture.

It is quite a different matter in *Fig 116* (a beach on Cap Fréhel, Brittany; 53 mm lens on 6 × 9 cm camera). Although this picture can also be clearly divided into distinct zones of brightness, the structures within these zones play an important role in the effect of the picture, so I have avoided the use of pure white or black. The darker background of the picture was achieved by

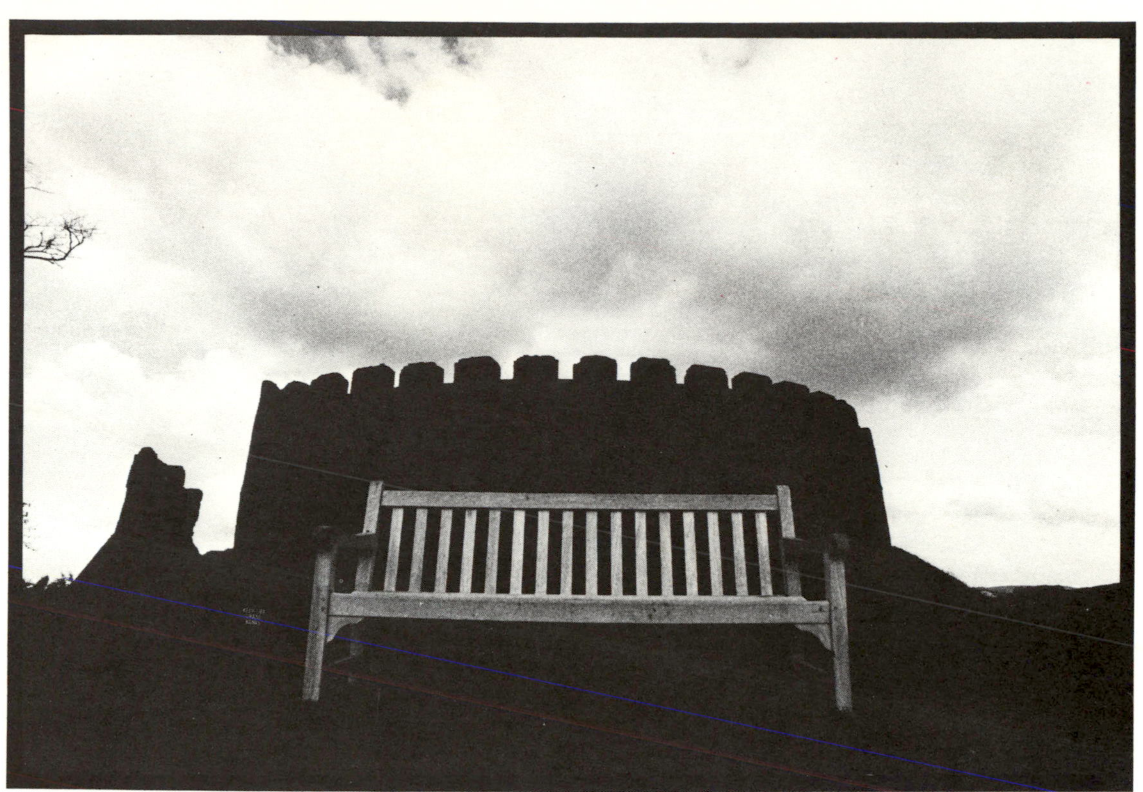

115

darkroom manipulation (post-exposure). I should really have preferred to wait for a moment during the taking of the picture when the rear portion of the subject was shaded by a cloud.

It was established in Chapter 17 that high-sensitivity film (400 ASA/27 DIN) has a wide contrast range. On the other hand, the contrast range of low-sensititivy film (50 ASA/18 DIN or less) is more limited. Obviously, these properties of different film stocks can be made use of in order to achieve such effects as those in the two examples shown here.

There is a problem connected with film sensitivity which can cause trouble especially in landscape photography. While there is a tendency—encouraged by dealer publicity—to use high-sensitivity film for low-light conditions and low-sensitivity film for bright ones, the converse may often turn out to be better. In southern regions especially, the sun's rays can be so strong that the contrast of light and shade can become too much for low-sensitivity film to cope with. In these conditions, under certain circumstances, a 400 ASA/27 DIN film can prove to be advantageous—even if, on account of the film's high speed, a neutral density filter has to be used.

The reverse naturally applies too. With dull lighting or at dusk (without artificial light sources), the subject contrast can be reduced to such an extent that a low-speed film can be much more useful—even if, because of the appreciably longer exposure times, a tripod has to be used.

To recapitulate, the correct lighting effect for the picture is just as important as the choice of the correct focal length or any other factor. There are three possible ways of influencing the lighting effect:

1 By choice of film stock (see above).
2 By selection of exposure time (determined by film type, lighting condition for the subject and desired effect).
3 By waiting—for a shadow to pass, for a change in lighting contrast, for clouds, for clear sky, for rain, snow, mist . . .

Personal experimentation is the best way to appreciate how strongly the impression of

116

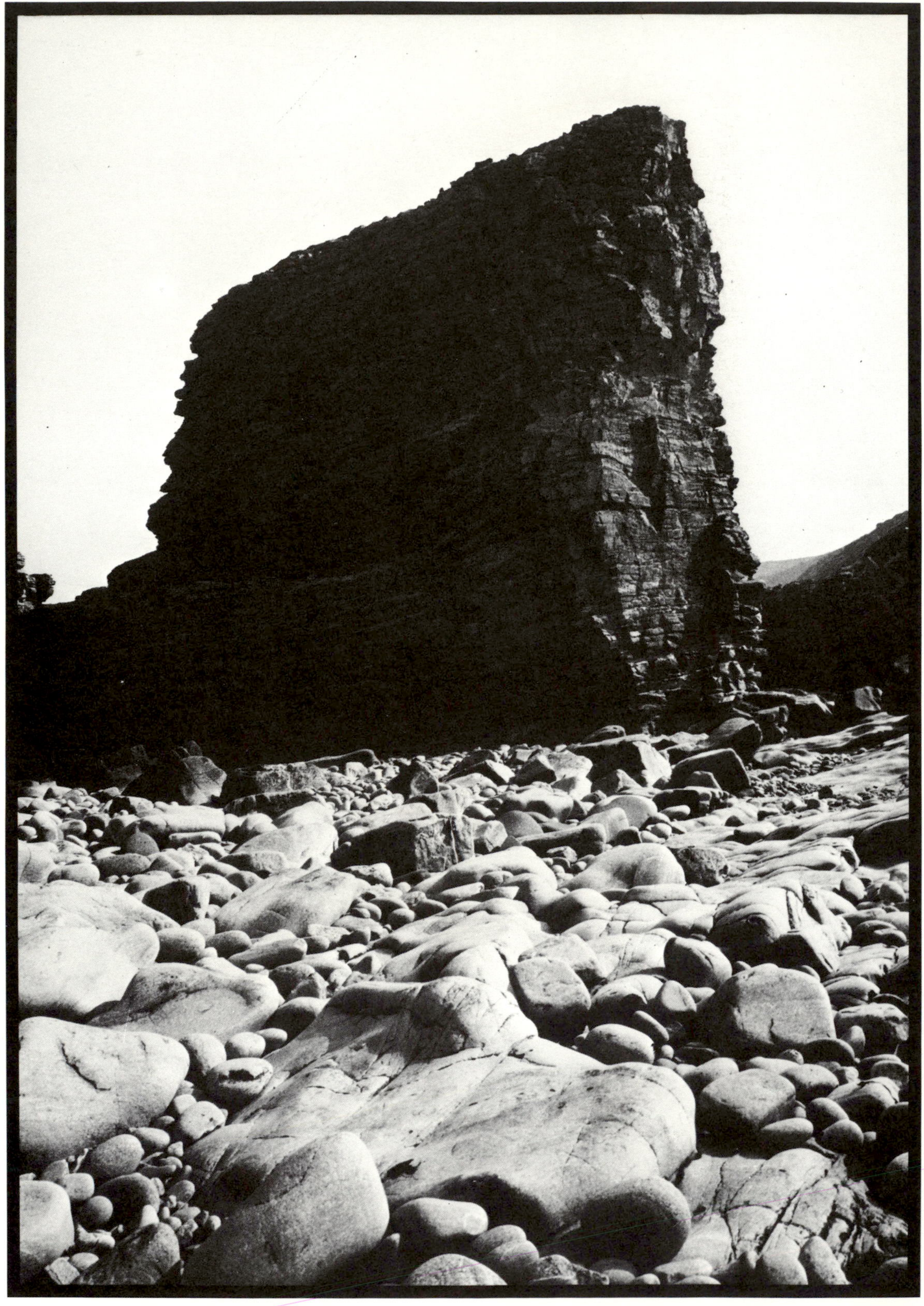

a subject can be affected by a variation in the lighting conditions.

These ways of changing the visual effect are naturally not confined to monochrome photography. The next two illustrations, *Figs 117* and *118*, show how the same effects can be applied to colour photography.

If reversal film is underexposed, the picture becomes darker; that is, the colours come closer to black. In addition, up to a certain degree of underexposure, the colours become stronger. This effect may be heightened still further by the use of a polarising filter (*see* Chapter 9), as may be seen in *Fig 117*. This procedure was employed here in order to create an impression of strong colouration, such as often happens when the sun comes out after a thunderstorm. (Lighthouse on the Isle of Møn, Denmark, *f*2.8/21 mm lens, polarising filter, taken at 1/60 sec at *f*16 instead of the automatically indicated 1/125 sec at *f*16.)

The opposite effect is obtained when reversal film is overexposed. The colours have a stronger white component, and the effect is more delicate and pastel. This was precisely the impression I received from the pale tones of this European fishing village (Fuerteventura) in the midday sun. In consequence, the exposure time for *Fig 118* was longer than the indicated value.

Please note—the correct value is what matters, not the indicated value! As discussed in Chapter 17, the light meter gives a false value for a subject which is not predominantly of a middle grey. Very bright subjects will be underexposed if photographed according to the meter reading. Hence the exposure time must be lengthened appreciably (for a subject such as in *Fig 118*, generally by about one stop). In order to reproduce the desired effect of pale pastel tones, the exposure time must be increased still more (or the diaphragm opened wider)—again by about one stop. Thus for the subject in *Fig 118*, instead of the indicated value of 1/500 sec at *f*16, 1/125 sec at *f*16 was used. (Camera lens *f*3.5/100 mm.)

In such cases, even for the experienced photographer, it is often extremely difficult to decide exactly on the right amount of overexposure or underexposure for a particular case. Accordingly, instead of becoming bogged down in profound calculations and tedious measurement, it is generally easiest to achieve your purpose by using several combinations of exposure and aperture in succession, and later selecting the picture which is most pleasing to you.

'Practice makes perfect' applies here too. If you know exactly what you are aiming at, you will discover quite quickly which technical means to employ in order to transform your ideas into photographic reality.

Figs 119—121 demonstrate the fact that parts of buildings are frequently more effective for making a photographic statement than general views of the same buildings. A general view can contain too many contrasting components, or even disturbing elements, to give a unified visual effect. A smaller section of the subject can make a stronger statement. For instance, if you find difficulty in composing a satisfactory picture using the suggestions offered here or using other ideas, it may be worthwhile moving in closer to the subject, to investigate whether a concentration on detail is more effective.

At this point it should be remembered that when working with the standard miniature format you cannot afford to lose any picture quality. Although in reportage, sport and wildlife photography it is often necessary to carry out corrections later by enlarging sections of photographs, these alterations should not be required in landscape photography. The photographer who later extracts portions of a landscape photograph merely betrays the fact that he was not working carefully enough when he took the photograph. And he pays for this with inferior picture quality.

If it really is difficult to decide which section of a scene to use, the best procedure is to take several photographs from several points of view, thus avoiding having to fumble about with the finished product later.

For reference, the technical data for *Figs 119—121* is given here: *Fig 119*, Island of Møn, Church of Elmelunde, *f*3.5/100 mm macro lens; *Fig 120*, Mont St Michel, Brittany, *f*2.8/21 mm lens; *Fig 121* as *Fig 124*, but with *f*2.8/21 mm lens.

117

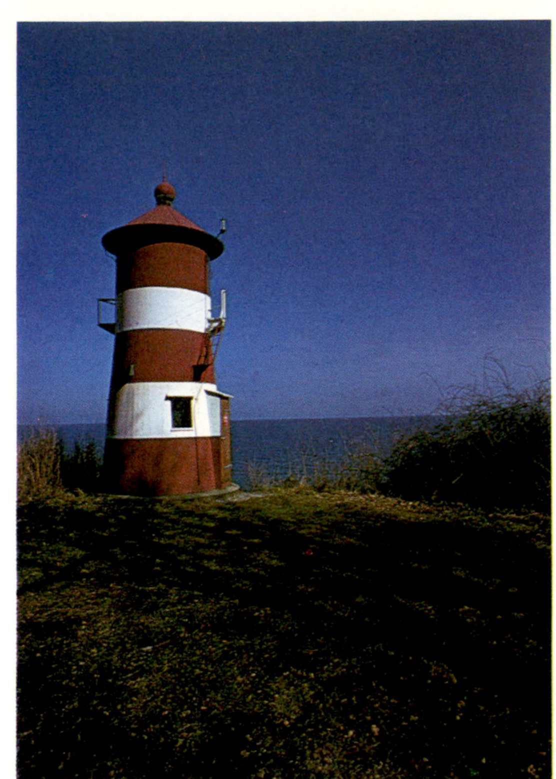

118

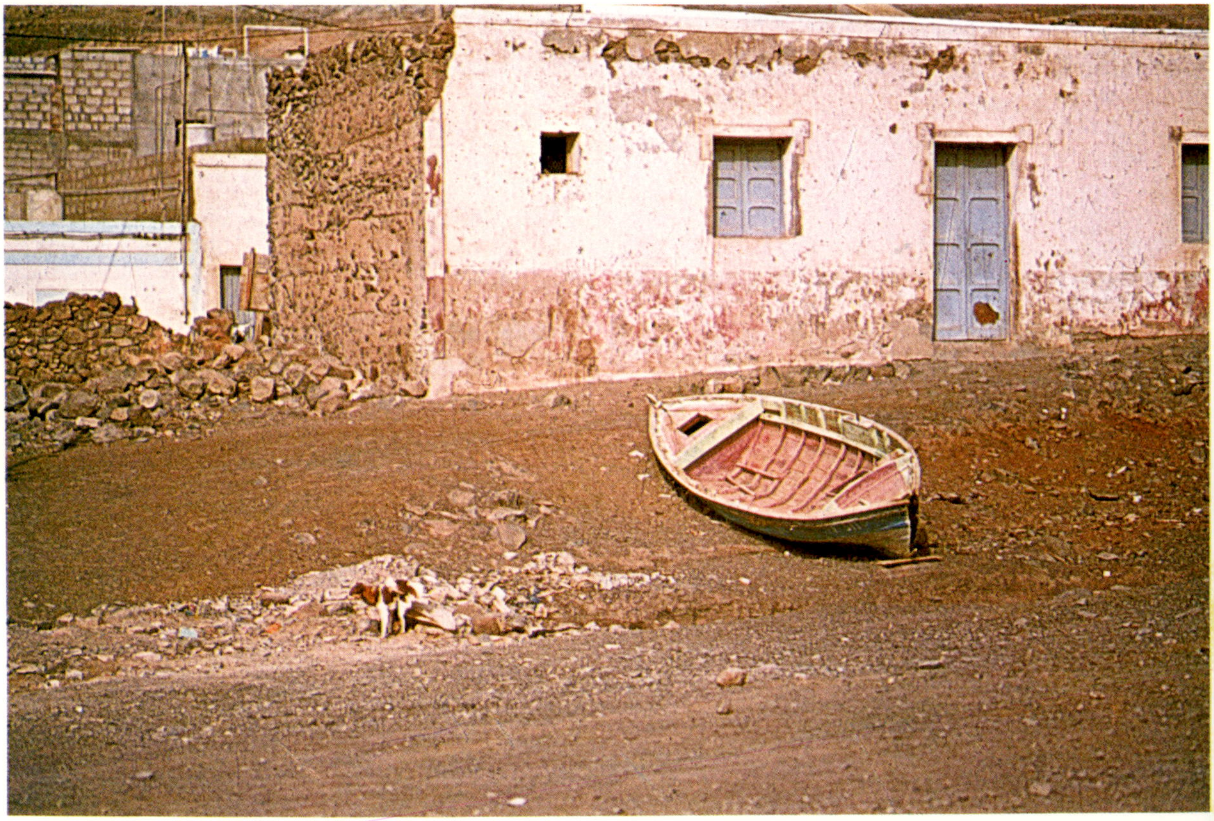

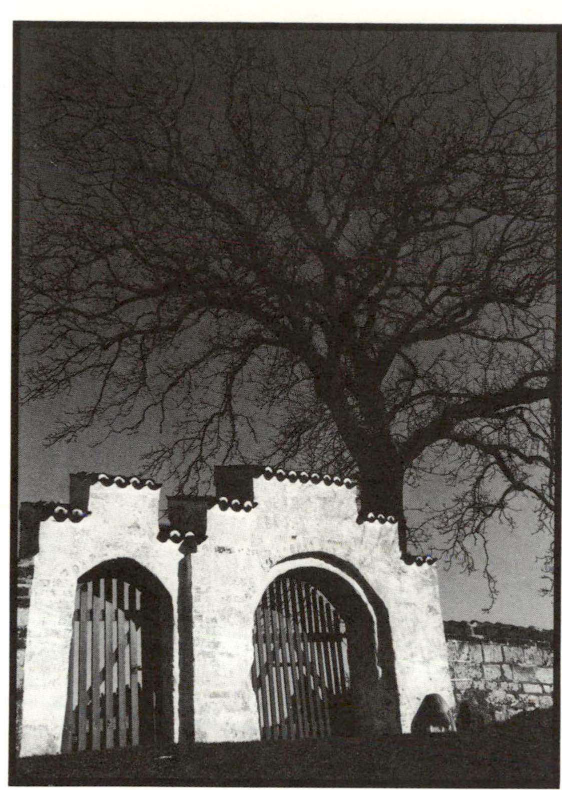

19

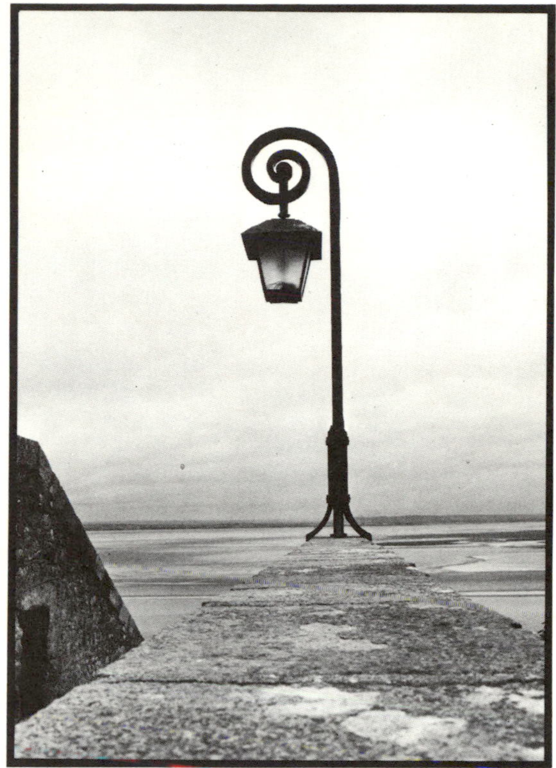

120

121

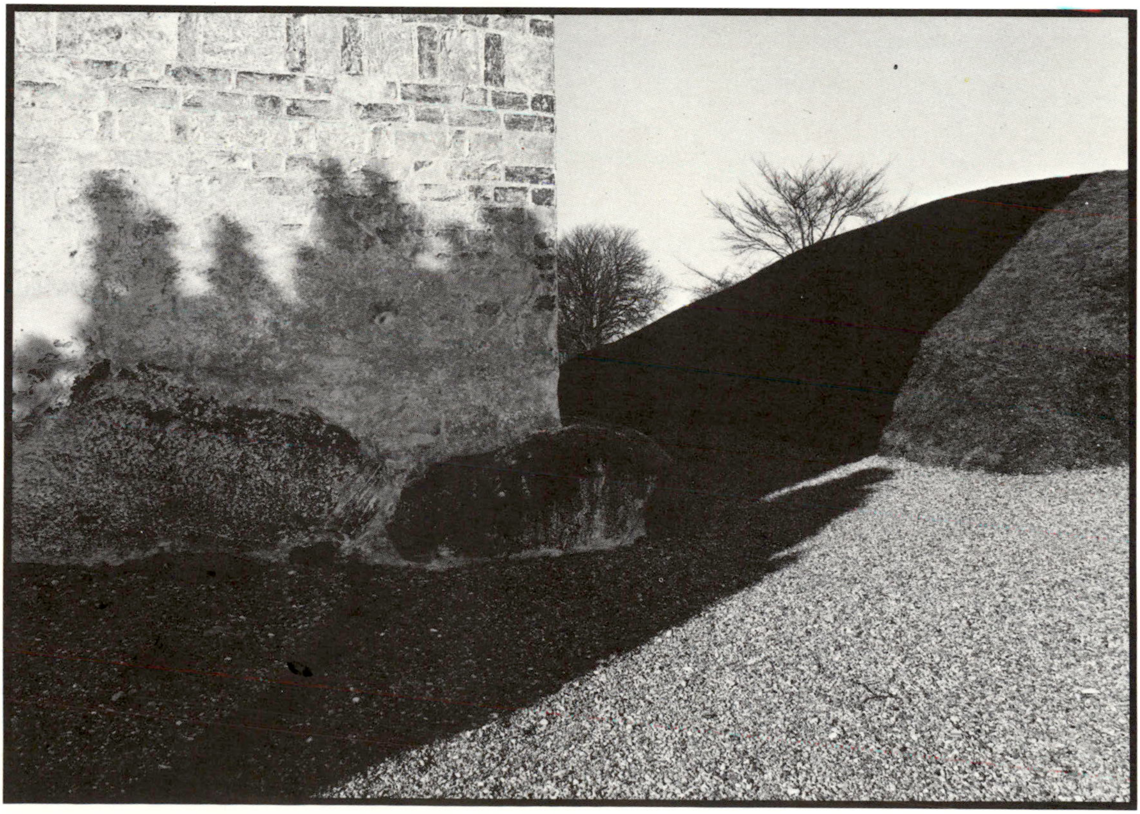

22: PORTRAITS

When you consider how many opportunities there are of photographing people—from family shots to formal portraits, from soft porn to the stylised nude, from people at work to formal weddings—and when you reflect further how many situations arise in which people play some sort of role (reportage, sport and so on), then you must come to the conclusion that this genre is an inexhaustible one, offering opportunities for an infinity of photographic statements and creative potential.

First of all, it is important when you are undertaking any portrait photography to make sure that you are not violating any laws of privacy of the particular country you are in. In some countries it is a serious offence to take, and especially to publish, a picture of anyone without having first obtained their permission.

Let us now devote our attention to the theme of the portrait. In order to discuss the theme of portrait photography, it is necessary to find at least a superficial answer to the question: what actually *is* a portrait?

A portrait is not a mirror, and the photographer is not an automatic passport picture machine. A portrait is not concerned exclusively with a physical likeness. It would be much more accurate to say that it should reveal the personality and character of the person portrayed. Here a second factor enters into consideration: a portrait is a combination of the dual impressions held about the model by himself and by the photographer.

The average person has some kind of concept about himself, and this concept is in turn part of himself. The portrait photographer, on the other hand, who for good or ill must be an observer of human nature, develops his own idea about the person whom he is going to photograph. The finished portrait represents the point of contact or the amalgam of the two concepts.

If the portrait turns out to be a poor one, then the point of contact must have been very tenuous. Perhaps the photographer regarded the subject as merely a means for expressing himself; or perhaps at the other extreme he omitted to involve his own concept in the picture, with the result that it became simply a representation of a physical entity and not the joint expression of two personalities.

Perhaps the most difficult idea for the beginner to grasp is that the portrait must be a picture bearing the imprint of two personalities. Nevertheless, this is indeed the case. Since the photographer alone creates the picture, the personality of the individual portrayed is realised only by the work of the photographer in transforming it into a picture. From this it follows again that a portrait does not necessarily consist only of the representation of a face, because the personality of the person portrayed reveals itself not only in his features, his posture and his bearing, but also in his clothing, its trimmings and his personal environment. This statement leads one to an initial piece of advice for anyone contemplating portrait photography. Do not use props, accessories and other items! Objects brought in from outside as aids to the presentation of your subject will have nothing at all to do with the personality of the model, and accordingly cannot assist in strengthening the picture as a portrait.

In my opinion the best portraits are simply taken in the customary environment of the person: that is to say, in his home or at his work. This applies even if the environment is not evident on the finished picture; it is a contributory factor, in that it helps the subject to reveal his personality more directly and spontaneously, truthfully and thoroughly.

Having considered all the above-mentioned factors and decided that you are to make a portrait in someone's home, the first concern must be with appropriate lighting.

If you are photographing during the day and not in the depth of winter, simply make use of the daylight which comes through the window. In this event, bear in mind that the intensity of the lighting rapidly diminishes as you move away from the window. In addition, especially in large rooms with dark walls or furniture, contrasts are quite

1 Model
2 Photographer
3 Fill-in screen
4 Window

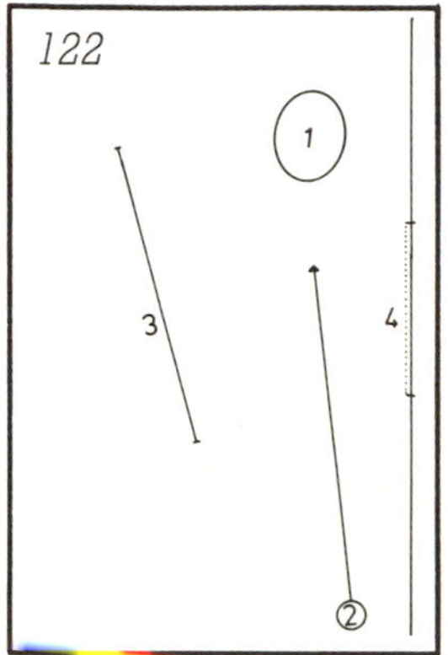

1 Model
2 Photographer
3 Flash unit
4 Fill-in screen

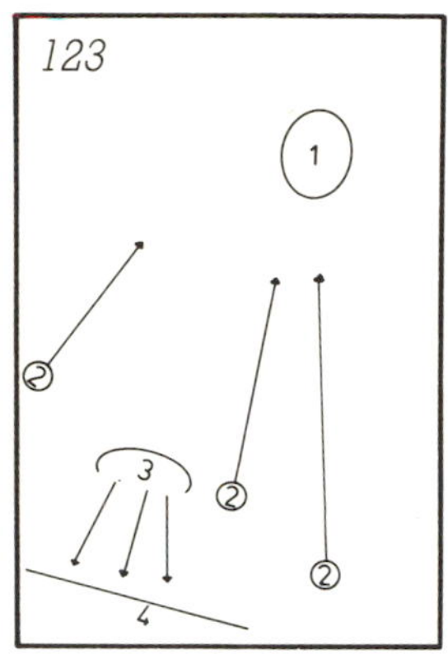

1 Model
2 Photographer
3 Main light
4 Fill-in light

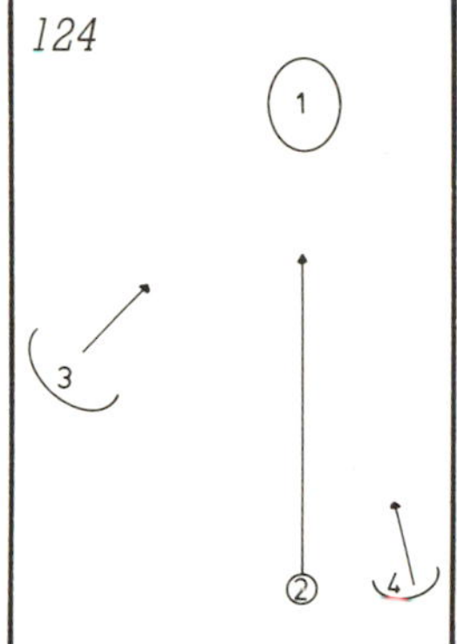

1 Model
2 Photographer
3 Main-light
4 Fill-in screen
5 Background light
6 Spotlight

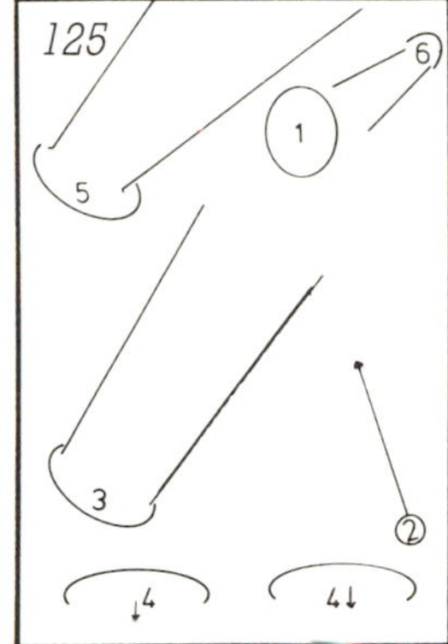

extreme. In these conditions a sheet of white card, or something similar, is helpful as a fill-in screen. A piece of cardboard (plain white or near it) measuring 70 × 50 cm would be suitable if you were intending to take a full-face or head-and-shoulders portrait; for a full-figure picture a rather larger sheet of card would be necessary. *Fig 122* shows how this operation works in practice.

I would emphasise strongly the fact that this type of lighting is not by any means to be regarded as merely an emergency device. Quite the contrary—as long as direct sunshine through the window is not involved, but instead perhaps a diffused northerly light, this type of lighting creates an atmospheric effect which is difficult to achieve in any other way.

Fig 126 illustrates a special case of this daylight illumination. The picture was taken from a house window, looking obliquely across a balcony. The sky was overcast and the balcony provided additional shade. In spite of this, no additional lighting was used, thus avoiding any loss of the effect (*f*3.5/100 mm lens).

Unfortunately, in many instances it is not possible to use daylight—and these are the times a flashgun must be used. Since nowadays almost every amateur photographer possesses one, and since these accessories, according to maker and design, have varying facilities and characteristics, only one example is described here. To find to what extent this applies to your own equipment, please refer to your instruction leaflet.

Never use direct flash. Never fix the apparatus to the camera and direct it straight at your 'victim'. Apart from the unpleasant shadows which are created, reflections can appear in the eyes, which in colour photography can give rise to the well-known 'red-eye' effect.

Always use flash indirectly. To illustrate this I shall describe how I work with my flash unit. The external sensor is at the camera position, while the flash unit itself is fixed to a tripod, with the reflector turned away from the model. At a distance of about 50 cm in front of the flash unit I place a crumpled sheet of aluminium foil, against which the flash is directed.

Fig 127 shows that this simple arrangement can create a faultless and interesting lighting effect. (*Fig 123* shows the plan of this lighting arrangement. The lens used was *f*1.4/50 mm.)

Indirect flash, as described above, uses up a good deal of power. One set of batteries has only sufficient power to expose two films. Apart from this, conventional flash units have another disadvantage: it is impossible to judge the effect of the lighting. For this reason the inexperienced photographer can be faced with repeated failures.

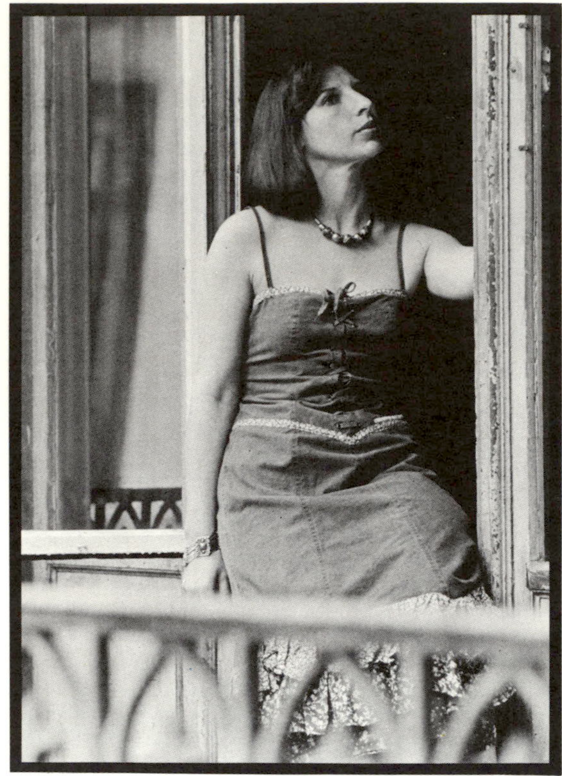

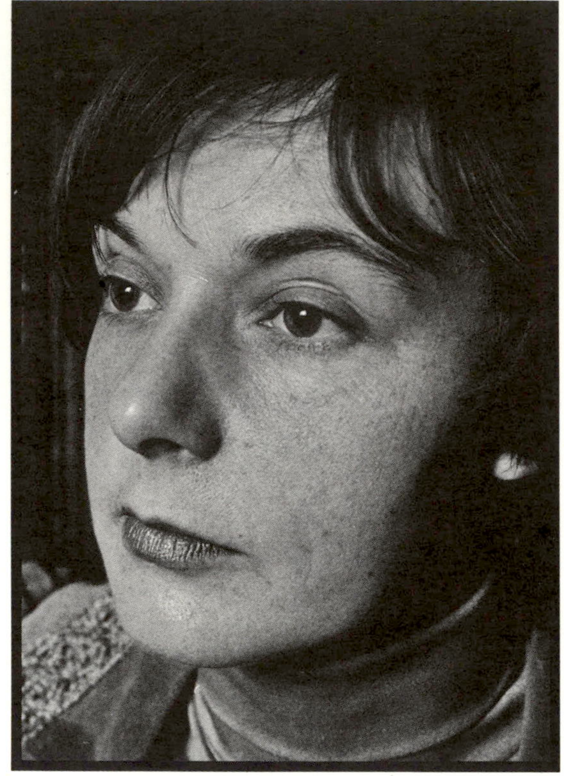

Accordingly, many people prefer floodlighting or, if it is available, an adjustable flash unit.

When using floodlights with colour film, always remember that different light sources have different colours, which have to be allowed for in the choice of colour film material (*see* Chapter 9). Since with artificial lighting more than one light source is generally used, the lighting must be arranged with very great care, as it has a decisive effect on the scene. Technically correct illumination should be regarded as only the very first step towards creative lighting, that is, lighting which is deliberately aligned to a specific effect. It is not only important from which direction the lighting is to come but the intensity of each individual light source must also be carefully assessed.

Fig 124 illustrates an example of simple 'standard lighting'. The main light is placed roughly at an angle of 45° to the left of and above the taking direction. The fill-in light is placed as close as possible to the camera. (Take care that no light falls directly on the lens as this causes reflections—*see* Chapter 6.) With this arrangement, if a 500 w lamp is used, for instance, at a distance of two metres, then a 100 w lamp is quite sufficient as a fill-in light.

If you are working for the first time with artificial lighting of this nature, it is advisable to take the trouble of having a 'dry run' with various arrangements of lamps, as this is the only way to obtain a clear impression of how the scene is affected by lighting arrangements. Along with the intensity and positioning of lighting units, there is a third factor to be taken into consideration. The kind of illumination (for example, directed or scattered light) also exerts a strong influence on the visual effect.

A method of adapting this kind of 'standard lighting', to achieve special effects, is illustrated in *Fig 115*. To produce this kind of 'effect illumination', experiment carefully with a willing and patient 'try-out model' before using it seriously. The first rule of lighting technique is invaluable here, that is, to operate one lamp after another. Only when you are fully satisfied with the effect of the first lamp should you switch on the second. The second rule is equally

128

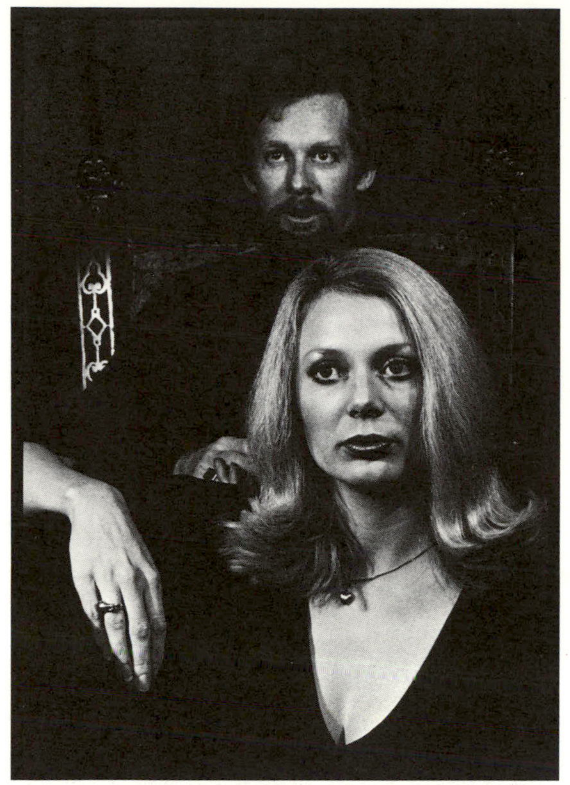

129

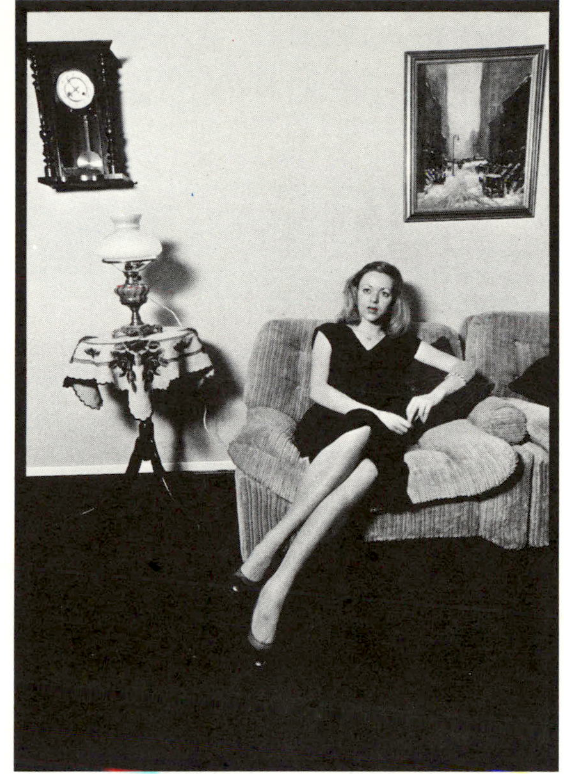

important, that is, to use as few lamps as possible. Every additional light source increases the danger of multiple shadows and reflections, and also makes the illumination less natural.

In addition, a complicated lighting arrangement makes it necessary to ascertain precisely the camera height and direction as well as the position and attitude of the model, with the result that spontaneity and flexibility are lost. Accordingly I generally prefer a very simple lighting arrangement with much use of indirect light, so that the model is left free during the sitting to change position, while at the same time I can adjust my stance without too much restriction.

Fig 128 was produced with the help of precisely directed lighting (*f*4/17 mm lens), while *Figs 129* and *130* exemplify my favourite kind of illumination, using a high proportion of indirect, soft light (both with *f*2.8/100 mm lens).

The type of lighting chosen, and hence the visual effect, depends in the final analysis on the outlook of the photographer and on the photographic situation; and for this reason there is little sense in my giving precise instructions to you. Instead, let us at this point examine briefly the camera outfit of a portrait photographer.

It is of course possible to take portraits with any kind of camera. If you have a choice, however, it is advisable to select a camera body with winder or motor. If you do not have to concern yourself with film transport, it is possible to concentrate a little more on the photography and also you do not have to remove the camera from your eye.

With regard to focal length, in general it is often suggested that focal lengths between 85 and 135 mm should be used in order to avoid facial distortion. This is not very sound advice, as it does not take into account the type of effect aimed at. In portraiture I prefer to work with three lenses: an *f*2.8/21 mm, an *f*1.2/50 mm and an *f*2.5/100 mm. Your attitude to this depends entirely on your photographic intentions—and on the persons whom you wish to portray. However, since, in contrast to general practice, I include in my recommendations short focal lengths for portraits, I must at least provide a few criteria for their use.

If you are photographing only a face, the

distorting effect of the short focal length is noticeable in misshapen features. A frontal view, for instance, will show a massive nose and projecting brow and chin. This effect naturally arises from the fact that with very short focal lengths, objects situated closer to the camera are represented as being disproportionately much larger than those further away.

While such distortions are best employed for caricature, there is a really sensible use of the wide-angle lens in full-figure portraiture. In *Fig 129*, because of the greater camera-to-subject distance, the distortion does not affect the facial features of the model, but confines itself to her legs and to the setting. This is an example of how the composition of the picture can be arranged in accordance with the original intention by means of a specifically chosen viewpoint.

In portrait photography there is also a psychological factor which plays a role in the choice of focal length. Long focal lengths make it possible to keep at a considerable distance from the subject, whereas with wide-angle lenses the photographer is almost within bodily contact distance. Here again the personality of the photographer shows itself in his selection of particular focal lengths and thus in specific visual effects.

So far the emphasis has been on technical requirements, but it is also important to consider how a 'portrait sitting' might proceed. Here again the kind of picture planned and the personal working methods of the photographer are vital features.

When I give you a brief account of my usual procedure, my intention is just to provide an impression of one way of working. Obviously, many photographers tackle things in a different way and produce different results from mine. My methods are certainly not better than others—it is just that they are better suited to *my* purposes.

For example, if someone with whom I am not acquainted approaches me and requests a portrait, the first step is for us to get to know each other. Then I show them some photographs.

I place a high value on this, because I agree to take a portrait only if I have a positive interest in that person. To help us get to know each other, I am happy to show portraits which I have made of other people. In the first place, they provide an excellent topic of conversation and secondly, my prospective 'victim' must be made aware of the kind of photograph I take. In just the same way that I might find myself declining to take portraits of that person, it may also occur that after this discussion he (or she) decides that my photography is not what is wanted. However, if this initial interview turns out to be satisfactory to both sides, an appointment is arranged—always either in the house or the workplace of the prospective model—and the work begins in earnest.

The lighting is so arranged that the model is able to move about freely and so that I can readily alter my viewpoint. The only influence I exert on the matter of clothing and make-up—generally indispensable with ladies—is if something photographically unacceptable might result from it. For example, many kinds of cosmetic produce a strong lustre on the skin which would dominate the features in a portrait; and some articles of clothing might fall into such ungainly folds in a chair that the figure looks deformed. I correct items such as those, but otherwise my associates in these photographic projects decide how they wish to 'present' themselves—I do not insist on having any further influence in that direction. During the photographic session I chat with the person. Often my wife is with me, and this is a great help, because then she does the talking. After four hours (or often as many as eight), I return home with between five and fifteen films exposed.

You will certainly want to know if such exertion is really worth while. The answer is not easy to give. If you merely want to have a photograph of someone, a record, then it is not worth while. A negative (or a transparency) is then sufficient, maybe two. But a portrait is meant to be more than this. If you agree with what I suggested at the beginning of this chapter, you will probably have come to the conclusion that it is worth the effort.

The outcome of such a 'sitting' is not just one picture, but a series of at least three, with a maximum of ten, each providing a different aspect of the subject.

At this juncture it is relevant to go into the matter of eventual picture presentation. This does not refer exclusively to pictorial effect; other influences are brought to bear on a picture, appreciation of which should be one outcome of the photographer's endeavour.

A picture which is allowed to lie around, perhaps folded and dog-eared, perhaps unretouched and covered with scratches and fingermarks, betrays to the observer that the photographer is indifferent about his pictures, and he will rightly conclude that those pictures are not worth seeing.

A really good photograph is a kind of masterpiece—and should be handled as such. Do not finger the surface of an enlargement. Mount it or fix it in an album or place it in an envelope, to prevent the edges and corners from becoming damaged. Retouch the picture (if necessary) carefully, or else make a new enlargement—flaws have no place in a picture.

Apart from this, give some thought to how the picture is to be presented—how big it is to be, what kind of surface the print is to have, whether or not it is to have a margin, and so on. All these matters play a part in the final effect of a picture, and hence they are not to be ignored. If you take the view that all this constitutes too much work, you should just consider how many really good photographs worthy of such effort you actually make . . .

The thought sometimes occurs to me whether I really have to handle a certain picture in the way I have just described to you; moreover, on thinking it over, whether it is really so good as I imagine. In this event I thrust the picture to one side, as it certainly will not be worth the effort. This is just as well, for while a poorly mounted good picture is at least not unpleasant to look at, a glorified piece of nothing can be an acutely disturbing object. In one sentence: picture and presentation should match each other. And with that I shall leave the subject and return to the actual theme of portraits.

So far I have mentioned nothing about child photography—a subject which kindles an interest in the breast of every proud father or mother. To go straight to the point, children are also people. Thus everything which has been said about pictures of grown-ups applies to child portraits. However, on account of the different way of life of children, and also because of their quite different behaviour, there are some

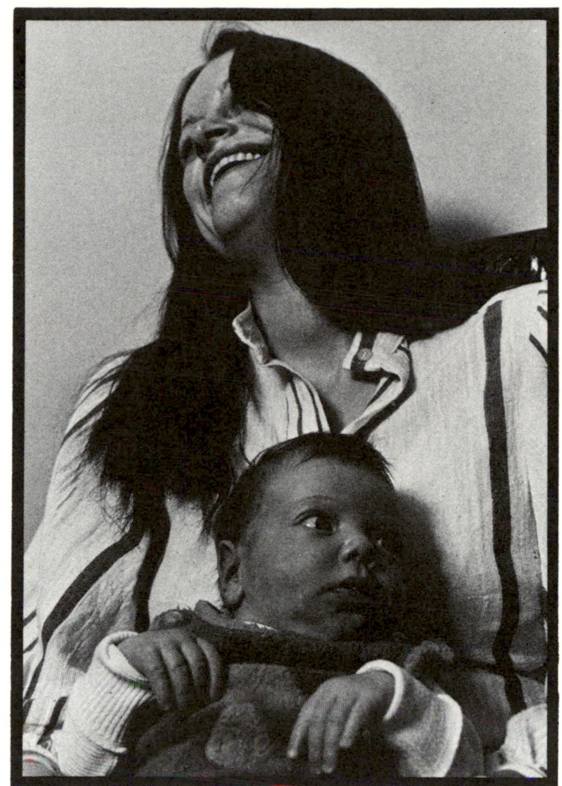
130

variations in procedure. There are also different subject areas, such as that of children at play.

Everyone realises that even at a tender age, children already have (and are) personalities. Accordingly they wish, and ought, to be taken seriously. Thus we should not confine ourselves to portrayal of the 'little ones' in their Sunday best for the benefit of proud parents, grandparents and sundry relatives—not just as 'little angels' to delight their mothers' hearts. Try occasionally to also create genuine 'portraits' of them—not so much of children as possessions: rather as people in their own right.

However, if you attempt to photograph them in a similar way to that described for adult portraiture, you might well be faced with frustration. The fact is that small children especially, in my experience, enjoy being photographed, but as a rule quickly become impatient and are easily diverted. You have to adapt yourself to the situation. Work rapidly, and above all stop at once if the children show the slightest signs of boredom. If they are obviously unwilling from the start, there is no point in preparing

131

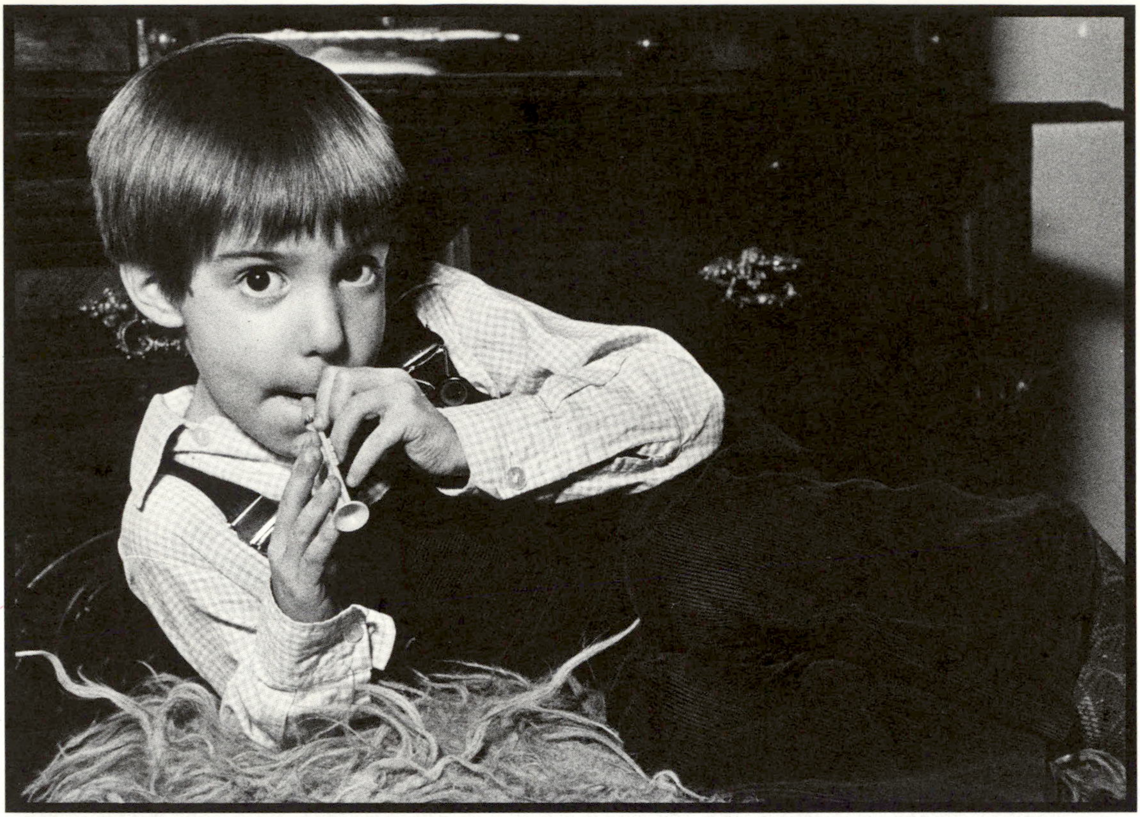

132

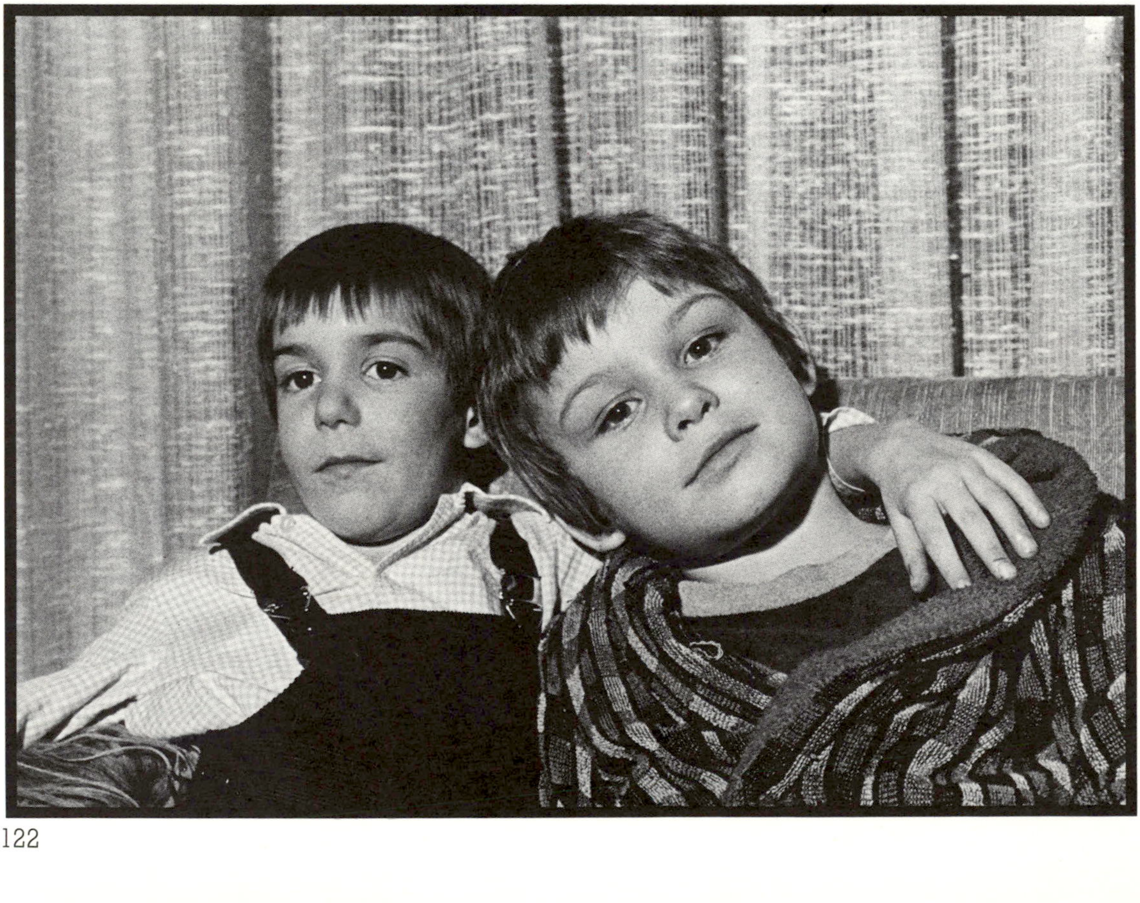

133

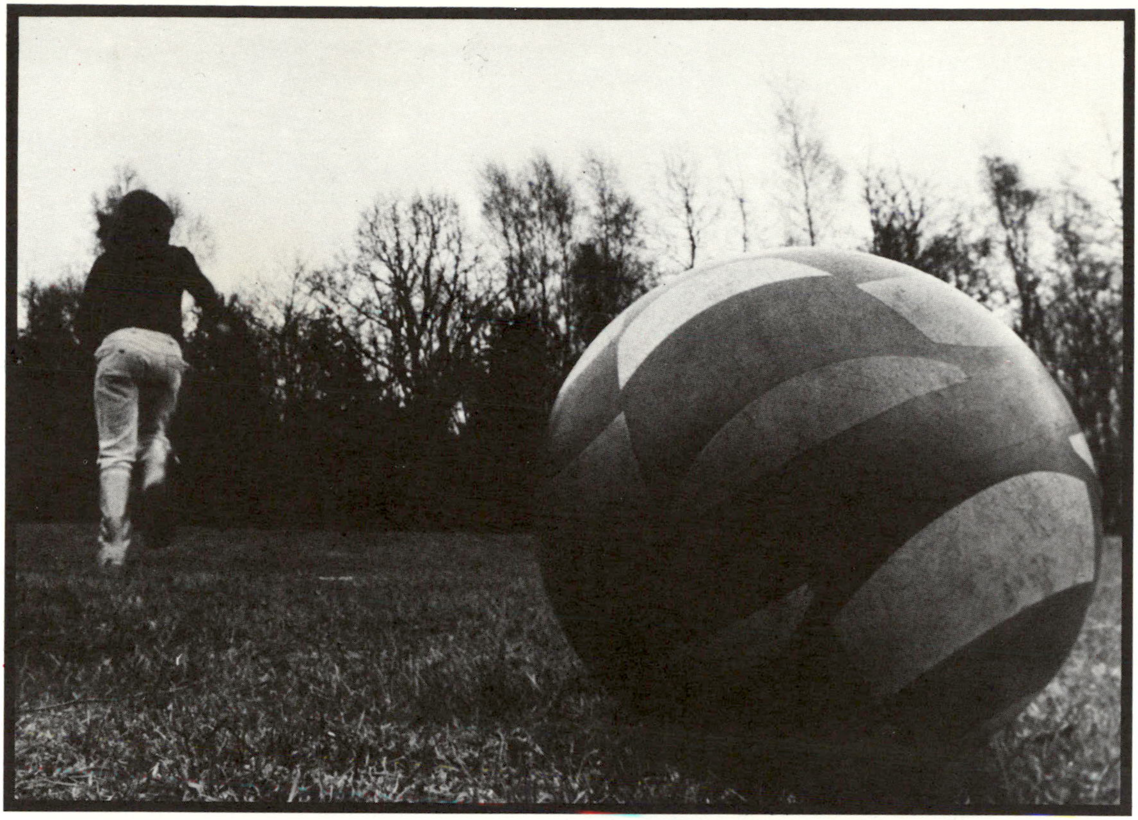

134

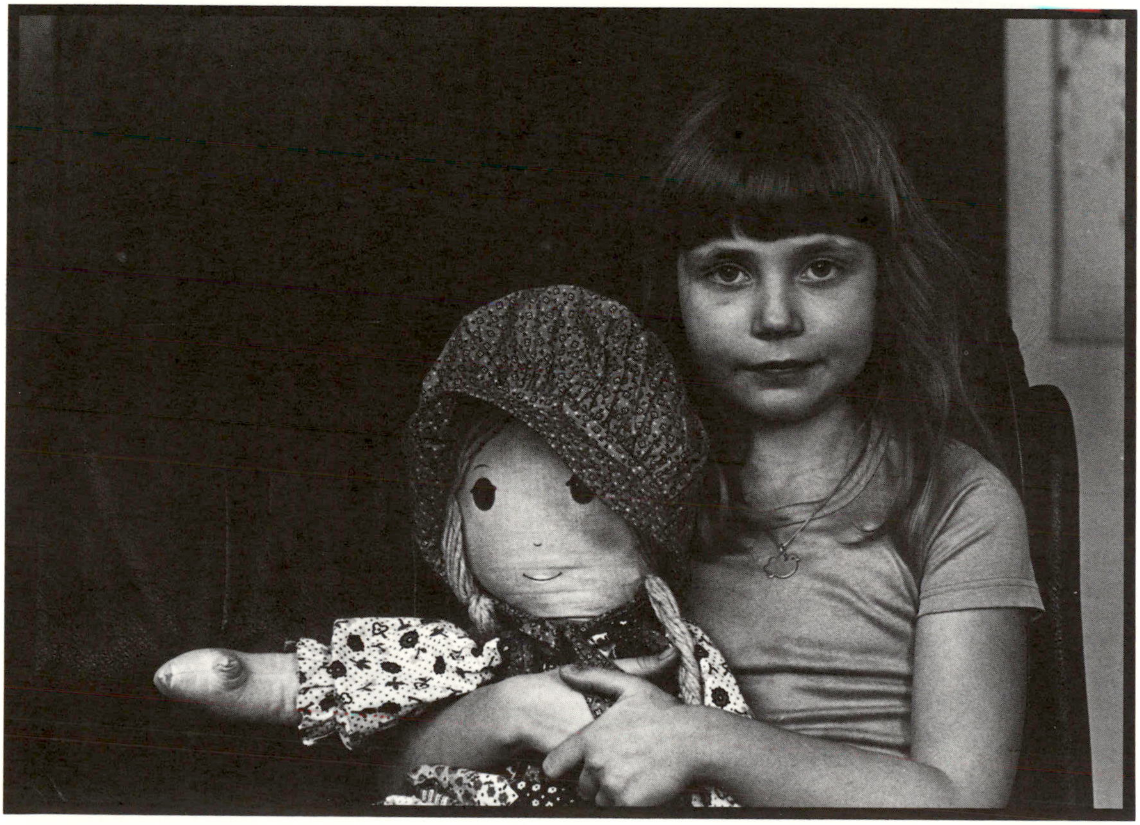

to take photographs of them.

As has already been suggested, this applies only if you have prepared a full 'photographic situation': that is, if you have set up a lighting arrangement, or made other preparations which require the child to get into position and be photographed. How such a situation is to develop depends entirely on the skill of the photographer. I can only assure you that photographic commands such as 'Sit still!' or 'Watch for the little birdie!' or 'Smile, please!' get you nowhere—or at best lead to a mutual display of bad temper.

For these reasons many people prefer to take child photographs in a casual situation—to observe photographically children at play. For this, in my opinion, there is absolutely no need to hide among bushes with a telephoto lens on your camera, or to conceal yourself behind furniture in the house. The presence of a grown-up festooned with camera equipment is generally very quickly accepted by children, and after half an hour has passed they act as if you were not present at all.

Figs 131 and *132* were produced in a genuine 'photographic situation' (*f*1.2/50 mm lens) with lighting arrangements and so on. In both cases I went about the job by first photographing the parents of the two boys, during which the children were told: 'You can have a turn too if you like!' In this manner I kept the interest of the children alive, and also, during the course of the evening, plenty of opportunity was provided of getting them in front of the camera in a friendly and uninhibited way.

The two following pictures, in complete contrast (*Figs 133* and *134*), are casual shots. The enthusiastic football players were completely oblivious of my presence and the young lady was so immersed in the game with her doll that within a very short time she had forgotten that I was there, or else was simply no longer interested. (*Fig 133*: *f*2.8/21 mm lens with angled viewfinder. *Fig 134*: *f*2.5/100 mm lens.)

Which photographic situation you decide on—extempore shot or planned portrait—depends on the personal inclination of the photographer. But in both cases there is a difference from 'grown-up photography'. Children are smaller than adults, and hence take up a smaller part of the picture. For this reason, think over carefully whether to photograph from what might be called a 'grown-up perspective'—from a high eye-level angle—or perhaps from the eye-level of the child. The end result is quite different.

To close the chapter I must mention an event which can happen to anyone who aims at producing genuine portraits. There have been certain cases, sometimes reported in the press, where photographer and model have come into a conflict. The model has felt his or her integrity to have been impugned, while the photographer has insisted on his right to portray in the photograph, using the means available, what he felt to be characteristic of the model. In such a situation you might simply add a gloss, acting according to the old master-painter's principle: 'Make the ladies thinner and the diamonds thicker'. By doing this, however, you are deserting the field of portraiture. Accordingly, in my view, you must avoid such a poor compromise.

It is possible to deal with this difficulty in advance by making a habit of insisting on your right of refusing to make portraits of all-comers; it simply becomes a matter of making all possible consequences clear at the outset to the parties concerned. However, should the misfortune occur, remember that you are not dealing with things but with people, whose dignity you must respect—even if you think you are in the right. To put it plainly, if there is a clash of opinion about certain photographs, you can simply take them back and destroy them. With professional work there is naturally a second question; an assignment, once arranged, has to be paid for even if the result is not accepted.

Fortunately, this is a problem which the amateur does not have to be too concerned with but it does no harm to be aware of these possibilities. Which amateur, after all, would not be glad to earn money (and recognition) with his photographs?

23: THE NUDE

It is said that nude photography is particularly difficult. But if this allegation is applied simply to the photographic technique involved it will be found to be totally false.

In the first place, nude photography may be regarded as a special form of portrait photography, in which case all the comments which I made in the previous chapter on that theme apply. Although portraiture entails special difficulties, these certainly do not stem from technical considerations. They arise rather from the essential 'harmonisation' between photographer and model. This also applies to a high degree to nude photography, if the nude photograph is to embody a representation of the personality of the model.

Secondly, nude photography can be said to be often a branch of landscape photography. In this case the nude would have to be integrated into the landscape or perhaps form a contrast to it. This applies to the formal aspect of the picture as well as to its message; but again no special technical problems are involved.

In the third place, the nude may form a so-called 'study' in itself, ostensibly as a purely formal representation of the human body. Here too no photographic difficulties apply particularly to this province.

The particular difficulties associated with nude photography are found in quite a different region. The portrayal of the naked body—just like the clothed body—entails, at least in contemporary cultural circles, a strongly positive or negative erotic element; and the person who does not accept that this is the case may get into real difficulties. It is not possible simply to disregard the erotic component in nude photography. Quite on the contrary—because it is necessarily present (in a positive or negative sense) in every portrayal of the naked body, it has to be implicated in the visual structure and planned statement. The person who asserts that he or she can create or contemplate nude photography beyond or without eroticism is either not honest with himself (or herself) or else misconstrues the real effects of nude pictures on the viewer. Accordingly, the whole uncertainty about nude photography resolves itself into a moral question which each person must answer for themselves. Since I do not intend or desire to offer assistance in this respect, I shall leave the matter at that. Instead I should like to consider another aspect of the subject.

Just as a portrait entails a penetration by the photographer into the 'spiritual intimacy' of the person portrayed, so nude photography postulates an entry by the photographer into the 'physical intimacy' of the model. For this reason alone, because many contemporaries hold the latter to be a major moral error, it is very important that photographer and model come to an understanding about the type of photograph that is to be taken and the use to which it will be put afterwards.

If we are not talking about a man-and-wife relationship, it is absolutely essential that the entire agreement be put down in writing—even if photographer and model are the best of friends! In those situations the strangest things have happened, and in order to avoid dissension it should be a basic principle never to display a photograph (even 'privately' to a third party) if no written authorisation has been given.

Equal attention should be paid to location. As a general rule you may take nude photographs anywhere—as long as you are not caught . . . But joking aside, it is generally true in most countries, that you should not cause what is termed 'public annoyance'. That is to say, if you take nude photographs in your own house, and an irate neighbour is able to observe what you are doing through a window, then you are causing public annoyance and may have to reckon with court proceedings. The lesson to learn from this is that you should take nude photographs only in places where as far as possible you are safe from the gaze of ill-disposed people—perhaps in naturist areas, in which nobody is shocked at nudity.

A third point worth considering is that of beauty. There are persons who are of the opinion that nude photographs should be taken only of 'beautiful' subjects. (That is like

135

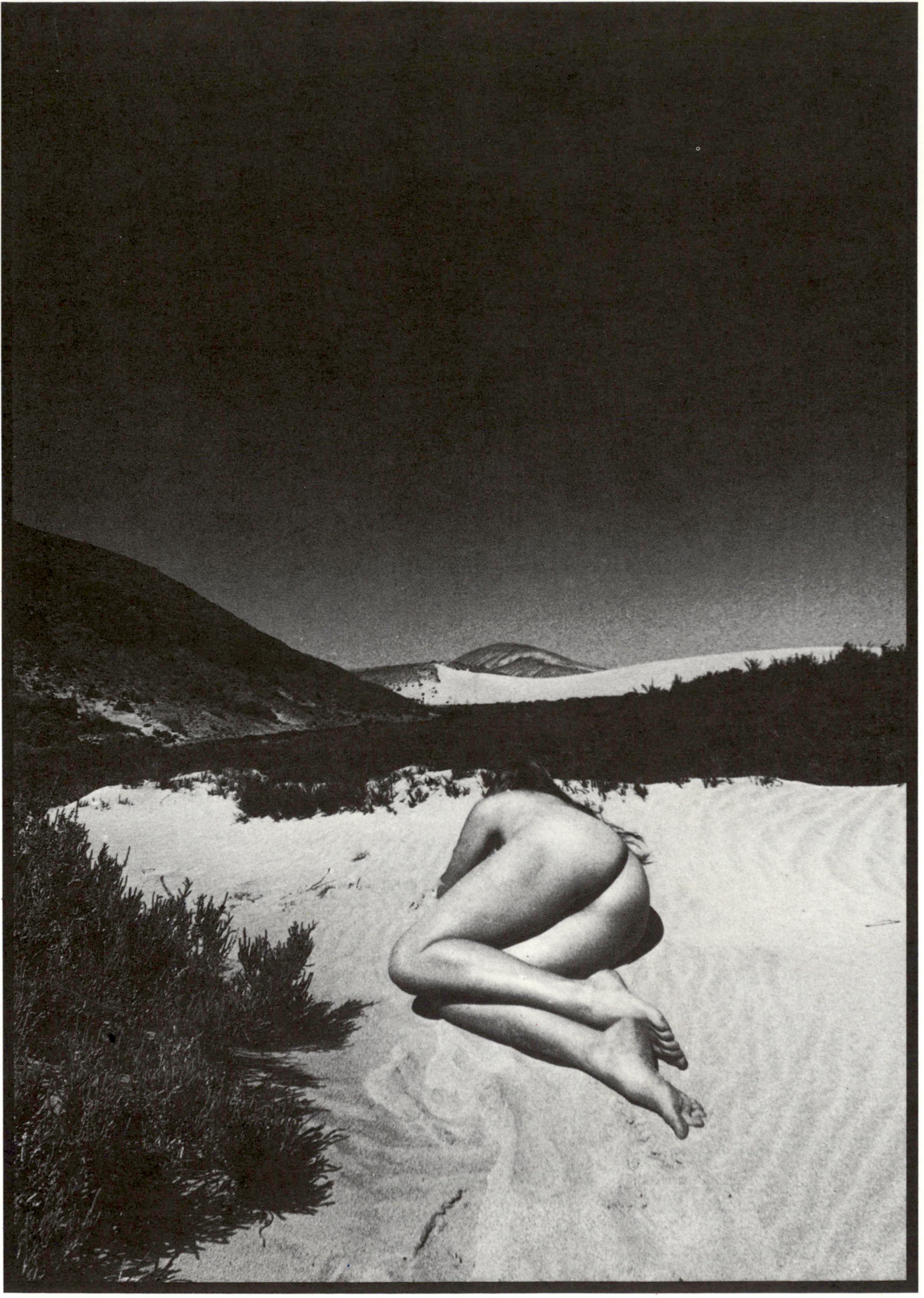

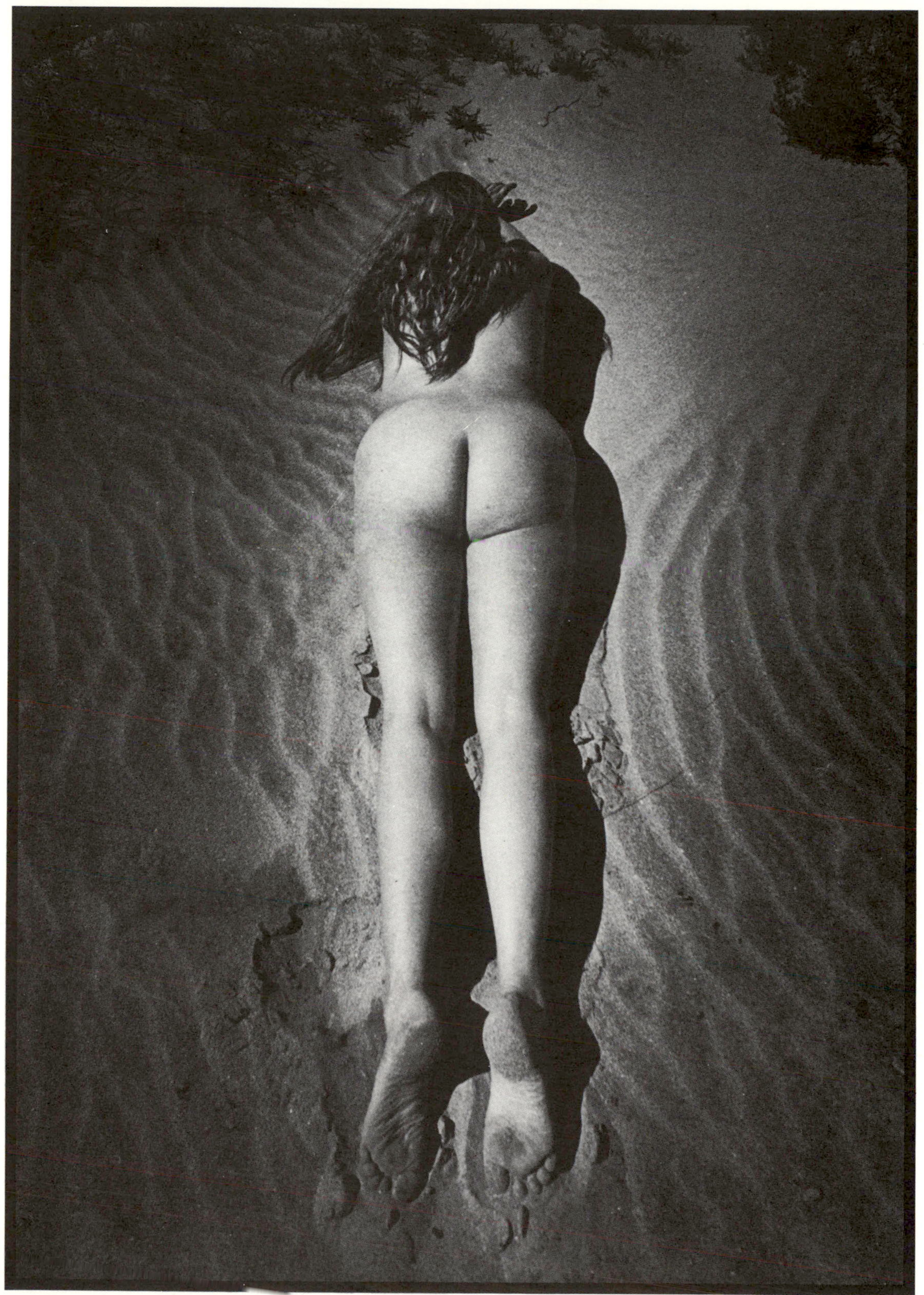

137

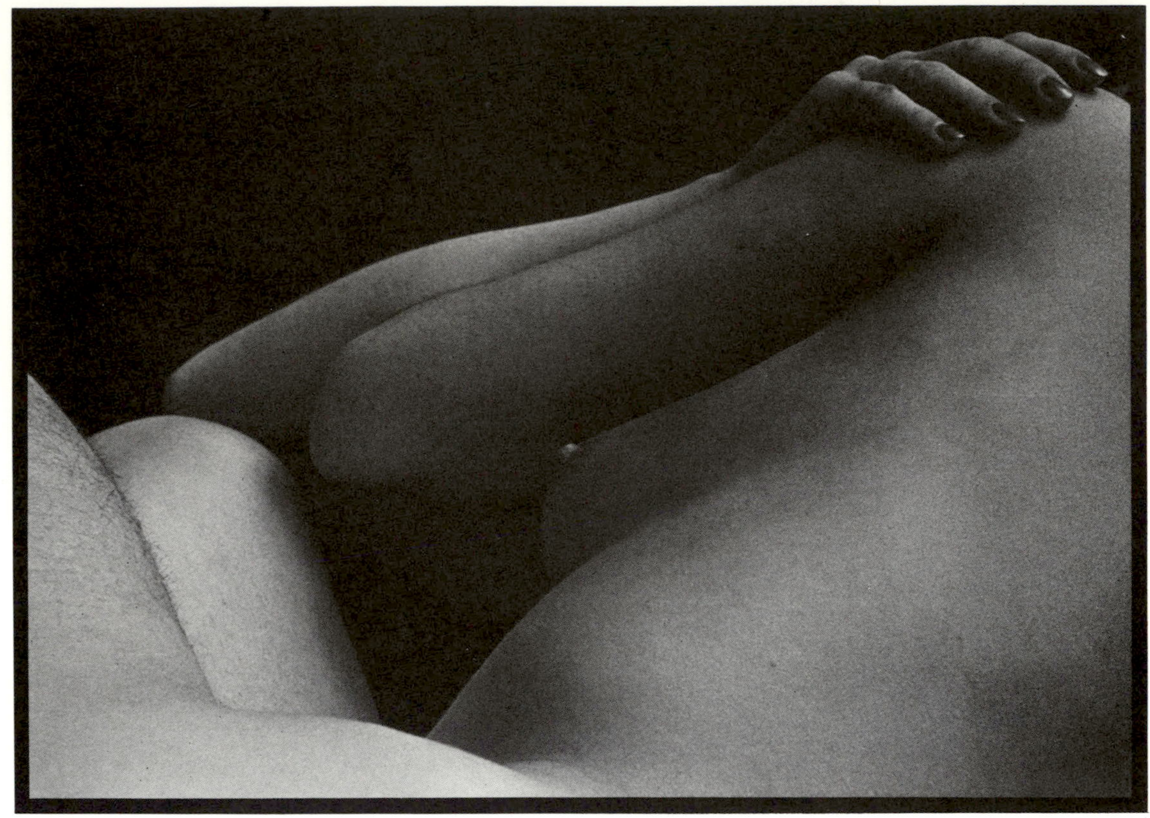

saying that in portrait photography you should confine yourself to beautiful faces.) Apart from the fact that ideas about who or what is or is not beautiful can differ radically, the suggestion applies only to a very small part of the field of nude photography. If you are intending to produce pin-ups or photographs for magazine covers, you will doubtless conform to certain saleable (and ephemeral) 'criteria of beauty'—but otherwise you have a perfectly free choice.

You can either base your interpretation on the model's appearance and character, in which case the visual effect and statement will have to be oriented towards this, or else you can have a specific aim in your mind and select a model to suit that purpose.

In this connection it is apposite to say a few words about the recognisability of the model. Particularly when you are looking for a model from among close relations or good friends, you often have to give an undertaking that the photographs will not allow recognition of the model. From this precondition emerge large numbers of pictures of cramped poses and strange props, whose sole reason for existence seems to be the concealment of the model's face. If you find yourself having to produce this kind of photograph, do not regard the 'facelessness' of the model as a handicap, but instead use the circumstance positively for visual effect.

As a demonstration of this, *Figs 135—137* show pictures in which the facial features of the women portrayed are not visible—but I have avoided giving the impression that the photographer had something to hide. *Figs 135* and *136* show two ways of integrating nude and landscape (both taken with a camera using winder and angled viewfinder, *f*4/17 mm lens); whereas *Fig 137* was taken indoors (camera with winder, *f*3.5/100 mm lens, lighting conditions as in *Fig 124*).

24: CLOSE-UP AND MACRO PHOTOGRAPHY

Although 'moderate' close-ups are possible without the use of various accessories, and although the photographic industry these days provides highly advanced facilities for macro photography, this subject area is nevertheless still avoided by many amateurs.

There are two main reasons for this. Firstly, the possible subjects for this photographic milieu are exceedingly small in size. They do not obtrude themselves upon us: on the contrary, it is necessary to consciously go in search of them. Secondly, close-up and macro photography has always been known to involve certain technical difficulties. It should, however, be realised that the advanced facilities already mentioned render it extraordinarily easy to photograph the smallest of objects. It is necessary only to know when and how to use these aids.

In this chapter these two factors are examined more closely. To begin with, however, it is important to clarify the question of what close-up and macro photographs actually are. There are various definitions, often very complicated. The generally accepted definition is as given below: macro photographs consist of all photographs in which the subject is represented on a scale between 10:1 and 1:1 (that is, between 10 × and life size); whereas photographs of a larger magnification than 10:1 (that is, in which the subject appears more than 10 × larger than life size) fall into the category of photomicrographs.

Let us now turn to the first two illustrations. *Fig 138* was taken with an *f*4/17 mm lens, while *Fig 139* involved an *f*2.8/21 mm lens. The photographs are similar in that they were both taken with lenses which seem inappropriate for the taking of macro photographs. With lenses of this kind, and without other accessories, it is feasible to enter the macro region. The *f*2.8/21 mm lens used makes photography possible within a very limited focal range, from 0.25 m on a scale of approximately 1:6, making full use of the available depth of field at an aperture of *f*16, and extending as far as a scale of 1:5. With an *f*4/17 mm lens, you could approach a scale of 1:8.

As these data are perhaps not particularly striking, I should like to clarify things further. If you were to enlarge the transparency of *Fig 139* to 30 × 20 cm, the main subject of the picture would be about as big as it was in reality. Or to put it the other way round, if you were to photograph a subject 30 × 20 cm in size with a 21 mm wide-angle lens, this would appear on a transparency (or on a negative) reduced by about nine times; that is, on a scale of 1:9.

A comparison of *Fig 138* with *Fig 140* (taken with an *f*3.5/100 mm lens) shows that the associated perspective effects with wide-angle and telephoto shots are retained in the macro region. Unfortunately this does not apply to depth of field. In the close-up region—that is, from a scale of 1:10—depth of field depends entirely on image scale. It is illogical to alter focal length in order to achieve depth of field. It is very sensible, on the other hand, to select various focal lengths in order to exploit or strengthen the perspective effect of the subject, because, as a comparison of these two pictures shows, these effects can differ greatly.

It should be noted that with image scales approaching natural size, the region of sharpness becomes so limited that all other components recede into unsharpness. Also, in the macro region it is not necessary to confine yourself to ultrawide-angle lenses, such as those mentioned. Very many wide-angle lenses are so designed that they can be used to go below the image scale of 1:10. This applies also to standard lenses and some of the telephoto type. If these scales, possible without the use of accessories, are not sufficient, the simplest—and cheapest—procedure is to use supplementary lenses.

The best supplementary lenses are not simple 'close-up lenses', but achromatic lenses, each composed of two corrected elements. Provided that a few precautions are taken, these produce pictures of such fine quality that it would be quite wrong to regard the lenses as mere makeshifts. These achromatic lenses should, however, not be used in the following cases: with macro lenses of 100 mm, and with all lenses with

138

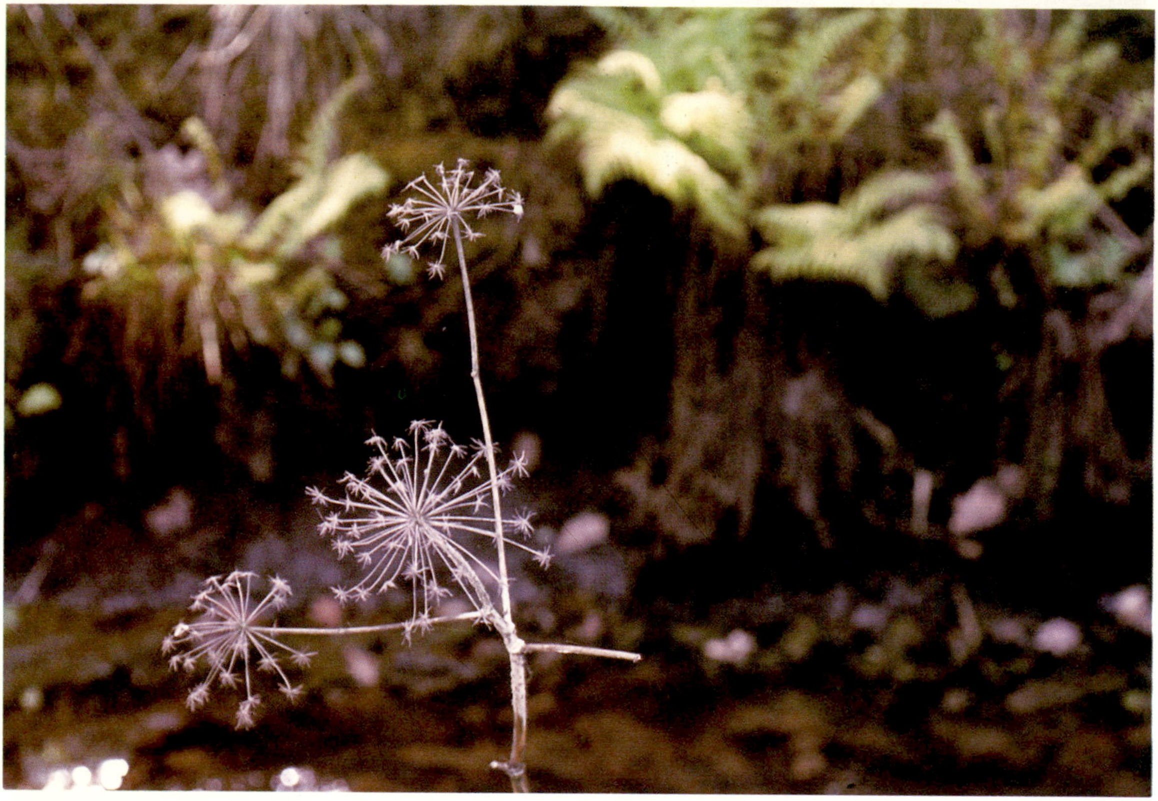

139

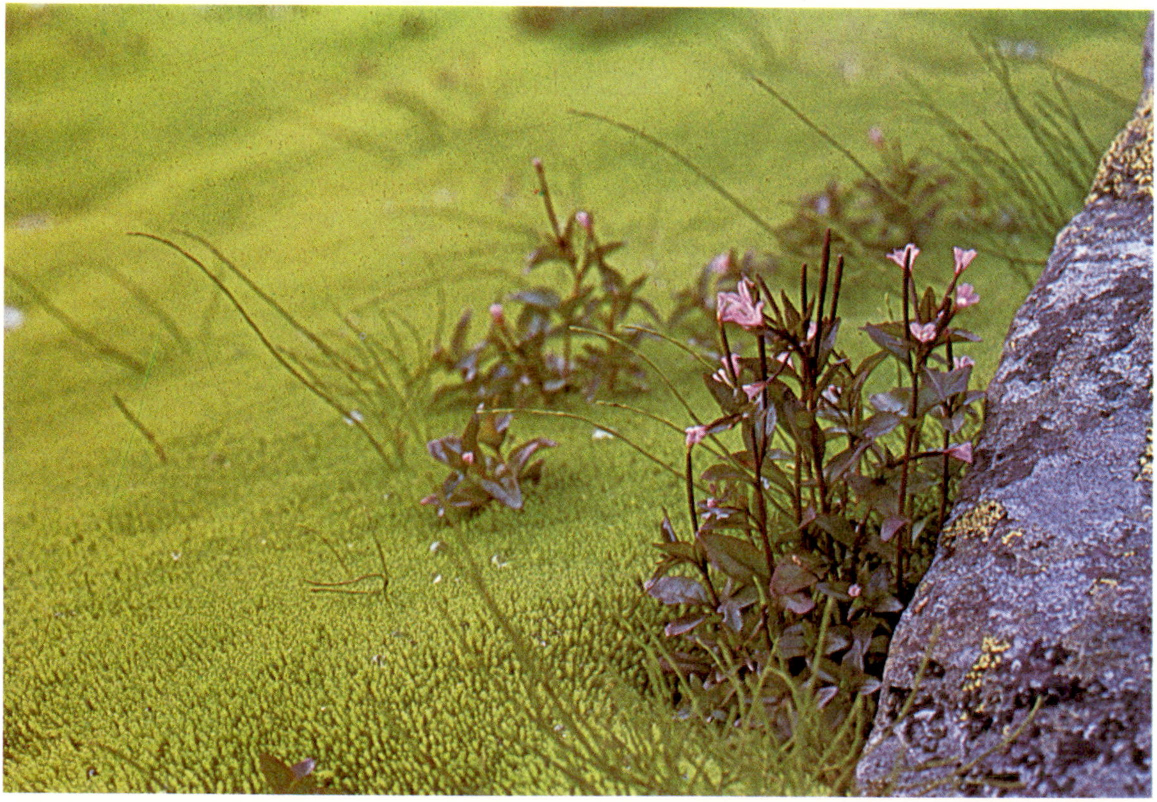

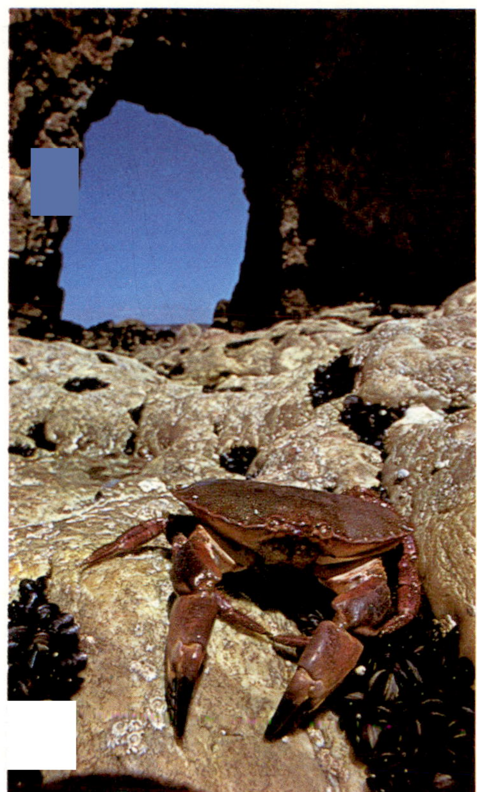

141

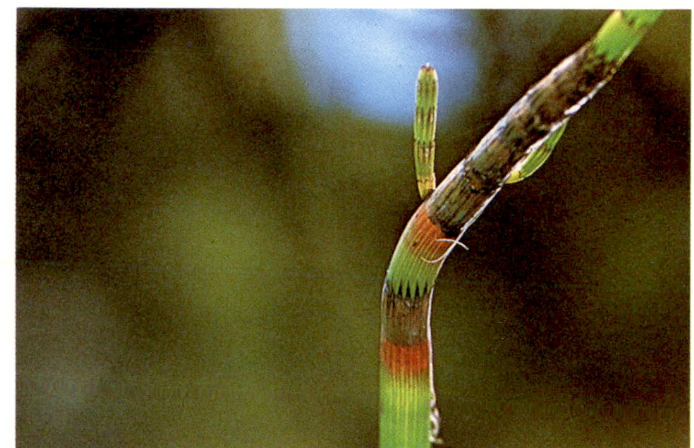

142

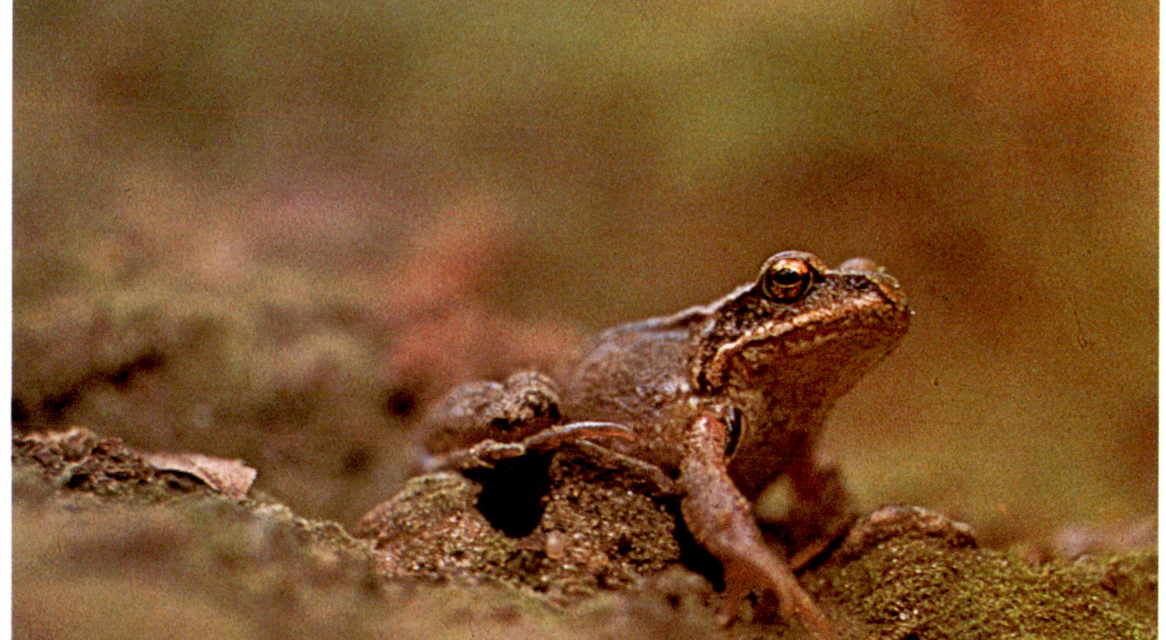

'floating elements'. If apart from that you take care to photograph, if possible, at an aperture of *f*8 or *f*11, or *f*5.6 at the most, there should be no problems in taking close-up photographs. With a standard lens of 50 mm focal length and a No 2 achromatic supplementary lens, an image scale can be achieved of 1:3; and with an *f*8/100—500 mm zoom lens and a special achromatic supplementary lens to fit its circumference, a scale of 1:2 can be approached! The latter combination is not as foolish as might appear, as it has certain advantages.

Fig 141 was produced using this combination. Although the image scale amounted to almost 1:2, I was able to photograph from a distance of about 160 cm—an advantage not to be underrated, when you consider that this horsetail plant was growing in the middle of the water, and if I had been compelled to move in closer I should have had wet feet. This long working distance is especially advantageous with wildlife photography, for it is not normally possible to approach so close to a butterfly, for example, as in *Fig 138*, where the subject distance was about 20 cm.

Close-up work offers such an infinite profusion of fascinating subjects that even the person who is not particularly interested in these should at least carry an achromatic supplementary lens in his camera bag. The expenditure is small (in both money and weight), and the possibilities which you purchase are incalculable. The person who intends to explore this subject area further would do well to consider special macro equipment, the use of which is demonstrated in the following examples.

Macro lenses of the *f*3.5/50 mm and *f*3.5/100 mm types perform excellent service in the region of their focal length. In addition, they are specifically designed for macro photographs up to a scale of 1:1. Both types of macro lens, as they are, can extend as far as a scale of 1:2, and it is possible to obtain adaptors enabling them to reach a scale of between 1:2 and 1:1.

Special macro lenses are distinguished from standard lenses mainly in that they have the necessary optical corrections to produce first-class results at close range. For reproduction and scientific purposes they are therefore indispensable; but on account of their excellent performance and convenience of operation they hold an interest for the amateur too.

For most photographic purposes, the 100 mm macro type of lens is particularly suitable, because with it you can work at a greater subject distance than with the 50 mm type, producing pictures on the same image scale. This greater subject distance is not required merely when you want to photograph small creatures, such as the frog in *Fig 147* (*f*3.5/100 mm macro lens, using angled viewfinder), but also when using some form of artificial lighting. Since lighting for many macro photographs forms the greatest problem, sometimes the only one, some discussion of this area is valuable.

First of all, with big image scales a certain amount of light loss must be taken into account. For example, using a macro lens for a scale 1:1 the light loss amounts to two stops (at an aperture of *f*11, a shutter speed of 1/30 sec instead of 1/125—although the camera automatically attends to this). In addition, because of the extraordinarily limited depth of field at extreme scales, you are forced to work with relatively small apertures. (For an image scale of 1:1, the depth of field at *f*5.6 amounts to a mere 0.75 mm, and at *f*22 only 2.9 mm!) Another point is that danger of camera shake is specially great with macro photographs. This is simply because all movements of camera and subject are magnified. For instance, if your subject is moved a distance of 1/10 mm during exposure by a breath of wind, at a scale of 1:10 the effect on film is of a movement of 1/100 mm—a value which lies so far from the diameter of the circle of confusion that it is not noticeable as unsharpness. On the other hand, if the same movement occurs when a scale of 1:1 is involved, a blur of 1/10 mm will be seen on the film, and the picture will appear totally unsharp.

Thus it is easy to see why artificial lighting generally offers the only possibility of using small apertures and at the same time sufficiently brief exposure times. When working at home, you can use floodlight for this purpose, while for photography 'on location', you always have to rely on flash. Thus a greater subject distance has two benefits. Firstly, you are better able to arrange the lighting if between the front of the lens and the subject there is the greatest possible amount of space. Secondly, by having a large subject distance, the lens or the camera itself will be prevented from casting a shadow on the subject. The latter of course applies also to photography in natural light. In my opinion, however, you should not be misled into making a practice of using flash for macro photographs in the open air. I try on the contrary whenever possible to work with natural light, as I find that most subjects lose realism when artificial lighting is employed. Bear in mind that we are not referring here to scientific photography, with which it is essential to portray delicate fragile objects as clearly and distinctly as possible. In creative photography the main concern is to develop a visual statement by the use of a certain subject and, therefore, a type of lighting which gives a clear and distinct image is not necessarily appropriate. (Similarly, in portrait photography, it is not the amount of light but the kind of light that is important!)

In the open air, therefore, if you are not going to use flash, two very useful accessories are generally required. First and foremost, the tripod here comes into its own—especially if it can be lowered to ground level—for there is a proliferation of macro subjects on the ground. (Do not forget the angled viewfinder!) For those people who are too lazy to carry a tripod around, I can suggest a substitute which I have tried out and thoroughly recommend. In the lid of my photographic case I have cut a small hole and stuck to it a small, cheap tripod screw. Thus in an emergency I can screw my camera directly on to my case, and there I have a really solid substitute tripod.

The second accessory, practically representing a 'must' for macro photography in natural light, is a windshield, which can be used to protect the subject from being moved by the breeze. This consists simply of a piece of glass or transparent plastic material fixed to a cardboard frame. A sheet of cardboard can be used instead, but not if wind and light are coming from the same direction.

The mushroom still-life photograph, *Fig 143*, was produced in the following way. The camera (with winder and angled viewfinder, *f*3.5/100 mm lens, scale about 1:2) was screwed firmly to the photographic case, and the subject was protected from the wind by a sheet of thick plastic material. Despite the exposure time of 4 sec (at *f*8), the photograph is perfectly sharp. To prevent any possible camera movement, a cable release was used. Any form of artificial lighting would have completely destroyed the special mood of the subject.

Neither of the modes of working just described can be employed with wildlife photographs (unless indeed you are photographing a snail!)—a bee is obviously not going to wait long enough for you to make a lot of elaborate preparations. By the time you have put up your tripod and unpacked the windshield, it will be too late. In spite of that, you can try using high-sensitivity film and special wide-aperture lenses before finally giving in and resorting to a flash unit. Some of these special fast lenses are such that very short exposure times can be used, and their quality is so good that they can be used at wide apertures. (This refers to genuine macro lenses with focal lengths of 10—25 mm and *f* stops of about *f*1.2—8. They cannot be used for magnifications of less than 1:1.) These lenses can also bring you to the fringe of photomicrography. Magnifications of 20:1 become a possibility. In comparison, the shortest lenses for 'normal' photography used on a bellows unit would only allow magnifications of about 10—11 times.

Fig 144 portrays part of a flower magnified about 12 times, taken with a motorised camera by daylight using *f*1.9/12.5 mm lens. The next picture (*Fig 145*) was photographed with the same equipment, but using an *f*2.8/28 mm lens in reverse (about four times magnification, by daylight).

Although the opportunity seldom presents itself of working at such scales, *Figs 144* and *145* show that in the area of macro photography fascinating subjects are to be found, which may be photographed without a great deal of additional equipment. With a bellows attachment, a reverse ring and a normal lens it is possible to cover the entire domain of macro photography and also investigate the micro world.

For a more detailed and thorough approach to macro photography I would recommend the reading of the appropriate technical literature. For those readers who intend only occasionally to dabble in this area, however, perhaps the foregoing notes will suffice. The intention was simply to

143

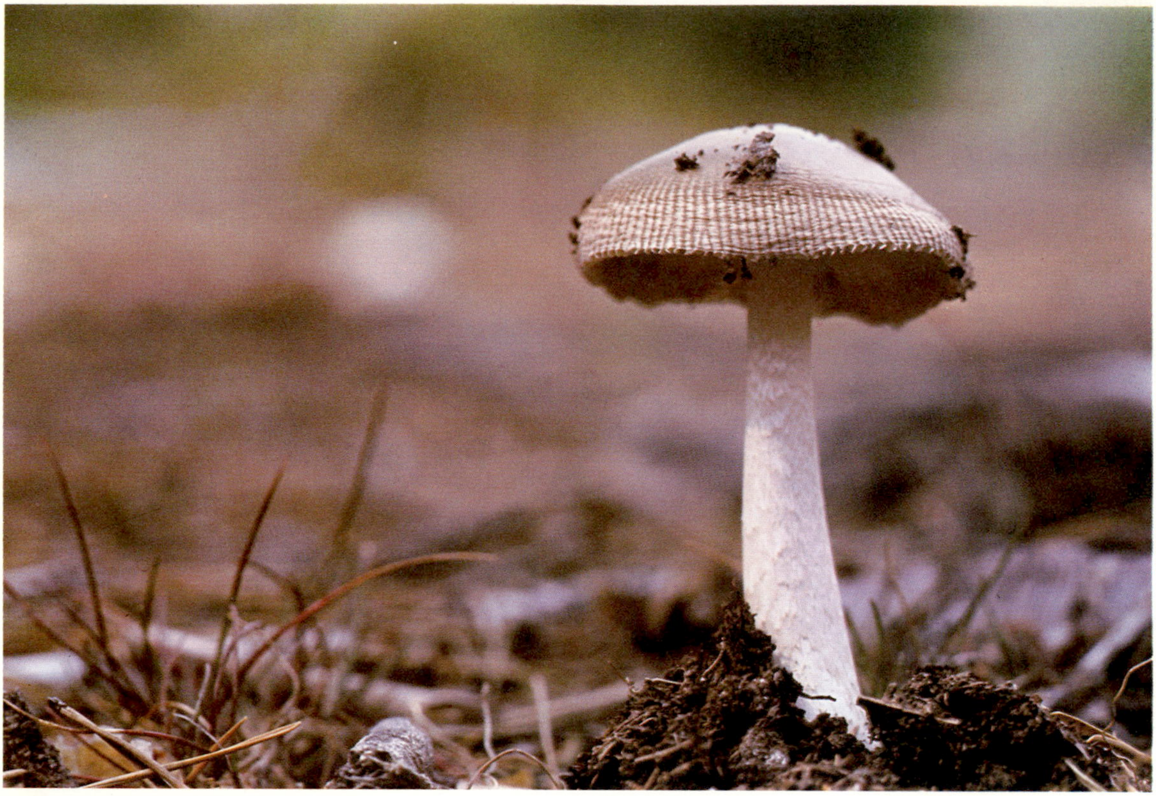

144

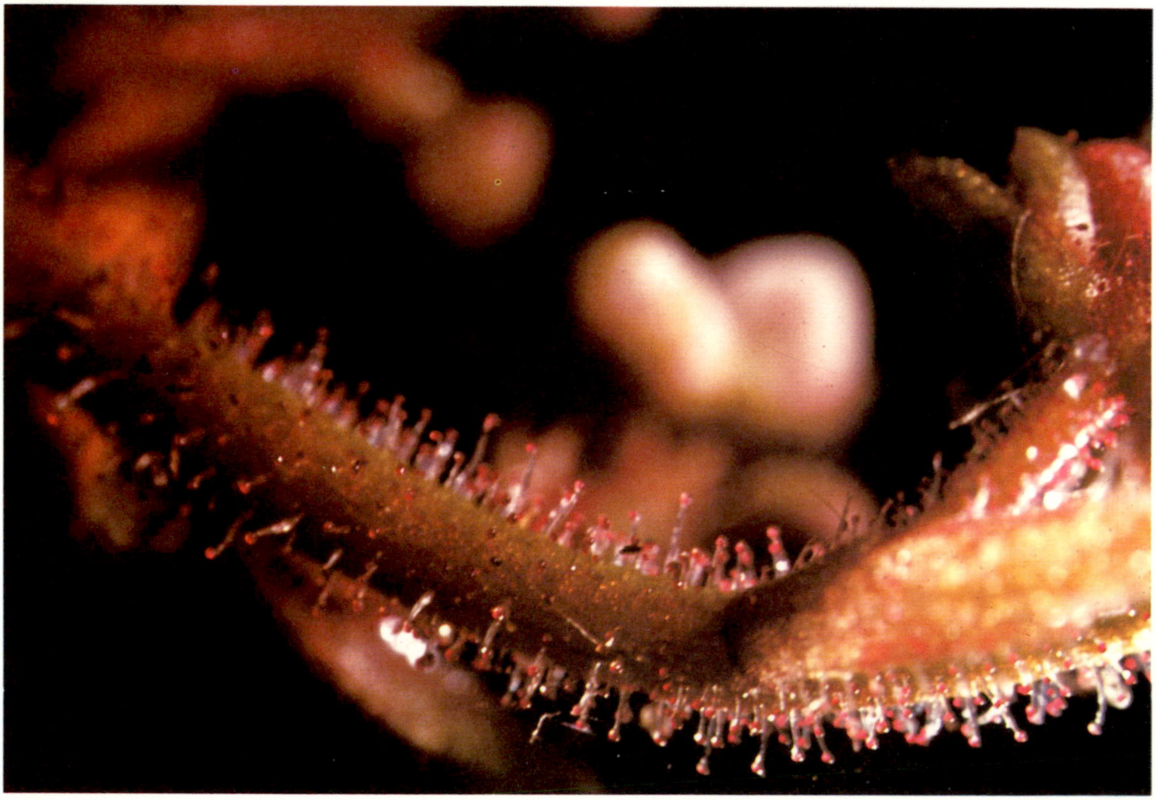

145

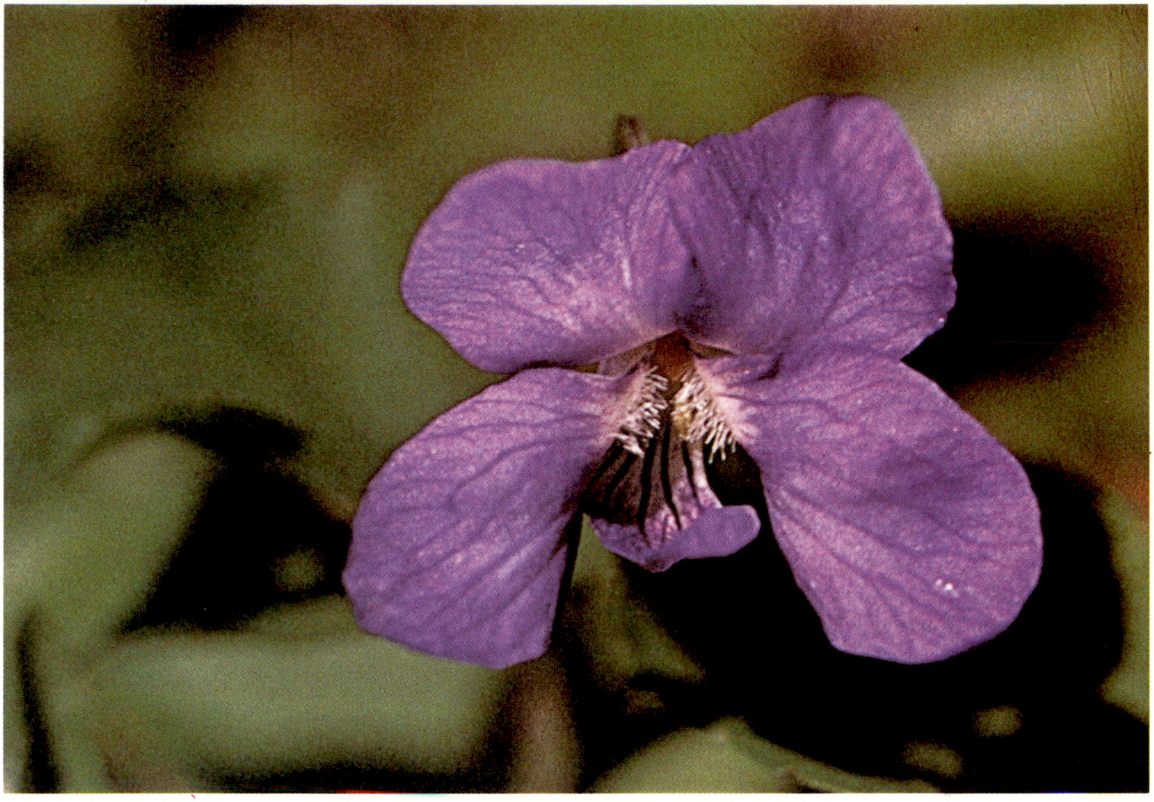

146

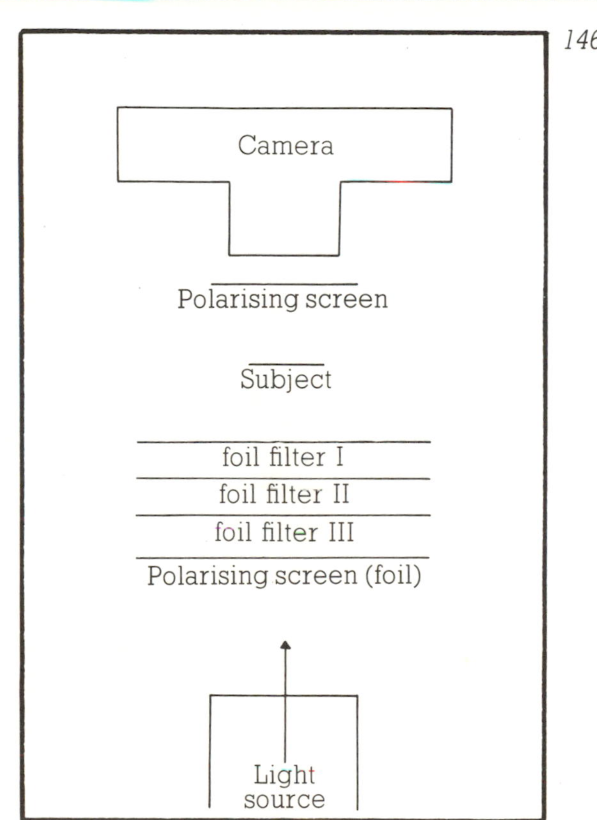
Camera
Polarising screen
Subject
foil filter I
foil filter II
foil filter III
Polarising screen (foil)
Light source

indicate something of the profusion of themes in this specialised photographic region, and to suggest how straightforward it is to make a start. I shall now content myself with offering some suggestions about equipment.

For occasional close up photographs, supplementary achromatic lenses are sufficient. These give good results without trouble, if you follow the suggestions made above. The most elegant type of macro photography is with the use of special macro camera lenses: say an *f*3.5/50 mm and an *f*3.5/100 mm. As a universal and particularly economical piece of equipment for the close up range, a bellows unit is to be recommended, as it can be used with conventional lenses. It is somewhat more complicated to handle than a macro lens. As all these pieces of apparatus are useful to have, the best plan is to start with the simplest and cheapest (the achromatic supplementary lens), and add to your equipment according to requirements.

The use of polarising screens is also relevant to this subject. The double refracting of photographic material in polarised light is associated with macro photography because the objects photographed in this way are generally very small. Subjects composed of transparent plastics and crystals are concerned here—objects that are normally colourless but in polarised light suddenly take on an astonishing abundance of hues.

Here are some examples of quite simple objects photographed in this way. *Fig 147* comprises a section of the cover of a storage box for polarising screens. The subject of *Fig 148* consists simply of pieces of colourless plastic film stuck at random across each other. *Fig 149* is a triple exposure of a torn piece of kitchen foil. The fourth photograph (*Fig 150*) exemplifies the classic subject for this kind of photography—it is composed of photographic fixing liquid crystallised on a transparency glass. In these examples I have quite deliberately confined myself to simple objects which are readily available to everyone, in order to show that you are free to give full rein to your fantasies and your experimental enjoyment, and also to show that interesting results are possible without great expenditure.

In *Fig 146* I have sketched out the arrangement for producing 'photo-elasticity' pictures. First a light source is required. For this purpose any kind of lamp can be used and an opal screen (ground-glass screen), or a light box or something of that sort. If you do not possess such a refinement, use a table lamp placed at a distance with its light directed upwards by means of a shaving or make-up mirror. Above this light source a foil polarising screen is set up (as a 'polarising agent'). Over that in turn is the subject to be photographed, and the second polarising screen is fixed on to the camera (as an 'analyser'). The camera outfit with bellows or macro lens is set at the desired magnification scale. (The illustrations were produced at an image scale of between 1:1 and about 7:1. An angled viewfinder was used, and an *f*3.5/50 mm macro lens.)

I do not propose here to go into constructional details, since this depends too much on the filters and other components employed. However, these examples were created with the aid of a set-up simply made of black cardboard, adhesive tape and two-constituent glue.

To work with this arrangement, one of the two polarising filters has to be rotated in such a way that the field appears as dark as possible (at the 'maximum extinction' setting), so that the doubly refracted subjects radiate in their finest colours.

You may find that these colours do not turn out to be so varied and vivid as you have observed in other examples. In order to achieve that, the photographic arrangement must be amplified a little. If you insert another 'filter' composed of flexible, colourless PVC between polariser and subject, this immediately produces quite a new effect. By rotating the polariser or the foil screen, or both at once, the colours are weakened or strengthened and also—most important of all—changed. Entirely new colours are formed, and by using several filters at a time, these can be altered again. Try it for yourself to see the multitude of variations possible in one object when it is handled in this way.

The material for making this screen is a transparent PVC sheet (Ultraphan). This material is used chiefly in model construction, and thus can be purchased (cheaply) in large hobby shops. However, if you are unable to find any, wide self-adhesive, plastic strips in 5 or 10 cm widths are a possible alternative.

Usually, macro photography is in colour, and seldom in monochrome. This is mainly because when subjects are photographed at various distances in these scales, there are large areas of unsharpness in the pictures. Such unsharp areas are more acceptable, with most subjects, in a coloured structure than in an effect made up of mere shades of grey. Of course, this simply shows that these pictures have not been composed carefully enough, because in a well-planned composition all components should contribute to the final effect—and this applies also to unavoidable areas of unsharpness.

The last four illustrations in this chapter show that composition can be handled in such a way that the apparent disadvantage of partial unsharpness can become a creative element. Many subjects which in colour merely have the effect of biological or zoological illustrations suddenly, in monochrome, reveal another meaning. This is particularly interesting, because in this subject area I started with the assumption that our concern was not with scientific and documentary photography but with the constructive and creative kind.

At this point it is useful to define what the difference actually is between these two areas of photography.

In scientific and documentary photography, the concern is exclusively with providing quite concrete, purely factual information about certain aspects of objects or processes. The involvement of the photographic medium has the purpose only of communicating this information as clearly and distinctly as possible. In contrast to this, the structural media employed in creative photography have a direct effect of their own. The subject provides the opportunity of making a positive statement, which by purposeful use of the structural media is either evoked for the very first time or else at least strengthened appreciably.

This implies that in creative photography, the specific media of photographic structure are themselves carriers of meaning. Since for these two systems completely different criteria are involved, it can quite possibly occur that a macro photograph taken for one purpose will appear to be quite meaningless in the other. Here again, before taking the photograph, it is important to have a clear concept as to which is your objective.

In reality, the differentiation between these two types of photography is by no means a simple matter, and there are also points of contact and overlaps. However, as this book is not concerned with media theory but with photography, I trust that these remarks have made things clear enough for present purposes.

47

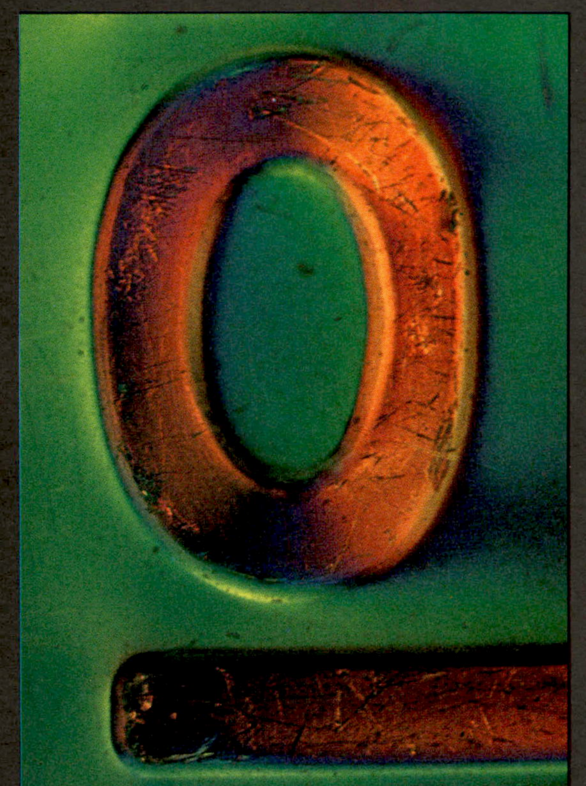

14

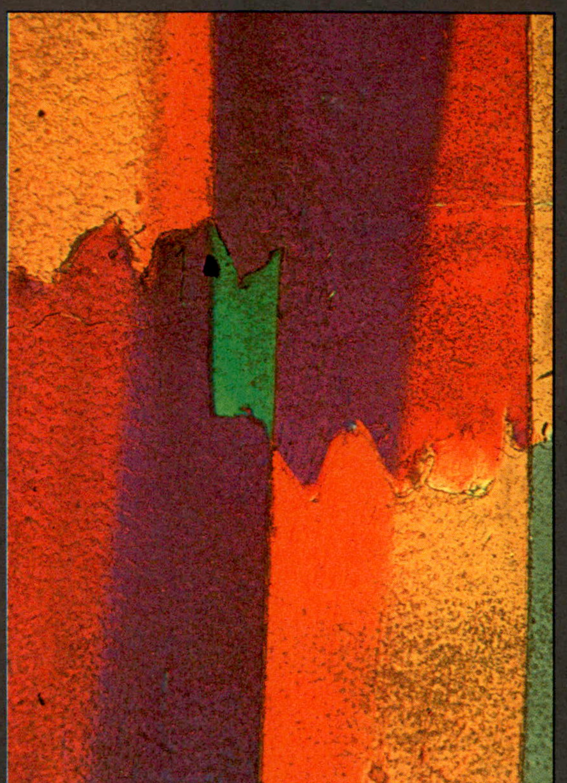

49

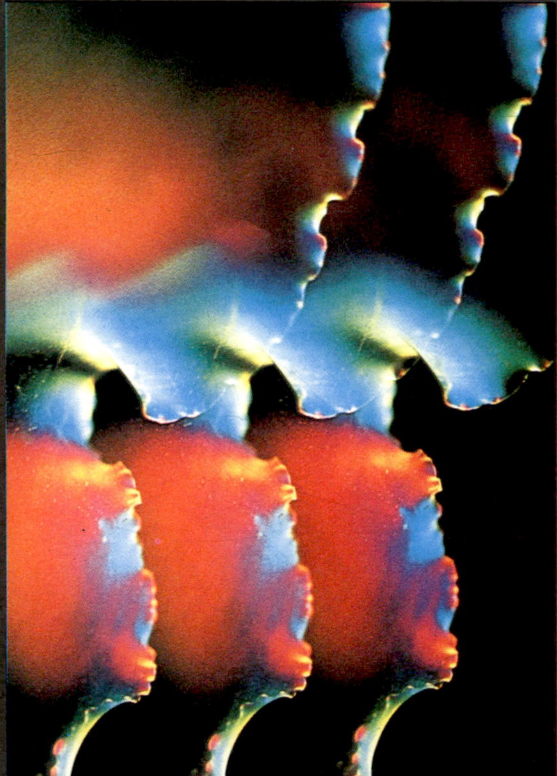

15

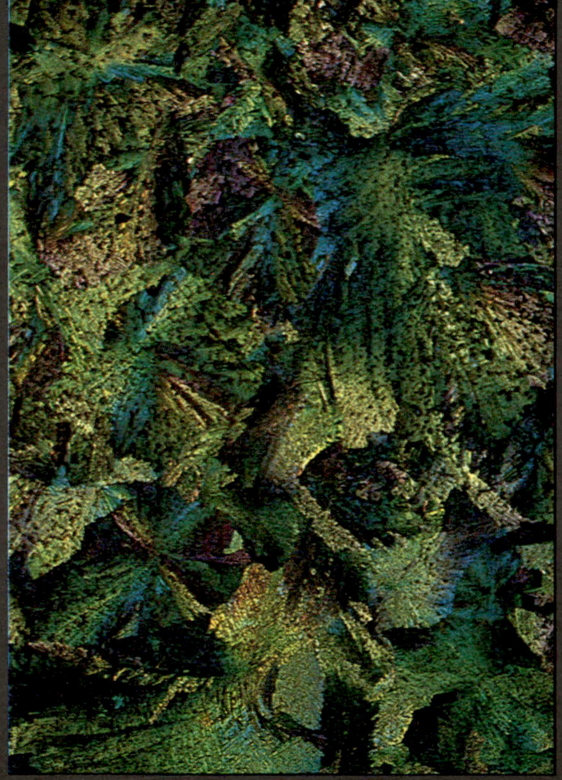

51

152

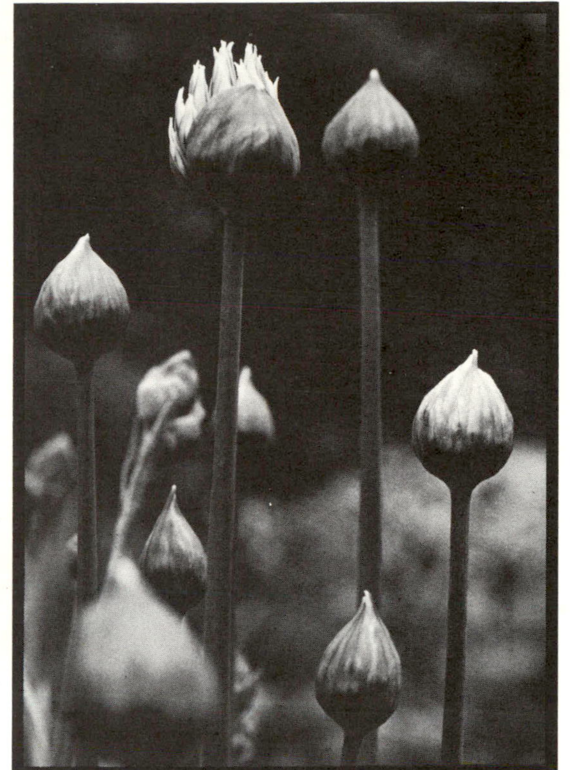

3

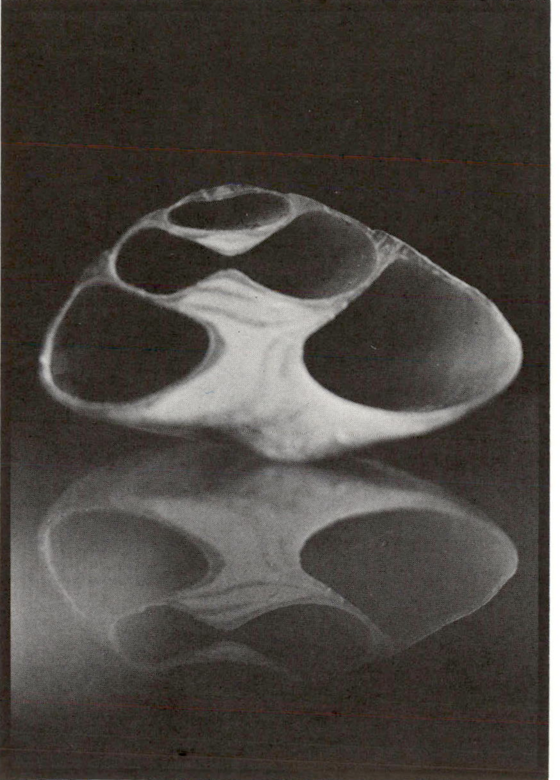

154

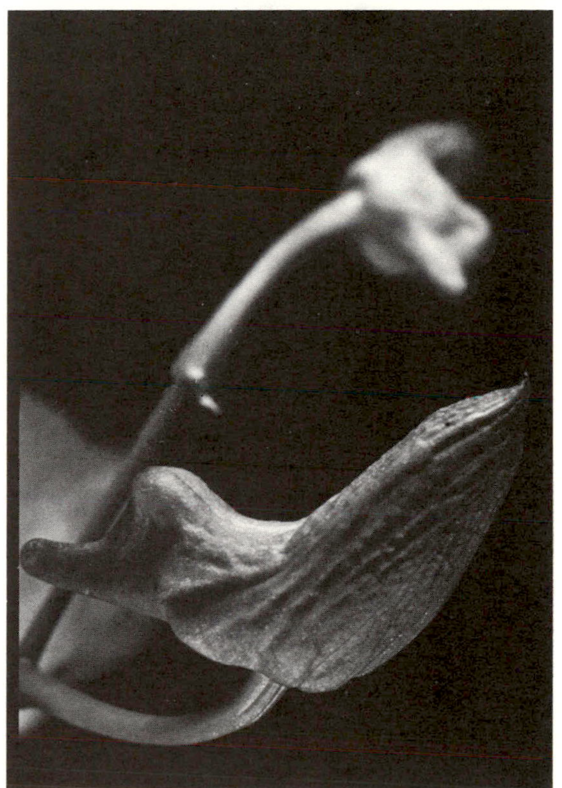

25: THEMES—AND A CONCLUSION

In the foregoing chapters I have made an attempt to place before you in word and picture three of the most significant thematic areas in photography. There is an endless list of possibilities—and indeed there are photographic books which list everything and give advice on all subjects to photograph from 'A' for 'Afternoon Mood' to 'Z' for 'Zoological Gardens'. Such a procedure does not seem either useful or sensible, because anyone who has grasped the fundamental technical and procedural methods described in this book should be in the position of being able to tackle problems as they arise.

Admittedly, when a mist shrouds the scene, it is initially easier to look up some clever book, make the lighting adjustments recommended therein, fit the appropriate filter and apply yourself to the 'Rules of composition for misty photographs' . . .

One thing is clear: if you take this approach you will certainly be able to take some successful photographs of the misty scene—but you might as well have handed over the task of taking the photograph to the author of the handbook as well. I have said this often already, but it is so important that I must repeat it once more: a photograph is an expression of personality. And if you have taken a photograph, it must express your own personality and not that of X or Y . . .

For example, at one time David Hamilton was an extremely fashionable photographer, and in every photographic journal and at every amateur photographic contest dozens of Hamilton-type photographs were to be seen—none of which were the work of Hamilton. Nevertheless, many originators of these photographs were proud of this, and would exclaim: 'Look at that—I can do it too!' The only answer to this is: 'Very good—and what can you do on your own?' It is always better to make your own mistakes than to imitate the success of others!

On the other hand, that is not to say that everyone has inevitably to do different things from everyone else. This only engenders a sort of cramp, which would probably take one of the following forms:

1 **Technique:** there are people who believe that a novel technique—be it a new filter, a new darkroom process or whatever—is a guarantee of magnificent photographs. The belief is false, for two reasons. Firstly, innovations have the characteristic of being very quickly used by other people, so that photographs which owe their existence to an innovation have the effect, at best, of a short-lived astonishing and quickly forgotten novelty. Secondly, even if such a photograph were for a short time unique and stimulating, it would not remain so for long. If everything which was new and rousing was also good, then our evening television news would be a feast of pure joy.
2 **Subject:** there are those who believe that a specially exotic or unusual subject guarantees outstanding photographs, although it really is not difficult to make a picture of the summit of Everest which is as bad as a photograph of your own backyard—if that kind of Mount Everest photograph really causes admiration and astonishment, this is most certainly not on account of its fine photographic quality!

The point about exotic subjects indeed embodies a (photographically) highly dangerous factor, since it is all too easy to be tempted to photograph something strange and unfamiliar without considering if the picture produced for this reason actually has anything to say. Concepts like 'strangeness' and 'unfamiliarity' are very personal ones: what is new and sensational for one person could be 'old hat' for someone else.

There is another photographic misconception of a similar kind. Many people find their own photographs specially good because they constitute a record of a personal achievement. If you perhaps bask in the glory of the knowledge that a special photograph was the outcome of a perilous climbing expedition, or perhaps represented the conquering of an incredibly tricky technical problem, this says nothing at all about the photographic quality of the photograph. For the beholder, the only thing that counts is what he sees! A photograph might be good as a novelty, or as a document about a distant place, or as a record of a personal achievement. But it shares these properties with many other things, and hence this says nothing about the photographic quality of the picture.

A photograph is not a representation of reality. I illustrated this point in the first part of this book with reference to certain photographs, but as it is of vital significance, I return to it here.

We are all only too well aware of the war photograph with its shocking documentation of human misery. Any photographer who journeys to a war-torn centre of contemporary crisis is a realist—because he communicates reality as it is. Another one, who five metres away from the first photographer captures the image of a beautiful flower, is quite clearly an escapist . . .

Do you really accept that? If you do, then think again a little. On the face of it, the two subjects quoted are of equal value. If you regard either one as of more significance than the other, this has nothing to do with its 'hold on reality', but instead with your own completely personal and ethical valuation of the subjects. You are substituting 'the thing in itself' for its relationship to you . . .

The reason why this point is so extraordinarily important is that if photography had been purely a representation of reality, then we would long ago have passed the stage of having portrayed the whole of reality—and thus all further photography would be pure repetition and accordingly worthless.

Photography accomplishes more than this. A photograph is a meeting between the personality of the photographer and a portion of reality—brought to fulfilment by the special agency of the photographic medium. It follows that photography will always be significant and fresh as long as new personalities emerge who use it as a means of expression.

I have no desire that anyone who takes up this book and skims through its pages should read these final paragraphs first of all and immediately drop it in horror. So I close my deliberations with thoughts on another aspect of photography.

Photography is fun. Photography can be an absorbing recreation; it can be an occupation practised because of its technical fascination; or it can simply be a means of capturing and retaining memories. It can serve us also in our profession, or, together with another hobby, as a means of documentation or as an instrument of scientific research.

The motivations which may lead a person to photography are as manifold as the persons who practise it. And none of these motivations are better or worse than any others. The important point is to ensure that the results of your photographic endeavours are always pictures in a real sense, and that the pictures are embodiments of your motivation.

In the second part of this book I have revealed something of my own motivations and of my kind of photography. From this point it is up to you to extract what interests you and make use of what you have extracted for your kind of photography.

If you have come to realise, from the first part of the book, that photographic devices are working tools which may be used according to your own inclinations, in order that you may realise your own conceptions—then as author I shall be well content—and I hope that as purchaser and reader you will be pleased too. However, if all this has been of no interest to you, I trust that the book will at least have fulfilled one purpose—as an informative source of basic practical knowledge.

INDEX